T0305188

Structural Reform in Open Economies

Structural Reform in Open Economies:

A Road to Success?

Edited by

Peter A.G. van Bergeijk

De Nederlandsche Bank N.V. and
Erasmus University Rotterdam

Jarig van Sinderen

Netherlands Ministry of Economic Affairs and
Erasmus University Rotterdam

Ben A. Vollaard

Netherlands Ministry of Economic Affairs

Edward Elgar
Cheltenham, UK • Northampton, MA, USA

Published by
Edward Elgar Publishing Limited
Glensanda House
Montpellier Parade
Cheltenham
Glos GL50 1UA
UK

Edward Elgar Publishing, Inc.
136 West Street, Suite 202
Northampton
Massachusetts 01060
USA

A catalogue record for this book
is available from the British Library

Library of Congress Cataloguing in Publication Data
Structural reform in open economies : a road to success? / edited by
    Peter A.G. van Bergeijk, Jarig van Sinderen, Ben A. Vollaard.
        Selected papers from the conference "The Effects and policy
    implications of structural adjustment in small open economies" held
    in Amsterdam, Oct. 23–24, 1997.
        1. Europe, Western—Economic policy Case studies Congresses.
    2. New Zealand Economic policy—Congresses. I. Bergeijk, Peter A.
    G. van, 1959– . II. Sinderen, Jarig van. III. Vollaard, Ben A.,
    1975–
    HC240.S768 1999   99–21716
    338.94—dc21   CIP

ISBN 1 84064 065 0
Printed and bound in Great Britain by MPG Books Ltd, Bodmin, Cornwall

Contents

Figures

Tables

Contributors

Willem Adema
  Social Policy Division, OECD.
Bart van Ark
  University of Groningen.
Eric J. Bartelsman
  Netherlands Ministry of Economic Affairs and Amsterdam Free
  University.
Peter A.G. van Bergeijk
  De Nederlandsche Bank N.V. and Erasmus University Rotterdam.
Per Callesen
  Danish Ministry of Finance.
Jakob de Haan
  University of Groningen.
Viv B. Hall
  Victoria University of Wellington.
Erling Holmøy
  Norway Statistics.
Martin Knudsen
  Statistics Denmark.
Lars Haagen Pedersen
  Statistics Denmark.
Toke Ward Petersen
  Statistics Denmark.
Dirk Pilat
  Science and Technology Division, OECD.
Jarig van Sinderen
  Netherlands Ministry of Economic Affairs and Erasmus University
  Rotterdam.
Peter Stephensen
  Statistics Denmark.
Peter Trier
  Statistics Denmark.
Ben A. Vollaard
  Netherlands Ministry of Economic Affairs.

Preface

Per Callesen

This volume, *Structural Reform in Open Economies*, contains a selection of papers from the conference 'The Effects and Policy Implications of Structural Adjustment in Small Open Economies', which took place in Amsterdam October 23-24, 1997.

The aim of the conference, which was organised by the Netherlands Ministry of Economic Affairs and the Danish Ministry of Finance, was to discuss problems and prospects of empirical assessment of structural reform. The conference brought together a number of ministerial policy advisers and university academics from a large number of OECD countries, though especially from the Northwest of Europe.

The idea to organise the conference came up after a seminar in Copenhagen October 1996 on 'The Use of Computable General Equilibrium Models for Policy Planning and Analyses'. In the process of building a computable general equilibrium model to be used by the Danish Ministries of Finance and Economic Affairs advice was sought from other countries, especially from the Netherlands, which has a strong tradition in the field of applied model building.

The Amsterdam conference invited papers on particular country experiences, on counterfactual model-based assessments of structural reforms and papers dealing with the effects of structural reform in particular areas. The origin of the conference was the common interest of the organisers in these issues. The editors have mainly selected papers from the conference covering the latter two aspects, but also some of the country-specific papers.

Structural reform is high on the agenda in many countries, even if it is not always clear what is meant by the two words. A workable definition may be policies that seek to improve the underlying path of growth, employment and saving-investments balances of the economy, especially raising potential output and the quality of that output by improving the functioning of markets and institutions. Particular reforms may be country-wide or cover specific markets, they may be large or small, and they may be gradual or big bang oriented.

The interaction between structural and macro-economic policies is a highly important aspect of structural reform. To what extent do growth and employment promoting structural policies require supporting macro-economic policies and conditions? What are the conditions for macro-economic policies to be supportive, and what is the division of work between structural and macro-economic policies when reacting to economic shocks?

Some have the view that structural policies are direct output and employment creating devices. Others see structural policies as improving the potential of the economy and the employability of the labour force, but underline the requirement of the right macro-economic conditions to exploit these opportunities. The latter approach may refer to the necessary demand management being generated by independent central banks reacting on output gaps and inflation. In some cases an economic recession seems to foster the necessary structural reform process as pressure for action increases due to the general dissatisfaction with the economy. In other cases strong recoveries and some inflationary pressures may be the necessary condition for reform as the immediate need for raising potential output is more obvious.

For dealing with shocks, flexible markets and strong institutions are vital, but the role of macro-economic policies (demand management policies) should not be forgotten. In one of his thought-provoking memos Paul Krugman complains that the latest decades of students of economics have been so occupied with micro-structural issues that macro-economic policy issues are either forgotten or severely downplayed – the consequence today being an inability to give proper advice. Macro-economic challenges thus appear, when the ideal world of independent monetary authorities being able to prevent slumps and overheating breaks down in special, but clearly relevant, cases. One such case is the present situation of Japan, where structural problems in the financial sectors have been aggravated by a demand slump and where low interest rates do not seem to have the expected effect. Another case is the fixed exchange rates and monetary union of European countries, where only the area-wide, but not country-specific, demand management problems can be dealt with by the monetary authorities. These are challenges for fiscal policies calling for sufficient underlying room for manoeuvre, but probably also for the timing of structural policies.

Structural reforms cover a much wider and less quantifiable set of instruments than macro-economic policies. The only relatively easy examples of economic instruments are replacement rates and tax rates. But structural reforms are much more than that. Some of the numerous examples are competition policies, regulation of entry barriers, non-tariff trade barriers, employment protection rules, eligibility and job search requirements for access to public transfers, the quality of education and training, the efficiency of various public sector agencies and labour supply effects of care for children and the elderly. A risk is that some of these policies are downplayed, because other instruments than replacement rates and taxes are difficult to quantify. Putting structural policies in a quantitative form usable for assessment of historical developments and cross-country comparisons is thus an important task.

The effects of the details in structural policies are not easily quantified and the link between them and between micro-economic and macro-economic effects is complicated. More conclusive results from the research on structural policies would be helpful and might smooth the policy process further. Such evidence may help change the weight between the expected gains often being widespread and diffuse at the macro-level and the perceived costs in terms of transition which often are more easily identified. It may also widen a view on structural policies (possibly being fed by an often too one-sided focus on replacement rates and tax rates) that they are something that moves on the trade-off between efficiency and equity rather than improving this trade-off.

How should structural reforms be undertaken, how should they be implemented and how should they be assessed? How can applied economic analysis improve the quality of structural reforms and inspire the decision-making process?

A basic condition is to provide a deep understanding of the macro and micro situation of the economy, including the interaction of these policies. On structural policies as such a variety of analytical methods ranging from soft to hard analyses exist.

Among the softer are benchmarking, finding best practices, getting inspiration from institutions and reform processes and related results in different countries. The major challenge in these areas is to find and adjust data that allow for relevant comparisons and to get clear and comparable understandings of the effect of different institutions in different countries.

In addition, studies on detailed labour and product market flows based on longitudinal panel data can inspire structural reforms, even though such studies are often mostly descriptive. Using micro-econometrics to estimate how certain policies affect these flows could show up to be highly valuable, the main problem though still being lack of sufficient data and time series.

Among the harder methods are econometric evidence on partial elasticities from micro- or macro-studies (national or cross-country), counterfactual analyses of economic developments based on large-scale economic models and the explicit modelling of structural effects in general equilibrium models. In addition to building and running the large models a major challenge in these exercises is to explain the assumptions behind the model-based results and to adjust the models for missing links between policy instruments.

The conference in Amsterdam was particularly successful in dealing with country-specific reform processes, research on specific structural topics and advanced modelling exercises. Hopefully this volume of selected papers will inspire further work on structural policies and structural reform.

1.   Structural Reform: The Issues

Peter A.G. van Bergeijk, Jarig van Sinderen and Ben A. Vollaard

Structural reform is today's tune. Privatisation, deregulation, liberalisation, globalisation, new tax structures, labour market reform, competition policy and other supply side policies are part and parcel of the modern economic policy maker's analytical tool box.

One reason for the popularity of these structural policy measures derives from the idea that such policies are able to improve on the long-run performance of the economy. Many politicians increasingly recognise the need to constantly upgrade the economy to make the economic system as flexible and efficient as possible while the public at large also appears to be well aware of the problems at stake.

Another reason is the demise of the Asian model, in particular the problems of Japan and South Korea. The recent experiences of these countries have shown the need for flexibility and adaptation of the economic system. Traditional macro-economic policies such as Keynesian spending policies (including tax reductions) and monetary relaxation appear to offer no solutions. The Asian problems are to a large extent of a structural nature, and reflect both an inadequate system of corporate governance and a sub-optimal functioning of product, labour and financial markets, in some cases leading to protectionist outcomes. Indeed, economic agents in the Asian countries are not stimulated by this manner of economic policies. Traditional policies do not appear to restore the confidence of market participants: multipliers tend to be low and Ricardian equivalence seems to hold, resulting in higher macro-economic savings rather than an increase in private consumption and investment.

Unfortunately, the policy maker that seeks some guidance when he or she contemplates structural reform measures often is not much helped by the debates in either the popular or the academic press: the exchange of views is best described by the *dictum* 'more heat than light'. Indeed, one cannot help but notice that these issues have been neglected for many years and that structural issues have only recently become the topic of serious analysis.

Moreover, the debates and analyses appear to take place on essentially a national basis with little or no cross-border learning effects.

Consequently, many debates on actual policy measures could benefit when the experiences of other countries could be taken into account. An important goal of this book is to bring together policy relevant analyses that were undertaken in a number of countries in order to shed some light on the empirical question of whether structural policies do matter. Actually, the present volume grew out of a conference that was co-organised by the Danish Ministry of Finance and the Dutch Ministry of Economic Affairs in Amsterdam in October 1997. That conference was organised because policy makers felt the need to improve on the available analyses, as Per Callesen explains in the preface to this volume.

One of the themes that emerged during this conference on the effects and policy implications of structural adjustment in small open economies was the difficulty of getting sound and convincing evidence on both the costs and the benefits of structural reform. Indeed, from a theoretical perspective measurement and analysis of the impact of intended structural policies is ambiguous and complicated while many logical and ideological traps exist. As Viv Hall points out in Chapter 2:

> Structural adjustment and structural change are not easy concepts to operationalise, either in terms of convenient measures or in terms of how such measures can be translated into economic benefits and costs and policy terms.

Publication in professional journals of such analyses that take into account political and conceptual aspects of structural reform policies appears to be rather difficult. This provides a disincentive for economists at universities to get involved in these issues; this may also offer an explanation for why the debates seem to be repeated in different countries.

All in all the empirical evidence on the macro-economic consequences of structural reform policies is scarce. This book aims to collect some of the evidence, providing an outlet for important policy relevant analyses related to structural reform. The book also gives an impression of the state of the art describing the techniques that have been used in the economic discourses in a number of industrialised economies. In doing so two 'success stories' are discussed in somewhat more detail: the experience of New Zealand where 'big bang' structural reform was initiated by Sir Roger Douglas and the so-called Dutch 'polder model' that features wage moderation as a key element in addition to structural policies. In order to broaden the scope of our analysis, reforms in Denmark and Norway are also taken into account. Drawing on these cases, this book details both the policy problems and the analytical issues at stake with respect to modelling and measuring structural change and illustrates how policy relevant questions have been investigated in a number of open economies.

A SHORT HISTORY OF STRUCTURAL REFORM POLICY

Given the paucity of empirical evidence *pro* structural reform, it is quite amazing that such policies have become part and parcel of the economic debate in the 1990s. The roots of this discussion date back to the 1970s. Indeed, structural reform as an element of economic policy was first put on the research agenda in the early 1980s when policy makers in most OECD countries started to recognise that the Keynesian recipes that prevailed in the 1950s, 1960s and 1970s were unable to cure the problems posed by lagging growth and high levels of structural unemployment. Initially the attention of policy makers focused on budgetary issues. High and rising deficits and unsustainable public debt positions explain this initial focus to a large extent. However, structural weaknesses were more and more recognised to be the apparent sources behind the lagging of economic performance, especially in Western Europe. Increasingly it was understood that (international) competition and dynamic entrepreneurship are the driving forces for cost minimisation, innovation and adaptations to changes in the (world) economic system. Consequently, structural reforms related to taxation, the structure of government expenditure, the functioning of labour markets, capital markets and product markets, regulation, as well as the openness of the economy became focal points of the discussion among policy makers. Naturally the policy agenda influenced research agendas, first in policy related institutions and later in academia. This book takes stock of much that has been learned since and identifies areas where progress in both analysis and policy is still possible.

Obviously much has already been achieved over the last decades both in terms of actual policies implemented and in terms of analysis. In 1983 the OECD published its seminal report *Positive Adjustment Policies: Managing Structural Change* and in 1987 this was followed up in the influential study *Structural Adjustment and Economic Performance*. Since then structural policies have been monitored on a more permanent basis by the OECD's Economic Development Review Committee, which annually reviews its member's economic developments, prospects and policies. Since 1987 the OECD country studies contain a section on structural issues and policies. It appears that many industrialised countries are making progress in combating market imperfections, liberalising product markets and increasing competition. In the early 1990s national economies to some extent tended to converge in the direction of greater reliance on market forces.

However, it is not only the OECD that follows and analyses structural change and reform. Also the European Union has shown a keen interest in structural issues and has importantly stepped up its efforts to analyse this aspect of economic policy. The Union now devotes substantial attention to rigidities, distortions and institutions on both product and factor markets in its broad economic policy guidelines. These guidelines reflect on the whole spectre of economic policies (fiscal policies and structural issues) and constitute the 'real economy counterpart' of the single European monetary policy. The importance of structural measures in the context of European Monetary Union is shown by the fact that the broad economic guidelines are prepared in close collaboration by the Economic and Financial Committee (EFC, the former Monetary Committee) and the Economic Policy Committee. The resulting documents form the basis for a constructive discussion amongst the European Finance Ministers in the EFC.

The set of macro-economic aspects of structural reform that constitutes the focus of this book is by no means the end of the agenda. It is important to look further and to consider micro-economic issues in addition, for example related to the topic of corporate governance. Clearly the experience of Japan illustrates the need to consider in more depth the structure of firms, their relations to financial institutions and the banking system.

Small Open Economies

All in all structural policies are considered to be important in many mature OECD economies and are actually being implemented. Thus structural reform is an ongoing process. This book focuses on a subset of OECD countries, namely the so-called small open industrialised economies: New Zealand and the North European economies Denmark, the Netherlands and Norway. The reason for this focus is threefold.

First, and admittedly this is a rather practical reason, we are best aware of the situation in this group of countries. They form a rather homogeneous group of industrialised countries that are customarily being used as a basis for comparison. In other words, these countries are a natural benchmark for the comparative policy analyses that have been done in these economies during the processes of formulating structural policies.

Second, it appears that structural reform is an essential element in the policy mix of these economies at the end of the 1980s, while the large economies have been less involved in structural reform. Willem Adema and Dirk Pilat in Chapter 4 point out that '[t]he policy response to inflexible labour and product markets has, however, been insufficient in many OECD countries' (in addition to the countries studied in this volume: the United Kingdom and Ireland). Indeed, a remarkable similarity exists between New

Zealand, the Netherlands and Sweden as it appears to have been the slow growth experience in the 1970s and early 1980s that stimulated policy initiatives aimed at structural reform in these countries. However, these countries have made a different degree of progress in implementing reform measures.

Third, the problems of small open economies to a large extent differ from the policy questions encountered by the bigger (and often less open) economies. One might argue that small open economies are in a better position to implement structural measures since the impact on their own business cycle tends to be less than in the case where large economies adjust their economic structures. For example, the demand effects of changes in the tax system tend to a larger extent to leak abroad in small open economies *vis-à-vis* large economies. Moreover, whereas small open economies cannot influence the stance of the world economy, they are often substantially exposed to the process of globalisation. Indeed, they have no other option but to constantly adjust their economic system. Actually, this divergence in policy perspective was one of the motivating reasons for the conference from which the present volume grew. At a more pragmatic level, small open economies lack the financial means and economic leverage to implement policies aimed at specific industries and, consequently, have to focus on generic measures. They opt, for example, for trade liberalisation rather than for so-called strategic trade policies.

Still, the policy experiences of these countries offer valuable lessons for larger economies that are contemplating structural reform. They provide interesting real world experiments for the academic economist and make the policy maker aware of the problems that are encountered in preparing the grounds for structural reform.

POLICY RELEVANT QUESTIONS

What kind of information do policy makers need to evaluate structural issues? It would seem that structural issues that are often micro-economic by their very nature need a new analytical approach. Traditional macro-economic tools cannot provide satisfying answers to many relevant questions. The roots of the idea of structural policies as a separate field of research and an individual element of economic policy making go back to Tinbergen's (1955) *On the Theory of Economic Policy*. In this seminal study Tinbergen makes a distinction between quantitative policy, i.e. changes of policy instruments within a given economic structure, and qualitative policy, i.e. changing qualitative elements of the economic structure, for example related to market structure, ownership or openness. Tinbergen focused on the realm of quantitative policy; this is a logical choice given the pioneering character of this early attempt to mathematically formulate some problems of economic policy making and to provide a numerical illustration related to government activities in the Netherlands. Still Tinbergen offers a number of observations on qualitative policies that are relevant for the discussion in this book. First and foremost is his recognition that qualitative policy is difficult to analyse because of our limited knowledge of 'human behaviour under different structural conditions'. Moreover policy makers that are often guided by an 'aversion of the complex' will not easily engage in structural reform policies as new grounds need to be broken while difficult analytical issues are at stake in evaluating considered qualitative policies. Still structural reform measures need to be considered, as their potential economic and social impact is substantial.

Given Tinbergen's assertion, the question emerges what kind of information policy makers need when they consider qualitative changes in their economy and how, i.e. by what type of studies, this demand can be met. The papers presented at the conference 'The effects and policy implications of structural adjustment in small open economies' and the consequent discussion illustrate that policy advisers have sought the answer by deploying several techniques:

- Purely deductive analyses.
- Modelling exercises mainly based on econometric investigations.
- Other empirically orientated techniques such as growth accounting.
- Comparative analyses.

Deductive Analyses

Often a deductive analysis is the centrepiece of the policy proposals that have actually been on the table in many countries. Probably the best example is the case of New Zealand that is discussed by Viv Hall in the present volume.[1] The importance of deductive analysis should not surprise the reader. After all the functioning of markets is the core business of economics since Adam Smith published his *Wealth of Nations*. So economic theory provides a strong and often convincing basis for considering and evaluating policy proposals. However, a purely theoretical analysis will often not do in the policy debate and reference to actual distortions or sub-optimal performance of industries, generally speaking, needs to supplement the deductive approach. Problems need to be identified clearly and some indication of the order of magnitude of the problems will have to be supplied in order to convince policy makers and the public at large that structural reforms are worth the trouble, i.e. that economic improvement is sufficiently large.

Modelling

One way to combine theory that is embedded in a structure of well-specified equations and empirics is to analyse structural reforms in economic or econometric models at the level of the macro-economy. Most often the approach involves the identification of market distortions at the industry level and developing alternative scenarios for core parameters such as the level of price responsiveness, the mark up of prices over costs and variables that reflect changes in underlying productivity. An advantage of this approach is that such a counterfactual approach allows one to determine the potential scope for improving the functioning of the economy, as well as the costs of the intended changes in the economic structure.

Measurement

Clearly, modelling exercises only become possible after the proper empirical identification of the problems at hand. Consequently, many modelling efforts have initiated econometric research aimed at uncovering the impact of different economic structures on economic performance, both at the level of individual industries and at the macro level of national economies. One theme, however, that also runs through the contributions to the present volume is the difficulty of actually assessing the impact of structural reform.

Comparative Analyses

The experience of other countries constitutes a final and valuable source of information about the (potential) impact of structural reform measures. In order to assess whether an economy or particular industries in an economy operate at the sub-optimal level, one needs a yardstick. Often this yardstick is provided by benchmarking, i.e. comparisons with best standard practices in other countries and/or industries. The idea of learning from other countries obviously is at the heart of this book as it analyses developments in Denmark, the Netherlands, New Zealand and Norway. Bringing these analyses together provides for a sharper analysis and to some extent may help to prevent one from focussing on the specifics of the policy maker's experience rather than on the common elements that constitute genuine lessons for structural reform processes in general.

While a balanced, comprehensive and scientifically sound evaluation of the actual impact of structural change may still be a bridge too far, it appears possible to discuss and analyse the available preliminary evidence of pro-competitive effects. Interestingly, the participants in the discussion seem to strike a different balance between the level of evidence that is required as a basis for sound policies. So, on the one hand, in Chapter 7 Bart van Ark and Jakob de Haan argue that the Dutch miracle is essentially based on improvement in international competitiveness as a result of wage moderation. They find no conclusive evidence that other aspects of structural reform, such as deregulation of labour and product markets, greatly enhanced economic performance in the Netherlands. On the other hand, in Chapter 4 Willem Adema and Dirk Pilat argue that while product market reforms have indeed been too recent to judge their effectiveness, labour market performance has improved substantially due to structural labour market reforms. Their analysis does not indicate that it will enable the Netherlands to reach a structurally higher rate of growth than other Northwestern European countries. Per Callesen (1997) assesses that sufficient evidence exists on the broad links between policies and actual economic performance. On the basis of the available evidence he confidently concludes that Danish structural policies are on track. Noteworthy is the intermediate position of Viv Hall in Chapter 2. He recognises that the available evidence is definitely not perfect, but at the same time he is 'cautiously optimistic on the sustainability of recently improved economic growth' and clearly willing to plead for further structural reforms on the basis of this, alas imperfect, scientific base.

ACADEMICS AND STRUCTURAL REFORM

In academia structural change has drawn the attention of many authors and inspired creative approaches. In addition to measurement issues, the available theoretical studies mainly deal with three topics related to the implementation of structural reform policies (cf. van Bergeijk and Haffner, 1996):

- Credibility and (time) consistency.
- Sequencing (the optimal order of reform).
- Political economy aspects.

Credibility and (Time) Consistency

The credibility of the intended structural policy measures is in itself a necessary condition for success, as is consistency of macro-economic policies (see, for example, Edwards, 1989 and Funke, 1993). Since the main objective of any structural reform programme is to reallocate resources into more efficient economic activities, it is essential that private expectations about (future) public policies are in accordance with the policy maker's plans. That is: announcements related to structural policies should be as credible as possible. An obvious requirement is that intended structural policies are sustainable in both the medium term and the long run, since otherwise the public will expect policy reversals (see for example Rodrik, 1989).

Sequencing

Sequencing has been characterised by some as 'arm chair theorising', but actually setting priorities is an important element of policy both when structural reforms are implemented step-by-step and when reform packages are considered. A related question is the speed of adjustment where New Zealand provides an example of 'big bang' reforms, while the Danish, the Dutch and the Swedish cases may provide evidence of a more gradualist approach.

Generally speaking, the advice is to achieve a stable macro-economic environment – characterised by low inflation, healthy public finances and balanced external accounts – before embarking on micro-economic reforms and to achieve openness to international competition as an important means to anchor structural reform initiatives. Transparency about both the costs and the benefits of reform strategies is advocated alongside realism about the expected (timing of) losses and gains in order to gain public support and credibility. Indeed, from both an economic and a political perspective, a broad, transparent and medium term approach is needed, as partial attempts to reform are difficult to implement while the effectiveness of policies ultimately depends on their medium term consistency and credibility.

Political Economy Aspects

The standard neo-classical approach argues that reform will take place whenever a change of policy benefits the representative voter. The government is assumed to be well informed and altruistic and to maximise social welfare subject to administrative and technological constraints. Also the voter is perfectly informed about the costs and benefits of the set of available policies. Unfortunately, this framework cannot explain why in the same economy some reforms succeed while others fail. Interestingly, failures and successes are often comparable in terms of proposed policy alternatives. Obviously other – non-economic – factors need to be considered as well.

Williamson (1994) has analysed several reform packages that were implemented in the 1980s and early 1990s, taking into account both economic and political aspects. His findings suggest that some common-sense assumptions are not supported by actual policy experience: for example structural reforms tend to be implemented by the whole political spectre (not just the right-wing) and are not only undertaken early on in the term of office of a new government. In other cases, the findings are more in line with a priori expectations. Obviously, structural reforms have a bigger chance to succeed if social consensus exists about what needs to be done.[2] Strong leadership also contributes to successful structural reform.

However, one of the most important determinants for the success of structural reform policies appears to be the existence of a crisis. A crisis provides for a sense of urgency, damming the influence of special interest groups, and so-to-say shocks countries out of traditional policy patterns. The importance of underpinning the need for structural reform by unsustainable macro-economic imbalances and micro-economic problems is clearly illustrated by the cases of New Zealand and the Netherlands. Both the Dutch and the New Zealand reform packages appear to have their roots in the policies of the 1970s that became increasingly inappropriate. For example, Viv Hall indicates that structural reforms in New Zealand received their initial momentum from a trigger mechanism of chronic economic problems, a major economic and constitutional crisis and decisive leadership. Note, however, that in Denmark the most important structural reforms took place during strong recoveries. The tax reform that is discussed by Martin Knudsen et al. in Chapter 6 is an example.

SOME NUMERICAL EVIDENCE

In addition to theoretical analyses modelling teams at universities and policy research institutes have investigated the potential consequences of structural reform numerically, showing substantial potential gains. Following Browning (1994), Peter van Bergeijk and Hugo Keuzenkamp (1997), for example, estimate the so-called non-tax wedge - the theoretical tax equivalent of market distortions like monopoly, monopsony or regulation - at 10 to 25 per cent of GDP in the Netherlands (see Table 3.3 for more details on the Dutch non-tax wedge). Often these analyses follow a partial equilibrium approach neglecting dynamic and second order effects of the considered structural policies. Erling Holmøy, however, clarifies in Chapter 5 that such analytical simplifications carry a price tag. He shows that a partial equilibrium approach that does not consider the influence of structural reform on shadow prices overestimates the welfare gain by more than 30 per cent compared to the general equilibrium approach. Still his finding of the Norwegian welfare potential of a good 20 per cent of GDP is substantial by any standard. Obviously, the upshot of Holmøy's analysis is not that policy analysts should use a partial framework in order to come up with the large numbers that may motivate policy makers to embark on the road of structural reforms. The message is that a comprehensive modelling framework is essential in order to make policy decisions as realistic and informative as possible.

Some recent examples of modelling exercises that provide insight into the empirical consequences of considered structural policies are Lipschitz et al. (1989), Norman et al. (1991), van Sinderen et al. (1994), Industry Commission (1995), Goff (1996), Nieuwenhuis et al. (1997) and OECD (1997h).

Table 1.1   Macro-economic effects of deregulation, privatisation and improved functioning of product and labour markets (cumulated deviations from base run or historic simulation)*

Country	GDP	Employment	Source
Australia	+++	++	Industry Commission (1995)
Germany	+	+	Lipschitz et al. (1989)
	+++	+	OECD (1997h)
France	+++	++	OECD (1997h)
Japan	+++	Nil	OECD (1997h)
Netherlands	+++	+++	van Sinderen et al. (1994)
	++	++	Haffner and van Bergeijk (1997)
Norway	+++	+++	Norman et al. (1991)
UK	++	+	OECD (1997h)
US	++	+	OECD (1997h)

Note: * Nil: -0.1 per cent to 0.1 per cent; +: 0.1 per cent to 1 per cent; ++: 1 per cent to 5 per cent; +++: > 5 per cent.

Table 1.1 provides the results of 10 modelling exercises with six different models aimed at determining the expected impact of structural reform on the economy. A caveat is in order as the countries that are studied in the table, the policy measures that have been considered in the exercises, and the tools that have been used in the analysis are quite heterogeneous. Hence, the results should be interpreted with caution, as indicated by the qualitative characters in the Table. Moreover, the reader should be aware of the limitations of the models. Econometric analyses of this type cannot cover aspects that by their very nature cannot be quantified (such as 'confidence', 'mentality' or 'conservatism'), but may be very relevant for the success of any policy that is considered.

The OECD (1997h) modelling exercises have been based on INTERLINK, a traditional econometrically estimated structural model. The Industry Commission (1995), Lipschitz et al. (1989), van Sinderen et al.

(1994), Haffner et al. (1997) and Norman et al. (1991) use general equilibrium models. General equilibrium models have a strong micro-economic underpinning and may be less vulnerable to the so-called Lucas critique that structural reforms influence the expectations of economic agents and hence the structure of the model. However, since general equilibrium models lack an explicit treatment of the exchange process such models might be less suitable for analysing questions related to the functioning of product markets (such as monopoly, regulation and other distortions). Whereas general equilibrium models sketch the long run, structural models (such as INTERLINK) provide information on the short and medium term dynamics of structural reform.

In addition to the differences in the 'philosophy' behind the modelling exercises substantial differences exist with respect to the assumptions on which the calculations have been based. All modelling exercises start from a detailed empirical investigation of the relevant structural impediments (most often at the level of individual industries and sectors) and intensively use international comparative analyses (benchmarking). The assumptions regarding the extent of the considered structural reforms however are quite different. Now the measures are known *en détail* (as with the Australian Industry Commission), then potential measures have been listed (without any consideration of the political feasibility, as in the cases of Lipschitz et al., the OECD and Norman et al.). Sometimes no link between policies and the impulse in the model was established at all.

Despite these differences, the outcomes of the exercises show a strong agreement on the potentially substantial beneficial impact on production and suggest some improvement in the employment outlook as well. At a more detailed level, the numerical policy experiments suggest the existence of synergy between product market reforms and labour market reforms. These experiments corroborate Viv Hall's finding that it is the 'combined pressure of welfare, product and labour market reforms' that affect employment outcomes. Indeed, a common finding of the studies that are summarised in Table 1.1 is that structural reforms in product markets are strengthened by labour market flexibility and *vice versa*. The macro-economic findings offer a valuable piece of the policy puzzle, but for a comprehensive analysis more is needed. More conclusive results from the research on structural policies would be helpful and might smooth the policy process further.

PLAN OF THE BOOK

Three papers dealing with the cases of New Zealand and the Netherlands provide the starting point of the discussion. In Chapter 2 Viv Hall provides an insightful overview of the problems that initiated structural reform in New Zealand. He discusses the actual implementation of the 'big bang' policy package and its economic consequences and assesses the scope for further action. Likewise Jarig van Sinderen and Ben Vollaard elaborate on the more gradualist policy reactions that constitute the basis of the successful Dutch 'polder model' in Chapter 3, identifying areas where potential welfare gains can be reaped. In Chapter 4 Willem Adema and Dirk Pilat provide a comparative analysis of the New Zealand and the Dutch recipes pointing out similarities and differences between the different approaches. They focus especially on labour market issues.

Next come two Chapters that illustrate the use of applied general equilibrium models in analysing structural issues. In Chapter 6 Martin Knudsen et al. report on the use of the DREAM model that examines the long-run effects of changes in the Danish (tax) incentive structure in the context of an analysis that takes intergenerational effects into account. Erling Holmøy reports in Chapter 5 on the Norwegian MSG-5 model that has been used to analyse structural reform proposals. He illustrates how a general equilibrium model can be used to assess welfare effects of structural policy reforms that target inefficiency problems at micro-economic levels, which are normally not described in an operational computable general equilibrium model.

The final part focuses on measurement issues related to structural reform in the Netherlands, especially with respect to its impact on productivity. The focus on productivity is important from an analytical point of view since perceived differences in productivity drive the results of the macro-economic modelling analyses of structural reform. In Chapter 7, Bart van Ark and Jakob de Haan argue that the Dutch miracle mainly boils down to the so-called catch up effect in terms of labour market expansion at the expense of productivity. Using a vintage model, Eric Bartelsman in Chapter 8 is actually able to directly relate the increase in labour productivity to institutionalised wage moderation. The upshot of this discussion is that both the endogeneity of the wage formation policy and the effectiveness of moderate wages cannot be established with certainty. As Bartelsman states, '[a] different predication for total factor productivity may be hard to distinguish in practice because one does not know what the direction of TFP would have been in the absence of wage moderation'. Therefore it may still be too early to deliver a final judgement on the effectiveness of wage moderation in a small economy.

NOTES

1. See van Bergeijk and Haffner (1996), Bollard et al. (1996) and Evans et al. (1996) on the theoretical underpinnings of structural reform in New Zealand.
2. Callesen (1997) points out that this, for example, may require that structural reforms do not adversely affect equality of income. See also Adema and Pilat in Chapter 4 on social cohesion.

PART ONE

Experiences with Structural Reform

2. Reform and Experience in New Zealand

Viv B. Hall

INTRODUCTION

New Zealand has experienced more than a decade of significant economic reform. In this Chapter, I assess the progress that New Zealand has made in macro-economic and micro-economic areas over the past decade. Two basic views underpin my assessment. First, by 1984, New Zealand had developed unsustainable macro-economic imbalances and serious micro-economic problems.[1] Second, deep-seated macro-economic and micro-economic problems often take much longer to turn around and require more persistent corrective action than many originally envisage.[2]

The Chapter commences with a brief background to New Zealand's reform processes, followed by a selective evaluation of macro-economic performance to date. The focus is on economic growth, unemployment, inflation, fiscal and external imbalances, and debt sustainability.

Structural adjustment and other micro-economic empirical evidence is evaluated next, initially from a sectoral perspective, and then for goods and services markets and labour markets. The degree of progress on structural adjustment, productivity performance, performance of the public sector, the role of New Zealand's 'light-handed regulation' regime, and the role of the Employment Contracts Act receives particular attention.

Policy implications, including sequencing and so-called 'big bang' versus 'gradualist' issues, are then considered. The questions of sustainability of macro-economic progress to date, and directions for further significant micro-economic reform affecting goods and services and labour markets are also addressed.

BRIEF PERSPECTIVE ON THE REFORM PROCESS

New Zealand's wide-ranging economic reform processes now span more than a decade.[3] They had their roots in long standing, deep-seated macro-economic and micro-economic problems, and increasingly inappropriate economic policies[4], but had their immediate catalyst in the foreign exchange crisis of July 1984. They therefore received their initial momentum from the triple trigger mechanisms of chronic economic problems[5], a major economic and constitutional crisis[6], and decisive leadership.[7]

Some authors have characterised the reforms as 'big bang' in nature (for example Brash, 1996, p. 10; Bollard et al., 1996, p. 21). The term seems to receive its justification from both the rapid pace of reforms during the first two and a half years, and their especially comprehensive nature. Of course, many other OECD countries have carried out various types of reforms since the mid-1980s, but after considering the six basic areas of international trade, financial markets, the corporatisation, privatisation and deregulation of industries, tax reform, public expenditure and labour market policies, Henderson (1996, p. 10) concluded that '[i]f ... we consider all the six headings together, New Zealand clearly stands out ... no other OECD country has such a portfolio of liberalising measures to show.' He singles out for particular mention New Zealand's 'least distortive system of taxation', reductions in public expenditure relative to GDP that have proved 'more than temporary', and the Employment Contracts Act 1991 which 'represents a larger step towards greater freedom in labour markets than has so far been taken in any other OECD country'. Lloyd (1997, p. 117) has singled out the Reserve Bank of New Zealand Act of 1989 and trade policy as areas of reform which were particularly radical and innovative.

A summary chronological listing of the economic reforms can be found in Bollard et al. (1996, pp. 24-8).[8] Rather than be categorised as big bang, the reforms can alternatively be thought of as having occurred basically in 'two significant waves'. For example, according to Dalziel and Lattimore (1996, p. 92):

> In the first wave, the New Zealand dollar was devalued by 20 per cent and then floated on foreign exchange markets; financial markets were deregulated; product markets were opened up to greater domestic and international competition; government subsidies to private producers were phased out; income taxes were reduced and GST was introduced; government trading departments were corporatised into commercial state-owned enterprises; the privatisation programme began; monetary policy was directed towards achieving and maintaining price stability [via the Reserve Bank Act, 1989]; and the task was begun of bringing the public accounts into line with generally accepted accounting practice [the Public Finance Act, 1989]. In the second wave of reform after 1990, key components of

New Zealand's welfare state were restructured, and the labour market was deregulated under the Employment Contracts Act [1991]. [The Fiscal Responsibility Act came into force 1 July 1994].

So, against a background of the extent of reform to date and the challenges which still lie ahead, the current New Zealand Government's Coalition Agreement, and the country's MMP voting system, an important issue now is whether a third either revolutionary or consolidatory wave will follow.

It is also important to emphasise at this stage four other key elements: the 'intellectual underpinnings' of the reforms[9], the extent to which they have been market-based[10], the accommodating nature of what was then New Zealand's electoral and legislative system[11], and the fact that reform had to be carried out in an essentially 'stand alone' context.[12]

To this point in time, there seems widespread but not universal recognition that significant progress has been made. It is possible to identify early particular success stories, but more generally it has to be said that the adverse effects of the major macro-economic stabilisation policies were being felt at least through to the early 1990s, and that these had a somewhat swamping effect on structural adjustment processes. Cyclically strong economic growth since mid-1991 has meant that successes in macro-economic areas are now identifiable. But that same economic growth has, at least until recently, also continued to disguise the extent to which structural gains have been made, and the extent to which remaining micro-economic issues still need to be more clearly identified and addressed. Income distribution effects continue to be controversial. We now consider some of these issues in greater detail.

MACRO-ECONOMIC PERFORMANCE

It has been well documented that by the mid-1980s, New Zealand's macro-economic problems included chronically low economic and productivity growth, significant fiscal and external imbalances, high and variable average inflation rates, significant disguised and rising unemployment, and potential public and external debt sustainability problems. Major progress has been made in correcting these since then, but maintenance of the stable macro-economic policies so necessary to underpin future economic and productivity growth and improved living standards remains an ongoing challenge.

Like many other countries, New Zealand has successfully reduced unsatisfactorily high and variable inflation rates to underlying rates which have been low and stable since December 1991. This quest for ongoing price stability, initially within a 0-2 per cent target range and more recently within a 0-3 per cent band, was tackled from 1987 to 1990 by conventional monetary disinflation policies and thereafter within the framework of the now internationally well-known Reserve Bank of New Zealand Act (1989). Sacrifice ratios associated with this major inflation reduction show that New Zealand's cumulative output losses have been relatively high, somewhat greater than those for Australia over the same period, but below those for Canada.[13] It is also inevitable that there will continue to be a range of challenges to the delivery of ongoing price stability, and important amongst these for New Zealand at present is inflation in the 'underlying non-tradeables goods' sector (see Figure 2.1). Despite significant progress in some sub-sectors, the market based disciplines on public and private sector economic agents operating in many non-tradeables goods and services areas still seem relatively weaker than those that economic agents operating in tradeables goods markets have been forced to wrestle with so successfully in recent years.[14]

Despite only modest economic growth rates recently, in the region of 2 per cent per annum, New Zealand's unemployment rate of 6.7 per cent for the June quarter of 1997 (and more recently 7.1 per cent for March 1998) is relatively low by OECD standards. The area of unemployment can also be regarded as a relative success story for economic policies of the past decade.[15] New Zealand's previously negligible unemployment rates began to rise from 1976/77 and, affected by both the disinflation and structural policies associated with the reforms, reached a peak of 10.9 per cent in September 1991 (see Figure 2.2).

Figure 2.1 New Zealand underlying inflation: tradeables and non-tradeables components (annual percentage change)

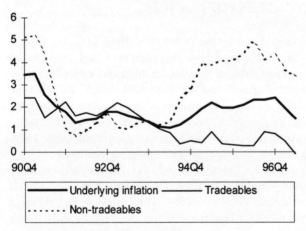

Source: Reserve Bank of New Zealand.

Figure 2.2 New Zealand total unemployment rate (quarterly data, seasonally adjusted)

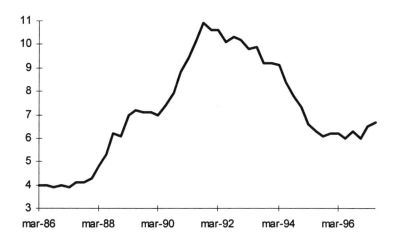

Source: Statistics New Zealand.

The analytical investigations done for the reform period are limited to date, but there are some useful preliminary insights. For example, Chapple et al. (1996) have examined the extent to which structural shocks associated with New Zealand's reforms might have been a prime reason for the rise in the aggregate unemployment to its peak of around 11 per cent. Much to their surprise, they found (p. 168) that it was primarily shocks from aggregate demand over the reform period rather than structural shocks initiated by the process of liberalisation which had been the dominant factor.[16] No research study has claimed conclusive evidence that New Zealand's Employment Contracts Act (ECA) has been the major contributing factor in unemployment falling from its peak. Nor is the ECA likely to have been the sole factor, as simultaneous cyclical growth and social welfare system changes will also have contributed. But the fact that Australia's economic growth has been similar to New Zealand's since mid-1991, and its unemployment rate has remained consistently above New Zealand's, help provide *prima facie* evidence that the ECA has probably contributed in a significant way towards improved unemployment outcomes in New Zealand. Similar views are expressed in Evans et al. (1996, p. 1880) and Kasper (1996b), and are consistent with counterfactual simulation results reported in Hall (1996a, section 5). But despite the encouraging aspects of these aggregate outcomes since 1991, including the fact that unemployment duration has also been declining from its peak, the non-accelerating inflation rate of unemployment (NAIRU) will probably remain around 6-7 per cent unless further institutional changes can be made to assist in reducing it further.[17]

With respect to fiscal deficits and surpluses, and net public debt sustainability, New Zealand has made significant progress in reducing a non-sustainable net public-debt-to-GDP ratio, from a peak of around 52 per cent in 1991/92 down to around 26 per cent for fiscal 1996/97.[18] Also, its government operating balance (excluding net foreign-exchange losses/gains) was turned around from a deficit of 4.6 per cent in 1991/92 to an estimated surplus of 5.0 per cent for 1995/96. This overall progress on the fiscal front has received favourable international attention.[19] Nevertheless, obvious current issues for New Zealand are its projected reduced operating surpluses[20], and the extent to which its projected net public-debt-to-GDP levels of between 20 and 30 per cent are optimal. I am not aware of empirical research which provides a satisfactory answer on the optimality question, and perhaps not surprisingly the Fiscal Responsibility Act of 1994 is framed in terms of 'responsible fiscal management' and 'prudent levels' rather than optimality.

New Zealand has run a deficit on the current account of its balance of payments for every year since 1974, and for the June 1997 quarter its deficit excluding payment for the frigate 'Te Kaha' is estimated to be around 5.8 per cent of GDP. The latter is uncomfortably close to the average deficit of around 6.6 per cent for the years 1982-87, despite the significant improvement from around 4 per cent to 1 per cent of GDP recorded between 1990 and 1994.[21] There are a number of key factors that can drive any country's current account, and in New Zealand's case one of the most consistently influential has been movements in its terms of trade. A particularly important factor in recent years, however, has been the rise in the deficit recorded for net foreign direct investment income, and that can clearly be related to the very significant investment in New Zealand over the past decade by overseas firms. Very considerable benefits can be associated with that foreign investment, though the net benefits do not yet seem to have been established conclusively through up-to-date empirical research. It should also be noted that there is insufficient research evidence to pass judgement on the extent to which structural adjustment associated with the reforms has influenced New Zealand's current account movements, relative to effects which may have emanated through terms of trade and other cyclical factors. The corresponding balance sheet position also gives little cause for comfort, though New Zealand's total overseas-debt-to-GDP ratio of around 80 per cent has been judged to be sustainable.[22] The government's foreign currency debt position is now approximately in balance, but despite this particularly favourable element, New Zealand's essentially private sector overseas-debt-to-GDP ratio is clearly very high by prudent international standards. The country will therefore remain vulnerable for some time to any substantial real and financial shocks, particularly those of an external nature.

Table 2.1 GDP growth rates of selected OECD countries (average annual percentage change, 1977-1996)

Period	New Zealand	Australia	United States	G 7	Denmark	Ireland	Nether-lands
1967-76	3.3	4.6	2.6	3.9	3.2	4.6	4.4
1977-84	1.7	2.9	2.9	2.8	1.9	3.9	1.4
1985-96	1.6	3.2	2.5	2.6	2.0	5.0	2.7
1993-96	3.9	4.2	2.6	2.0	2.7	6.8	2.3

Source: OECD (1994b, 1995a, 1996a, 1997h).

Real GDP growth rates for selected OECD economies are presented in Table 2.1. The figures here show that New Zealand's cumulative performance since the mid-1980s of 1.6 per cent per annum is still unfavourable relative to that of other comparable OECD countries. It was preceded by the slightly better, but still comparatively poor record of 1.7 per cent per annum for the eight year period 1977 to 1984. Together, those numbers support the view that New Zealand's *average* unsatisfactory growth performance is not a new (or post reform) problem, and should not be claimed as such. However (see Tables 2.3 and 2.4), New Zealand has recorded cyclically strong economic growth since its most recent business cycle trough in mid-1991. It shared this business cycle trough date with Australia and the United States, and in the six year period since then, the New Zealand and Australian economic growth rates have significantly outperformed those of many other comparable countries.

It is therefore not surprising that there remains considerable controversy in this area. There seems general agreement on matters such as New Zealand's historical growth performance having been relatively poor, there having been very considerable costs through to 1991 in the form of the output losses associated with correcting the major macro-economic imbalances, and on New Zealand's having lifted its performance very considerably since 1992. It also seems widely accepted: that '... there is still room for debate about the degree to which the recovery is structural rather than cyclical' (Evans et al. 1996, p. 1893); that '... it is still too soon to know whether New Zealand will join that small group of countries who have become 'growth success stories'' (Hall, 1996a, p. 66); and that '[t]o firmly establish a case either for or against having a sustainably better growth performance will require data for at least the peak (and subsequent trough) of the current business cycle' (Hall, 1996b, p. 12).[23] But there are also New Zealand economists who would agree with Dalziel (1997, p. 12). In the context of a detailed analysis of New Zealand's real per capita output data, he has recently argued that '... there is still no clear-cut improvement in the sustainable growth performance of the New Zealand economy ten to twelve years after the beginning of the reform programme ... [and] that substantial income sacrifices were incurred during the process (especially between 1987/88 and 1993/94) ...'. There seems to have been no significant research evidence published on the all-important counterfactual question of what economic growth rates might have been in the absence of the reforms.

Hall (1996b, pp. 3-7, 12) has examined the relative merits of the 'growth is now fantastic' versus the 'growth still feeble' ends of the spectrum. He has suggested first, that one can be at least cautiously optimistic on the sustainability of recently improved economic growth[24], and secondly that 'further progress is needed'. In the latter context, the challenge for New Zealand from now, therefore, is to be able to maintain *sustainably* higher potential growth rates somewhere in the 3.0 to 4.5 per cent range over the next decade. Views vary considerably on where in the range this can be. In depth research conducted by the Reserve Bank of New Zealand and the New Zealand Treasury has recently supported numbers of around 3 to 3.5 per cent per annum.[25] Others, such as Kasper (1996b, p. 12), have suggested figures around 4.5 per cent or above as potentially sustainable. To me, while 3 to 3.5 per cent economic growth rates are probably sustainable on the basis of policy progress to date, it also seems crucial that New Zealand should be aiming to achieve rates higher than 3 to 3.5 per cent if unemployment rates are to be reduced further and living standards are to be improved on a sustainable basis. Achieving those higher growth rates, though, seems unlikely if there are not further significant micro-economic changes and productivity gains, backed by commensurately improved domestic savings and sustainably high business fixed investment. Clear progress has already been recorded for some sectors, but New Zealand's overall experience to date suggests[26] that it takes more than six years of better growth and productivity performance to move from being an OECD cellar-dweller to maintaining sustainably higher trend rates.

In summary then, on the macro-economic front, New Zealand has made very significant progress over the past decade in achieving price stability, and in the unemployment and public debt sustainability areas. Maintaining hard-won fiscal surpluses will remain a challenge, and there remains both cautious optimism and controversy over the extent to which New Zealand has offset cumulated output losses and put itself firmly on sustainably high growth paths. Important for influencing the latter, as well as for assisting further progress on current account deficits and net external debt sustainability, will be recent and potential structural change and productivity gains. It is to these areas which the Chapter now turns.

STRUCTURAL ADJUSTMENT AND OTHER MICRO-ECONOMIC EMPIRICAL EVIDENCE

In this area, my selective evaluation of the evidence available is summarised under four headings: Structural Adjustment, Productivity, Goods and Services Markets, and Labour Markets.

Structural Adjustment

Structural adjustment and structural change are not easy concepts to operationalise[27], either in terms of convenient measures or in terms of how such measures can be translated into economic benefits and costs and policy terms. However, for the purposes of this Chapter, it is convenient to comment on the New Zealand evidence in the context of van Bergeijk and Haffner's (1996, pp. 12, 15) illustrative categorisation of 'two extreme approaches':

> [T]he case of New Zealand, where structural change was radically implemented without *a priori* analysis of the costs and benefits and where, as a consequence, large costs were put on the population. The second case is the Netherlands, ... where it is very difficult to initiate and implement structural adjustment policies because quantitative evaluation techniques are not sufficiently well developed ... Obviously, it is a wise policy to avoid the dangers that are inherent in the extreme strategies.

In their evaluation of structural reform in the Netherlands and New Zealand, Adema and Pilat (see Chapter 4) express the contrast in terms of New Zealand having '... implemented wide-ranging and deep structural reforms ...' and the Netherlands having taken '... a much more gradualist approach.' One of their key conclusions is that '... there are several roads to improved performance, and that country-specific conditions are an important determinant of the design of reforms to labour and product markets.'

I have no specialist expertise on the Netherlands experience and so make no comment on that. But from a New Zealand perspective, as stated above, there seems no dispute with New Zealand's programme of structural adjustment since the mid-1980s having been the most radical of any OECD country. But, it is also important to emphasise from recent empirical evidence that in New Zealand's case the 'large adjustment costs' are unlikely to be attributable solely or primarily to the structural adjustment reforms. Rather, and this is consistent with the van Bergeijk and Haffner view (p. 201) that '[t]he best foundation for micro-economic reform is a stable macroeconomic environment ...', the major adjustment costs in New Zealand's case have been associated with the period of cumulated aggregate output losses and increasing unemployment, and are almost certainly associated primarily with its having taken a significant number of years to reduce major macro-economic imbalances. Moreover, there has only recently begun to appear significant partial evidence on the structural adjustment issues. Some of this has provided encouraging evidence, though overall one has to say that to date the empirical picture remains incomplete and that much further detailed work is required.

At the aggregate level (though obviously reflecting sectoral data), two basic messages have emerged from the growth related work of Hall (1996a, 1996b) and the labour market study of Chapple et al. (1996). Hall's work presented simple real output based index numbers (Lawrence, 1984, p. 51) to assist preliminary judgement on whether any measurably different structural change occurred during the years 1978 to 1995.[28] The index numbers were calculated in both cyclical and non-cyclical form. They showed that structural change had been substantially greater in the 1985-95 period than for the years 1978-85, and that structural change during the contraction phase 1987-92 was more substantial than that during the expansion phase 1979-87. The quite high index value for the more recent expansion period 1992-95 is consistent with the rate of structural change continuing to be quite high in absolute terms and considerably higher than during the previous expansion. Chapple et al. (1996, pp. 151-6) used several structural indicators (including a Lilien index, a Beveridge-curve-based econometric analysis, and some mismatch unemployment indices). Their interim overall conclusion, with respect to the relative importance of demand and structural change as a source of unemployment over the reform decade, is that '... the importance of structural change has been exaggerated'. Their second key interim conclusion is that '... we have significant doubts regarding the claim that the increase in unemployment was due primarily to a shakeout from government or former government trading enterprises.'

With respect to evidence at the sectoral level of disaggregation, there remains much investigative work to be done. Some preliminary evidence on shifts in sectoral output shares is presented in Table 2.2.[29]

It is not surprising that there has been considerable variation in performance across sectors, but as yet there is no published analytical evidence identifying the possible reasons for significant differences.

Table 2.2   New Zealand real GDP by sector (percentage of total GDP, 1978-1995)

	Actual rates					Business cycle context			
	1978	1985	1995	78-95	85-95	79-92	79-87	87-92	92-95
						cycle	exp.	contr.	exp.
Agriculture	5.6	5.8	7.5	1.9	1.7	6.8	6.2	7.7	7.7
Fishing, Hunting	0.2	0.3	0.5	0.3	0.2	0.4	0.3	0.5	0.5
Forestry, Logging	0.9	1.1	1.2	0.3	0.2	1.1	1.1	1.1	1.2
Mining, Quarrying	1.4	1.1	1.8	0.4	0.7	1.3	1.1	1.8	2.0
Food, Bev., Tobacco	5.9	6.2	5.8	-0.1	-0.4	6.0	6.1	6.0	5.9
Wood, Wood Products	1.4	1.5	1.4	0.0	-0.1	1.3	1.4	1.2	1.3
Paper, Printing	2.6	2.8	2.5	-0.1	-0.4	2.7	2.6	2.8	2.5
Basic Metal Industry	0.9	1.1	1.4	0.4	0.3	1.0	0.9	1.2	1.4
Total Exportables	18.7	19.8	22.0	3.3	2.2	20.7	19.8	22.2	22.6
Textiles, Leather	2.3	2.4	1.4	-0.9	-1.0	2.1	2.3	1.7	1.4
Petroleum, Chemicals	2.1	2.3	2.4	0.3	0.1	2.3	2.3	2.3	2.4
Non-Metal Mineral Products	1.1	1.2	0.9	-0.1	-0.2	1.0	1.1	0.9	0.8
Machinery, Metal Products, Misc.	5.7	6.4	4.7	-1.0	-1.7	5.3	5.7	4.7	4.3
Total Importables	11.2	12.2	9.4	-1.8	-2.8	10.6	11.4	9.6	9.0
Total Tradeables	29.9	32.0	31.4	1.5	-0.7	31.3	31.1	31.8	31.6
Electr., Gas, Water	2.6	3.1	3.1	0.5	0.0	3.1	3.1	3.3	3.2
Building, Construction	6.9	6.0	4.3	-2.6	-1.6	5.5	5.8	4.9	3.8
Trade, Restaurants, Hotels	20.8	18.6	17.3	-3.5	-1.3	18.3	19.2	16.9	16.7
Transport, Storage	5.4	5.4	6.5	1.1	1.1	5.5	5.3	5.7	6.4
Communications	2.4	2.9	5.8	3.4	2.9	3.4	2.8	4.2	5.5
Financing, Insurance, Realty	10.4	11.6	13.6	3.3	2.0	12.3	11.4	13.8	13.9
Other Services	4.5	4.5	4.6	0.1	0.1	4.6	4.6	4.4	4.6
Tot. Non-Tradeables (excl. Dwell. and Gvt.)	53.0	52.1	55.3	2.3	3.2	52.7	52.3	53.2	54.1
Owner-Occ. Dwellings	4.1	4.0	3.9	-0.2	-0.1	4.2	4.1	4.2	4.2
General Gvt. Services	12.9	11.8	9.3	-3.6	-2.5	11.9	12.5	10.9	10.1
Tot. Non-Tradeables	70.1	68.0	68.6	-1.5	0.7	68.7	68.9	68.2	68.4

Sources: Calculations based on Philpott (1994, 1995) and Statistics New Zealand.

However, of potential note from Table 2.2 is that:

- The Communications, Financing, Insurance & Realty, Agriculture, and Transport and Storage sectors have all recorded noticeably increased output shares between 1978 and 1995, with well over half the increase coming between 1985 and 1995; and
- For the sectors that have recorded noticeable declines in their output shares between 1985 and 1995, there are a range of possible causal factors. These include their handling the contraction phase of the business cycle worse than the expansion phase, their failure to adapt successfully to gradually more demanding domestic and international market disciplines, and their being affected directly by the consequences of micro-economic reforms. Potential candidates for being in the latter category are: General Government Services (with 2.5 per cent of its 3.6 per cent decline in output share coming between 1985 and 1995); Machinery, Metal Products & Miscellaneous (with its 1.7 per cent decline over 1985-95 being greater than its 1.0 per cent decline over 1978-95); and Textiles, Apparel & Leather (with its 1.0 per cent decline during the reform period also being greater than its decline between 1978 and 1995).

So, as emphasised in Hall (1996b, p. 9, 1996a, p. 47), it will take further data observations and much more detailed investigation (including with some form of dynamic integrated sectoral-macro-economic model), before greater conclusiveness can be established on the role of micro-economic reform as a potential contributor to the substantial sectoral differences.

But what of any findings with respect to productivity gains and of structural change at more micro levels?

Productivity

Whilst there is no doubt that productivity is a fundamental driver of economic growth, international competitiveness and a country's overall living standards, it is also well known that at both the macro and aggregate sectoral levels, this is an area in which it is particularly difficult to produce robust empirical magnitudes and to draw credible conclusions. New Zealand is no exception, due in part to a wide range of legitimate measurement difficulties (e.g. Hall, 1996b, pp. 9-12; Janssen, 1996). These include the fact that the outputs for a number of 'service industry' sectors are defined by Government Statisticians as essentially the same as inputs, and therefore by definition cannot record substantial measured productivity gains.[30] Yet in New Zealand over the past decade, according to credible enterprise level measures, some of these service sectors have recorded vast improvements in quality and efficiency of delivery of output.

In a New Zealand context, then, it should not come as a surprise to others that there has been considerable debate about productivity performance over this period, and that there have been many claims that are flawed on methodological grounds. These include a number of attempts to tie good or poor productivity performance into specific events, or periods such as the period since May 1991 of New Zealand's ECA, with no appropriate adjustment for preceding and subsequent stages of the business cycle. My own methodological preference when attempting judgement on productivity performance has therefore been: to make appropriate adjustment for the stage of the business cycle; to evaluate total factor productivity (TFP) as well as a range of labour productivity measures; and to supplement measures derived from official data with suitable industry-specific and enterprise-level statistics.

Table 2.3 'Proximate sources' of New Zealand growth rates (1978-1995)

	Actual rates			Business cycle context			
	78-95	78-85	85-95	79-92	79-87	87-92	92-95
		pre-reform	reform	cycle	exp.	contr.	exp.
Compound Percentage Growth Rates							
GDP	2.0	2.4	1.8	1.5	2.5	0.0	4.8
Labour quantity	0.1	0.6	-0.2	-0.5	0.4	-1.8	2.7
Capital quantity	2.4	2.5	2.3	2.4	2.5	2.3	2.1
TFP	1.1	1.2	0.9	1.0	1.3	0.3	2.3
Labour productivity	1.9	1.8	1.9	2.0	2.0	1.9	2.0
Capital productivity	-0.4	-0.1	-0.6	-0.9	-0.0	-2.2	2.7
Percentage Points Contributions to GDP Growth Rate							
Labour quantity	0.0	0.4	0.0	-0.3	0.3	-1.1	1.6
Capital quantity	0.8	0.8	0.9	0.8	0.9	0.9	0.8
TFP	1.1	1.2	0.9	1.0	1.3	0.3	2.3
GDP	2.0	2.4	1.8	1.5	2.5	0.0	4.8

Sources: Hall (1996b, Table 3), calculations based on Philpott (1994, 1995) and Statistics New Zealand.

*Table 2.4   New Zealand total factor productivity by sector (annual
percentage change, 1978 - 1993)*

	Actual rates			Business cycle context		
	78-93 total	78-85 pre-reform	85-93 reform	79-92 cycle	79-87 exp.	87-92 contr.
Agriculture	4.68	3.10	5.99	5.49	6.47	3.88
Fishing, Hunting	7.42	3.70	10.21	7.64	13.59	-0.77
Forestry, Logging	4.31	2.51	4.79	4.43	3.59	5.01
Mining, Quarrying	2.04	-5.02	8.17	5.10	3.76	6.86
Food, Bev., Tobacco	1.91	1.80	1.83	1.75	2.84	0.03
Wood, Wood Products	0.04	1.96	-1.64	-1.28	0.31	-3.69
Paper, Printing	1.46	3.48	-0.38	2.03	3.29	-0.07
Basic Metal Industries	3.69	0.36	6.50	3.42	-2.22	11.65
Textiles, Leather	0.94	3.01	-0.80	1.16	2.71	-1.22
Chemicals, Petroleum	-0.77	-2.43	0.85	-1.62	-2.78	0.19
Non-Metal Mineral Products	2.30	3.88	1.16	1.31	3.07	-0.90
Machinery, Metal Products, Misc.	0.99	3.17	-1.02	0.66	1.91	-1.40
Electr., Gas, Water	2.22	3.20	1.34	2.74	2.75	2.69
Building, Construction	-0.68	1.19	-2.29	-0.62	1.29	-3.61
Trade, Restaurants, Hotels	-1.86	-1.56	-2.13	-2.12	-2.20	-1.98
Transport, Storage	3.97	3.06	4.82	3.84	2.32	6.30
Communications	6.26	4.05	7.36	6.18	4.93	7.22
Financing, Insurance, Realty	-1.38	-0.00	-2.61	-1.25	0.79	-4.49
Other Services	0.20	0.85	-0.53	0.37	0.30	0.14
General Gvt. Services	-0.37	0.92	-1.48	-0.37	0.81	-2.27

Sources: Hall (1996b, Table 6), calculations based on Philpott (1994, 1995).

Preliminary research evidence for New Zealand at the aggregate and
sectoral levels (see Hall, 1996b, pp. 9-11)[31], which recognises the above
important issues wherever possible, reports that:

- New Zealand's TFP performance at the aggregate level was 'markedly
  worse' than for other OECD countries for the period 1950-84 (Smith and

Grimes, 1990, pp. 141-6). As shown in Table 2.3, TFP has continued to be low *on average* at 0.9 per cent per annum for the 'reform and beyond period'; but when due adjustment of the average is made for business cycle movements, TFP is shown to be an unsurprising 0.3 per cent for the 1987-92 contraction phase, and an exceptionally high 2.3 per cent for the 1992-95 expansion phase of the currently incomplete business cycle. The latter rate provides promising but not yet conclusive evidence when compared with the 1.3 per cent recorded for the previous full expansion phase of 1979-87; and

• Not surprisingly, TFP performance has varied widely across sectors, and some sectors have been more affected by aggregate domestic and international business cycle movements than others. A full set of sectoral results appears in Table 2.4. While these sectoral figures can provide potentially useful insights, for the reasons already mentioned and because meaningful numbers for the current expansion phase cannot yet be calculated, they should be formed with more than the normal degree of caution. I confine myself here to pointing out: first, eight sectors show improved TFP performance when the average for 1985-93 is compared with that for 1978-85, whereas the average outcome for 11 sectors is worse. Secondly, by focusing on performance in the 1987-92 contraction phase, one can identify six star performers as: Basic Metal Industries; Communications; Mining and Quarrying; Transport and Storage; Forestry and Logging; and Agriculture. Further detailed research would be required to establish or reject causal linkages, but *prima facie* these sectors have all been directly or indirectly affected in significant ways by major micro-economic reforms and restructuring over the past decade, and by increased exposure to more internationally competitive trade and financial capital conditions.[32]

This evidence is far from conclusive, and there are clearly still big question marks over the extent to which New Zealand's productivity improvements to date can be sustained over time. But to me, it is evidence which is far more encouraging than a number of the gloomy conclusions highlighted in recent years from partial evidence.

Färe et al. (1996) have also undertaken a comprehensive study of productivity growth at the sectoral level. They utilised the Data Envelope Analysis technique, which allowed them to compute a constant returns to scale Malmquist productivity index to reflect TFP, and its efficiency and technical change components. There has been relatively limited experience in interpreting these measures empirically, especially for individual sectors which are compared to an aggregate best practice frontier for the New Zealand market sector. As a result, their individual sector results are currently seen as controversial and should be interpreted with considerable caution. Färe et al. conclude, however, that the economic reforms have had an overall positive impact on productivity growth performance of the New Zealand market sector, and that as one would expect the impact has been quite uneven across sectors. Technical change/innovation (including through openness to foreign knowledge and technology in a freer trade environment) were found to be key drivers of TFP growth, rather than efficiency change. The latter was regarded as being possibly hampered by labour market rigidities for the initial years of the post reform period. Particularly impressive improvements in productivity were associated with primary sectors selling their output primarily into export markets, and the 'Communications' and 'Transport and Storage' sectors significantly affected by various reforms.

There have been a small number of studies of productivity performance at more micro levels. Careful work has been undertaken for the telecommunications company, Telecom, by Boles de Boer and Evans (1996), and for the Electricity Corporation of New Zealand Limited (ECNZ) and the Coal Corporation of New Zealand Limited (CoalCorp) by Spicer et al. (1996).[33] The studies support a conclusion of these state owned enterprises (SOEs) achieving major gains in productivity over levels reached under previous government departmental structures.

However, whilst an examination of productivity outcomes is obviously important to any assessment of structural change, it is further important to examine in the next two sub-sections such other evidence as exists in goods and services and labour markets more broadly.

Goods and Services Markets

Not surprisingly, the evidence to date is piecemeal, but some important messages are starting to emanate and are considered here under four headings.

Traded versus non-traded goods sector adjustments
An important summary conclusion at the micro-economic level from Bollard et al. (1996, p. 22) is that the traded sector has had to adjust much more quickly and harshly than the non-traded sector. Whilst this adjustment has been due partially to the relative impact of structural reforms such as the removal of import quotas and other non-tariff barriers, and substantial reductions of tariff rates, it has also been due in a very major way to exchange rate appreciation effects associated with correcting fundamental macro-economic imbalances. Lattimore and Wooding (1996, pp. 350-1) have emphasised that resource reallocation following major trade reforms could have been expected to take some years to occur, and that while the post 1984

trade policy changes have provided some discernible positive trends, it is still too early to assess their full impact.[34]

Responses at the level of the firm

These include the closure and restructuring of existing firms, and can be related to the degree of openness of entry and exit. The importance of evidence at this level has recently been emphasised in an international context in McMillan (1997, sections 3-5). Early detailed case-study work reported in Savage and Bollard (1990, pp. 144-5) showed that while '... the surprisingly rapid rationalization process led by market forces ... led to considerable pain amongst firms and workers ... the adjustment process itself has been broadly effective.' At that point in time, which was of course prior to the ECA coming into operation in 1991 but after the passing of the Labour Relations Act of 1987, the most commonly cited policy constraint was reported as the industrial relations system. The most recent comprehensive study at the micro level has been that of Campbell-Hunt and Corbett (1996). After confirming (pp. 125-37) that by the end of the 1980s (the period also covered by Savage and Bollard), very few firms (10-20 per cent) had progressed beyond survival mode, they consider '... the weight of evidence ... suggests an escape from survival conditions since the nineties' and that '... management in New Zealand is now broadly comparable with that of the country's trading partners'. They suggest this is '... not inconsistent with what is known about the difficulties organisations face in responding to large-scale strategic dislocations', and caution that '... there remains a large number of organisations, approaching the majority, which show limited adaptation to the new environment.' Not surprisingly, then, they reach the conclusion (p. 133) that '... there is wide scope left for New Zealand firms to develop the foundations of sustainable advantage: in specialisation and networking; in building branded reputations with the consumer; in sustained product and process innovation; and in expanding the number of firms and overseas markets in which all of the assets of sustainable advantage are created.' On the question of the durability of the 'glorious economic summer' of the nineties being converted from a single 'season of excellence' to ongoing seasons of excellence, and after giving due weight to the fact that by definition ongoing sustainable advantage takes a long time to create, they conclude on balance (p. 137) that '... New Zealand managers are minded to press on with the organisational revolution of the nineties, and this must tip the balance in favour ...'.

The clear message from micro evidence at the level of the firm is therefore that sustainable successful structural adjustment is a process that can only be evaluated reliably over decades rather than years.

Performance of the public sector

Here too, in depth evidence has been relatively slow to emerge, but important empirical evidence is now available from Duncan and Bollard (1992), Duncan (1996), Spicer et al. (1996) and Evans et al. (1996, pp. 1872-7). The evidence is focussed on the outcomes of transformations of government (trading) departments or entities through corporatisation and/or privatisation, a process which has of course being going on in many other countries as well. In New Zealand, the legislative underpinnings for the public sector as a whole were provided by the State Owned Enterprises Act of 1986, the State Sector Act of 1988 and the Public Finance Act of 1989.

As in probably all other countries, changes in the education and health sectors continue to be controversial. Many have suggested that changes made to date remain far from complete, and it is also clear that there seems little available yet in the way of in depth empirical evaluation of degree of success.

In Duncan (1996, p. 416) it has been argued that the corporatisation and privatisation process of trading activities in both central and local government areas remains far from complete. Not surprisingly, the evaluative studies report considerable variation in performance, but the general tenor of them is of very significant success over relatively short time horizons. For example, Spicer et al. (1996, pp. 171, 203) have concluded that 'Overall, the New Zealand government's objective of gaining an improvement in the economic and financial performance of government owned enterprises by transforming them into SOEs does seem to have been achieved, at least for the organisations that we studied ... the successful transformations of these five government owned enterprises were not isolated cases.' Duncan (1996, pp. 416-9), from a more economics based perspective, points to the major gains in productive efficiency, and net gains to allocative efficiency and welfare to the economy as a whole, but is unable to offer any significant evidence on the perhaps potentially greater but difficult to measure dynamic efficiency effects.

Competition policy/'light-handed regulation'

New Zealand's competition policy, as enacted in the Commerce Act of 1986, features what has become known as 'light-handed regulation' in an economy-wide setting (see, for example, Evans et al., 1996, p. 1885, and Evans, 1996, pp. 7-8). There is therefore a presumption against industry-specific or price regulations, so as to minimise government and regulatory intervention and place reliance on actual and potential competition for the regulation of prices and monopoly behaviour. Evans (1996, p. 7) argues that actual and potential open entry to an industry are critical for the success of light-handed regulation, and that this form of regulation is more open than industry-specific regulation to achieving efficiency gains under conditions of rapid technical change.

The limited analytical empirical evidence presented to date is summarised in Evans et al. (1996, pp. 1887-90). There it is argued that light-handed regulation has had its most stringent test to date in telecommunications, and that based on evidence from Boles de Boer and Evans (1996), Ergas (1996) and Evans (1996) there is some initial presumption of the superiority of light-handed regulation in telecommunications. It is also suggested that the number of industries to which light-handed regulation is potentially applicable is quite wide-ranging. But as evidenced for example in the relatively slow movement to even the current state of competition in the electricity sector in New Zealand, in depth evaluation of light-handed regulation in a wider context will remain in its infancy for some time to come.

Labour Markets

Significant liberalisation of New Zealand's labour markets did not take place till the ECA became effective from May 1991, and so in this area too, evaluative empirical evidence remains in its infancy.[35] This is partly because of the limited time period which has elapsed since then, but also because the introduction of the ECA coincided with the most recent business cycle trough of mid-1991. It is well known that prior to the reforms, New Zealand's labour market system was highly centralised and heavily regulated, with a national awards system of wages, a legislated adult minimum wage and compulsory unionism. In almost complete contrast, it was replaced by the ECA, an Act defined 'to promote an efficient labour market', and designed to achieve a decentralised, more competitive wage setting system based on bargaining at the individual enterprise level. National awards and compulsory unionism were thereby removed. But as somewhat of a counterbalance, it also established a separate Employment Court and Employment Tribunal to assist in resolving contract disputes, and left in place certain statutory provisions for minimum terms and conditions of employment. The latter have since been the subject of considerable controversy, as have particular aspects of the ECA itself.[36]

As regards the evaluative empirical evidence published to date, some key messages in the areas of unemployment, the ECA, and income distribution are:

- As emphasised above in the section on Macro-economic Performance, Chapple et al. (1996) have established that unemployment rate changes over the reform period have been dominated by aggregate demand rather than structural change.

- Maloney and Savage (1996, pp. 210-11) have concluded that the economic reforms have had substantial effects on New Zealand's labour markets. But perhaps more importantly, they also consider that '... achieving better labour market outcomes requires a broader focus than just a reform of the labour relations system. It is the combination of welfare, product and labour market reforms (together with external pressures like changes in the terms of trade) that will alter labour market outcomes.' More specific amongst their labour market conclusions are that: almost all of the decline in unionisation in New Zealand since 1991 can be attributed to the ECA, with unionism also having become increasingly decentralised via single-employer agreements; and that within the context of real wage increases having been modest overall, '... employment growth (and real wage declines) occurred in industries experiencing the largest relative declines in unionisation in the post ECA period.'

- From a significant sized Survey conducted by the NZIER for its December 1995 Quarterly Survey of Business Opinion, written up in Savage and Cooling (1996), it was concluded (p. 33) that: the most notable labour market outcomes as a result of the ECA were said to be for larger firms and to have involved increased productivity and operational flexibility, greater training, and increased employment (especially part time and casual jobs), but also relatively small impacts on the firm's total wage bill, hiring and redundancy costs, and negotiation costs; the most common changes to employment contracts have been higher ordinary-time wages, lower overtime and penal payments, an increase in flexible work practices, reduced demarcations, increased multi-skilling, and increases in performance based pay. It was also recorded that three quarters of the firms regarded the net effect of the Act as positive for their overall performance, and that whereas firms were initially (in the 1993 Survey) focused mainly on cost-cutting and productivity gains, they have more recently put strong emphasis on increased training and higher wages for their employees.[37]

- The effects of the reforms on income distribution have been the subject of much partial, speculative comment. However, Easton (1996) has recently analysed this issue in the context of some degree of real wage stagnation and increased wage dispersion having started to occur prior to 1984 in both New Zealand and other OECD countries. Consistent with the labour market evidence cited above, he emphasises that macro-economic stabilisation measures increased unemployment and hence personal and household income inequality, as did flattening of the income tax scale in 1988, and measures in 1991 which reduced benefit levels and entitlements. He also suggests (p. 136) that '[i]f it is only market liberalisation, there is little evidence it impacted substantially on the aggregate economic distributions, although we noted some minor changes.' This can be seen also in the context of Stephens' (1996) economic analysis of social services, in which he concludes (p. 490) that 'The welfare state in New Zealand ... has been more enduring and resilient than many observers thought in 1991.'

In summary, the above still very much partial evidence on structural adjustment is consistent with the view that the greatest part of the adjustment costs can be associated with reduction of macro-economic imbalances rather than structural adjustment, that after more than a decade since major reforms were commenced there is significant evidence of positive effects, that key adjustments in the product markets have been taking and will continue to take very lengthy periods before sustainability can be assured, and that in both the product and labour markets the reforms have not been complete in their coverage.

SOME POLICY IMPLICATIONS

There is little dispute that the initial phases of New Zealand's economic reforms were closer to the 'big bang' than to the 'gradualist' end of the spectrum. There will, however, be debate for some time on whether the big bang approach has been justified in New Zealand's case, and on whether the sequencing of its reforms has been optimal.

My own interpretation of the evidence is that the big bang approach has been justified by the deep-seated and widespread nature of New Zealand's economic problems, by the resultant foreign exchange crisis of July 1984, and by the near certainty that continued adoption of previous piecemeal or gradualist approaches would have been insufficient. It is also clear to me from the New Zealand evidence that while some adjustments have taken place rapidly, one should not equate the adoption of a big bang approach with unreasonably rapid solution of fundamentally serious real sector and fiscal problems. Bollard et al. (1996, p. 19) and others have emphasised that, even after more than a decade of the reform process, the net outcomes for some areas of economic activity from New Zealand's big bang shock have been surprisingly difficult to measure. What this seems to suggest for other countries is that the degree of success of reforms must be linked with the magnitude of the problems faced and the estimated counterfactual outcomes, as well as the size and speed of the reforms themselves. Or put another way, even when a big bang approach is taken, it will take time for such well-recognised economic mechanisms as the non-instantaneous adjustment of inflationary expectations and other product and labour market rigidities to be worked through or changed through policy action.

On sequencing issues, a number of implications have emerged.[38] First, and perhaps least controversially, Maloney and Savage (1996, p. 211) found from their analysis of New Zealand's labour markets and policy that it is the combined pressure of welfare, product and labour market reforms, and external shocks that will affect labour market outcomes. Hence, it may be preferable to create pressure for reform through this combination of influences, rather than solely and initially through factor markets. Second, Lloyd (1997, pp. 124-5) has observed that New Zealand's reforms were different from conventionally regarded economic views on sequencing, i.e. they were back to front in the sense of fiscal stabilisation not preceding micro-economic reforms, and product and labour market reforms being preceded by reform of financial markets. However, one of the Evans et al. (1996, p. 1894) 'four important lessons' for other developed economies trying to improve their competitiveness is that, when a country is confronted by particularly major problems and has given due regard to the cumulated dynamics of the full reform processes required, the traditional sequencing literature '... need not dominate the practicable option of proceeding as rapidly as possible on all fronts'. Thirdly, perhaps the dominant particular suggestion in the small New Zealand literature on a possibly different sequencing has been that the radical labour market deregulation via the ECA may have come too late in the process (e.g. Spencer, 1990, pp. 255-7; Hansen and Margaritis, 1993, pp. 29, 34, 35). Evans et al. (1996, pp. 1871-2) have suggested that an earlier more flexible labour market combined with a faster reduction in the fiscal deficit could well have produced additionally beneficial effects through reduced adjustment costs. One clear advantage of the ECA having taken effect as late as mid-1991 was that it coincided with the most recently documented trough of New Zealand's aggregate business cycle. But would the benefits recorded to date have been as great at an earlier stage of the cycle? Whilst counterfactual evidence from a credible dynamic macroeconometric model is obviously not able to be totally conclusive, it can provide useful assisting evidence. Little such work of a counterfactual nature has been done for New Zealand, but results from the illustrative 'combined wages-productivity' shock reported in Hall (1996a, pp. 57-61) are not inconsistent with the arguments of those who have suggested there could have been significant real sector benefits from having introduced the ECA around five years earlier.

There seems considerable agreement amongst New Zealand's professional economists that, despite the cautious optimism expressed on progress to date, there is considerable need and scope for New Zealand's economic performance to be improved much further. Indeed, as well as there not yet being totally clear cut evidence on sustainably improved economic growth and productivity performance, recent events have shown that under current structural settings, New Zealand has not yet been able to sustain 4-5 per cent economic growth rates without generating unsatisfactory inflationary pressures. Not surprisingly, there is a wide range of views[39] about how fast policy and other changes in a 'third wave' of reform might take place, and in which specific areas they should occur. A selection now follows.[40]

The OECD (1996e, p. 39) has recently concluded that 'Over the past two years or so, [New Zealand's] policy efforts on the structural side have aimed at implementing, refining and complementing the initiatives launched in the late 1980s and early 1990s.' They refer specifically to consolidation of health and education reforms, restructuring of the electricity sector, and improvement of the financial management and accountability of local government, all of which have direct or indirect impacts on the growth and inflation performance of non-tradeables goods and services sectors.

With respect to the category of still unfinished structural policy business, it is not difficult to find either actual or potential candidates and proponents. For example, whilst the OECD (1996e, p. 2) has singled out in a broad sense '... skill development, trade protection, privatisation and health reform', it is perhaps more useful in the context of the current Chapter to list briefly some key possible candidates under the product market and labour market headings.

Further enhancement of product market competition could come from: the outcomes from the 1998 Tariff Review which will set a timetable to remove all remaining tariffs well within the 2010 deadline set by APEC[41]; further transformation of the processing and marketing functions of existing agricultural and horticultural Producer Boards[42]; the rolling back of increased costs of complying with central and local government legislation and regulations; and the corporatisation or privatisation of further central and local government 'commercial' entities.

In terms of further improving labour market efficiency and assisting in the further reduction of New Zealand's NAIRU, potential change has to be regarded in the context of New Zealand's now having one of the more deregulated systems of wage bargaining in the OECD. Some proponents of further change have been evaluating whether altering the existing forms of minimum wage and other provisions, and the current monopoly provision of accident compensation insurance through the Accident Rehabilitation and Compensation Insurance Corporation, could assist further on both the efficiency and NAIRU fronts. Current coalition government policy is for their review of existing industrial relations legislation[43] to be completed for the 1998 legislative programme. There is little surprise in the OECD's

(1996e, pp. 61-3, 87-8) synopsis of OECD Jobs Strategy recommendations for New Zealand. Its judgement is that in the area of workforce skills and competencies, New Zealand has fallen behind other OECD countries and that this is '... to a large degree probably responsible for its poor historical record of productivity growth.' New Zealand should therefore be giving highest priority to improvement of such skills and competencies. Productivity, the NAIRU, and overall living standards could all be enhanced further if significant improvement were to be recorded in these areas.

So, there obviously remain considerable challenges for New Zealand policy makers and other economic agents in the structural adjustment area.

CONCLUSION

Against the background of a set of macro-economic and micro-economic problems which were diagnosed as more deepset and wide-ranging than for other developed economies, New Zealand has experienced more than a decade of significant economic reform and structural change. During this time, many other countries have been reforming and adapting to varying degrees. New Zealand has made very significant progress over the 1984-1997 time period in most key macro-economic and many micro-economic areas, but still faces major challenges of sustainability and improvement on almost all fronts. The need for the latter is due variously to the relative ease with which macro-economic imbalances can re-emerge under lax policy settings, the still relatively inconclusive evidence on the sustainability of improved economic and productivity growth performance, a widespread desire to reduce the NAIRU further, and the likelihood that in recent years other countries' reforms have eroded a number of the comparative advantages New Zealand had achieved in key areas. In the absence of a further major crisis, another 'big bang' sequence of reforms seems unlikely, especially under New Zealand's current MMP electoral system. But the international and domestic economic evidence is certainly consistent with considerable ongoing adjustment being required.

NOTES

The views expressed in the Chapter are those of the author. They are not to be attributed, directly or indirectly, to any organisation with which he has associations. Without implication, I wish to acknowledge the excellent assistance of Alice Fong, and valuable comments from Mark Blackmore, Bob Buckle, Andrew Coleman, and an anonymous referee.
1. These were clearly documented at the time (e.g. New Zealand Treasury, 1984), even if not

universally accepted.

2. For discussion of this in the context of the economic growth performance of New Zealand, Chile and some other countries, see Hall (1996a, section 6). See also McMillan (1997), from a more micro-economic perspective and in a wider international setting.

3. This passage of time means that, following on from the relatively early consideration of the reforms in Bollard and Buckle (1987), a now fairly comprehensive set of economic studies is beginning to appear. Some of these contain major analytical work. The studies include Dalziel and Lattimore (1996), Evans et al. (1996) and Silverstone et al. (1996). Evaluative commentaries have also been written by Easton (1994), Henderson (1995, 1996), Brash (1996), Grafton et al. (1997), Lloyd (1997), McMillan (1997) and Brash (1998).

4. For example, Henderson (1996, p. 6) has recently expressed the view that '...by 1984 the direction and tenor of New Zealand economic policy, and the character of the system, had become out of line with the rest of the OECD...While New Zealand was not alone in being still a highly regulated economy, its economic policies in general, and the attitudes underlying them, bore an increasingly old-fashioned, antediluvian look.'

5. As indicated in the section on Macro-economic Performance, the chronic macro-economic problems included low economic and productivity growth, unsustainable fiscal and external imbalances, and high and variable average inflation rates. At the micro-economic level, the underlying problems included chronically inefficient resource allocation in most goods and services and labour markets, associated in particular with centralised controls and regulations over imports, prices, wages, interest rates and foreign exchange.

6. The July 1984 foreign exchange crisis and associated constitutional crisis are explained succinctly in Dalziel and Lattimore (1996, pp. 22-3) and Bollard (1994, pp. 98-9). Essentially, these crises commenced with a flight of capital from New Zealand following announcement of a snap election, continued with the Reserve Bank suspending trading in foreign exchange the day after the election, and lasted until the outgoing Prime Minister eventually conceded implementation of the 20 per cent devaluation of the New Zealand dollar agreed to by the incoming government. Dalziel and Lattimore (1996, p. 23) report that 'The Reserve Bank later calculated that the cost to the taxpayer of supporting the New Zealand dollar before the election, and of meeting its contractual obligations after the devaluation, was $797 million ...'.

7. Henderson (1996, p. 8) has emphasised the reinforcing nature of 'chronically poor performance' and the 'crisis in foreign exchange markets'. Deane (1995, p. 13) has suggested 'six lessons' which might be drawn from New Zealand's period of economic change. These include the needs: '... to start with a crisis or some other genuine stimulus to persuade people of the need for change'; and '... to get quality people to lead the process ...'

8. Different listings and accompanying descriptive commentary can be found in Brash (1996, pp. 10-32), Bollard et al. (1996, section 3), Evans et al. (1996, pp. 1859, 1863-70, 1895-1900), and Grafton et al. (1997, pp. 4-9, Table 1).

9. The intellectual underpinnings or underlying economic principles stressed by Evans et al. (1996, p. 1862) are '... the pursuit of: coherent policies on a broad front; credibility and time consistency; a comparative institutional approach; and efficient contracting arrangements'; while Bollard et al. (1996 p. 7) have singled out the 'new micro-economic' theories of contestability, principal-agency and public choice.

10. Lloyd (1997, pp. 118-9) has emphasised the 'simplicity' of reform methods and their 'least-interventionist' nature.

11. See Bollard (1994, pp. 86-7). New Zealand has a single legislative chamber in the Parliament, with no upper house, no state or provincial governments, and no written constitution. The then first-past-the-post (FPP) electoral system has, however, since been replaced by a mixed-member proportional (MMP) system.

12. As emphasised in Bollard (1994, pp. 73-4), New Zealand is a small country, geographically isolated in the South Pacific, with minimal international bargaining power. Unlike some of the small open European countries, therefore, it has not had the considerable advantage of

close physical and trade associations with a much bigger group of countries such as the European Union.

13. See Hall (1996a, sections 4 and 6) for details. It is also emphasised there that all disinflations have real output and employment costs, and that the ultimate benefits to output can take a long time to achieve. How great the associated benefits are, has yet to be computed for New Zealand.

14. See, for example, Janssen (1996, p. 13).

15. However, as emphasised in both Brash (1996, p. 4) and the OECD (1996e, pp. 52-3), while both Maori and Pacific Islander unemployment rates have also fallen since 1991/92, the rates for both groups currently remain around 15 per cent.

16. It is a technically difficult research exercise to separate the effects on aggregate unemployment into those that can be associated with aggregate demand and those associated with structural change. The associated empirical results are also often controversial. Chapple et al. (1996) have chosen and explained their methodology carefully, and have been appropriately cautious in drawing their preliminary conclusions.

17. This is clearly well below what it would have been immediately prior to the introduction of the ECA. I am not aware of any formal estimates but it is not impossible the rate could have been as high as around 10-11 per cent then. The OECD (1996e, pp. 48, 59) has recently argued New Zealand's NAIRU is at or below 6 per cent.

18. See, for example, the discussion and analysis in National Bank of New Zealand (1992).

19. See, for example, Shultz (1995, p. 7) and IMF (1996, p. 10).

20. Official (New Zealand Treasury, 1997, Table 2.1) operating-balance-to-GDP ratios are estimated to be a 2.6 per cent surplus for 1996/97, and projected to be 1.5, 1.8 and 2.3 per cent for subsequent years. The corresponding net-crown-debt-to-GDP ratios are 27.1, 25.5, 23.2 and 20.5 per cent. The NZIER's September 1997 *Quarterly Predictions* for the operating balance ratios from 1997/98 onwards are somewhat lower at 0.9, 1.1 and 1.7 per cent.

21. As of mid-1998, the current account balance is estimated to be around 8 per cent of GDP. Most forecasters now expect a steady but slow improvement from this figure.

22. See Colgate and Stroombergen (1993).

23. These views can also be considered in the context of the study of van Ark and de Haan in Chapter 7, which investigated the extent to which recently improved economic growth in the Netherlands has been primarily due to 'catch-up' rather than to outcomes from recent structural reforms.

24. A similar view is expressed in Bollard et al. (1996, p. 20).

25. See Reserve Bank of New Zealand (1996, p. 38) and New Zealand Treasury (1996, p. 22).

26. See Hall (1996b, p. 12).

27. Amongst the reasons for this is that structural change is usually a process which is spread over a considerable period, with any benefits (often unlike its costs) emerging over decades rather than years.

28. The attempted identification of potential causal factors from a general equilibrium and/or dynamic integrated macro-sectoral model was therefore left to future work. See, for example, the model-based work reported for Australia in Dixon and McDonald (1993), Murphy and Brooker (1994), and McKibbin (1994), and for the Netherlands in van Sinderen and Vollaard in Chapter 3.

29. This evidence can be read in the context of the evidence and commentary on sectoral economic growth rates presented in Hall (1996b, pp. 9-10), and the preliminary work on sectoral employment shifts which can be found in Hall (1996a, pp. 49-51).

30. This can seen in the context of the recently expressed view of Wagner and van Ark (1996, p. 20), that 'The extension of comparative productivity studies to services, which represent an increasing share in output and employment of economies of advanced nations, should now be a top priority on the productivity research agenda.'

31. Janssen (1996) has also recently reported on New Zealand's labour productivity performance

in the context of TFP growth.

32. On the latter, see for example Färe et al. (1996, pp. 97-8).

33. Specifically, Spicer et al. (1996, pp. 170-1) conclude that for the five SOEs they studied, 'In general, ... asset productivity increased substantially and so did labour productivity ... operating efficiency (as measured by SALES/ASSETS and other input-output ratios) is higher than previously.'

34. They consider that 'discernible trends' are appearing '... especially in agriculture and manufacturing with its shorter production lags' and that '... trade data available through 1993 and 1994 is only of limited usefulness in assessing the full impacts of the changes ...'.

35. Major pieces of published work are those of Chapple et al. (1996), Maloney and Savage (1996), and Kasper (1996a). These can be usefully read in conjunction with the OECD's view (1996e, section III), the comparative evaluation of labour market reforms and performance in New Zealand and the Netherlands presented in Chapter 4, and the detailed information presented in Harbridge et al. (1997).

36. For example, there continues to be residual differences of opinion between the ILO and the New Zealand Government which are likely to remain unaddressed (see Harbridge et al., 1997, pp. 6-7). There have been a number of studies which have argued that labour market efficiency would be improved further by the abolition of the Employment Court and of minimum wage provisions. In March 1997, the Coalition Government increased adult and youth minimum wage rates significantly, and there have been suggestions for an industrial relations framework under a revised Act (see Bowden, 1997).

37. Whilst this evidence based on 562 respondents is encouraging, it should also be seen against the summary view expressed in Campbell-Hunt and Corbett (1996, p. 128) that '[h]alf of all employers have shown no interest in using the new freedoms in the ECA to improve, or even to change, the nature of the workplace relationship.'

38. Succinct representations of New Zealand's sequence of reforms are available in Bollard et al. (1996, p. 10, Figure 1) and Evans et al. (1996, p. 1859, Figure 2).

39. See, for example, Savage and Bollard (1990, pp. 50-4), Dalziel and Lattimore (1996, Chapter 10), (OECD, 1996e), and Campbell-Hunt and Corbett (1996, 130-137).

40. The material in the remaining part of this section was prepared in October 1997. It should now be read in the context of a number of significant micro-economic policy measures set out in the 1998 Budget Speech (Peters, 1998). These measures were designed to further improve the efficiency of goods and services and labour markets, and the interface between social welfare benefit payments and labour market behaviour. Specifically, the measures included: tariffs on motor vehicles, which had been up to 22.5 per cent, to be removed from 15 May 1998; Producer Boards being requested to provide details by 15 November 1998 of their plans to operate in a deregulated environment without specific statutory backing; the removal of restrictions on parallel importing of goods protected by copyright; confirmation of the sale of further government owned non-strategic assets to proceed on a case by case basis; and as from 1 July 1999, employers and self-employed people to be able to choose between the ACC and private insurers for coverage of accident injuries. At the interface between social policy reform and the labour market, the measures included: the sickness benefit to be lowered to that of the unemployment benefit from 1 July 1998; the unemployment benefit to become the 'Community Wage' from 1 October 1998; and from 1 February 1999, persons receiving the domestic purposes benefit or the widows benefit to be subject to work tests. So, whilst these measures do not on their own constitute a 'third wave' of reform, they do provide clear evidence of the desire to continue with ongoing micro-economic adjustment of significance.

41. See Peters (1997, p. 9; 1998, p. 9).

42. See, for example, Evans et al. (1996, pp. 1890-3).

43. The key initiatives outlined in the Coalition Agreement are summarised in Harbridge et al. (1997, pp. 7, 61-2).

3. The Policy Experience of Structural Reform in the Netherlands

Jarig van Sinderen and Ben A. Vollaard

INTRODUCTION

About two decades ago the Dutch economy found itself in a depressing state. Low economic growth and - by Dutch standards - high inflation were combined with deteriorating public finances, growing unemployment and very low corporate profitability rates. At the end of the 1970s, policy makers paid little attention to the proper functioning of markets. Economic policy was infected by the so-called 'scala mobile', a vicious circle of inflation and nominal wage demands. However, in the early 1980s this policy was challenged by grave economic problems and was replaced by a 'moderate supply-side policy' characterised by cutbacks in government spending and wage moderation. After 1983, economic growth picked up, unemployment fell steadily, and the health of government finances improved. The recovery process took some 15 years to realise. In the second half of the 1990s, in particular, the remarkable recovery of the Dutch economy drew the attention of many observers. It is often referred to as the 'Dutch miracle' (see for example the *Financial Times*, 23-10-97). What brought about the change from a 'paralysed' economy into a 'running' economy? In this Chapter, we focus on the contribution of structural reform policies to the improved economic performance. In the Dutch case, structural reform was aimed at:

- Redefining the role of government;
- Increasing incentives and reducing distortions created by the tax and transfer system;
- And, more generally, increasing the efficiency and flexibility of the economy.

The programme of structural reform in the Netherlands had two fundamental characteristics. First, the structural reform policy was characterised by a sequential strategy, in which the most acute economic problems were attended to first. Second, it was pursued in co-operation with the 'social partners', i.e. the employers' organisations and trade unions. These organisations agreed to moderate wage growth and to shorten the working week. An explicit role was given to the social partners, although policy-makers kept their own responsibilities.

This Chapter is structured along the lines of the subsequent steps that were taken in the structural reform process. After discussing the structural dilemmas of the early 1980s, we focus on the reorganisation of public finances and social security, the policy of wage moderation and the improved functioning of labour and product markets. To give an overall picture of the macro-economic benefits of the structural reform policy, we conclude the Chapter with some tentative calculations on the basis of a semi-general equilibrium model.

Figure 3.1 Key economic indicators for the Netherlands (annual percentage change, 1980-1997)

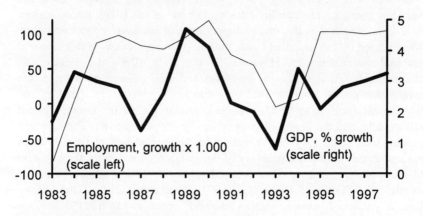

Source: Netherlands Bureau for Economic Policy Analysis (1998a).

STRUCTURAL DILEMMAS

In the early 1980s, the Dutch economy was characterised by low economic growth, deteriorating public finances, high inflation and gradually rising unemployment (see Figure 3.1 for the key economic indicators). Government spending as a percentage of GDP was among the highest of the OECD countries, with a bias towards social security spending. Public consumption and investment as a percentage of GDP were slightly below the OECD average. Between 1980 and 1984, the number of jobs declined by almost half a million, which was 10 per cent of total employment. Considering regulation, the high minimum wage depressed the labour-market opportunities at the lower end of the wage structure. Regulatory constraints on hiring and firing employees added to corporate reluctance to take on new workers when the economic climate improved again. As a result of the generous social security schemes and eligibility requirements, the number of people claiming sickness, disability and early retirement benefits exploded. The OECD has calculated that broad unemployment (including those in subsidised employment and benefit claimants) increased to more than 25 per cent of the labour force in 1985 (OECD, 1998d, p. 33).

Figure 3.2 Ratio of inactive to active people (percentage)

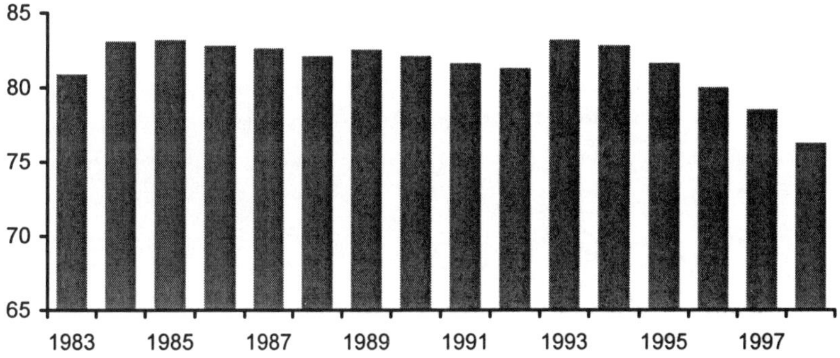

Source: Netherlands Bureau for Economic Policy Analysis (1998a).

Moreover, the combination of high social security allowances and high tax rates necessary to fund these programmes had a negative impact on demand for, as well as the supply of, labour. These factors led to a significant under-utilisation of the labour force, a large proportion of long-term unemployed in total unemployment, and, in general, low labour market participation rates. The ratio of inactive to active people remained at high levels in the 1980s, so that the recovery in the Dutch economy did little or nothing to benefit inactive persons during the 1980s (Figure 3.2). Partly as a result of low participation rates, the growth of GDP per capita lagged behind the growth rate in other EU countries (Figure 3.3). In 1983, the investment ratio was below the average for the EU and well below that for the US. In the second half of the 1980s, this position gradually improved (Figure 3.4).

Figure 3.3 GDP per capita, ranking of the Netherlands in EU-15

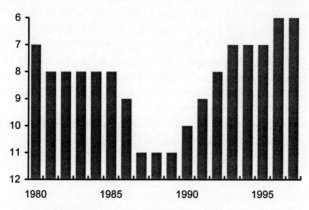

Source: Eurostat.

Figure 3.4 Gross investments (percentage of GDP, 1983-1998)

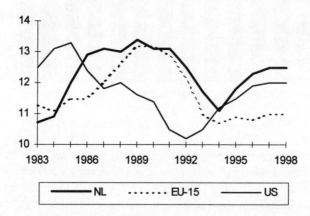

Source: Netherlands Bureau for Economic Policy Analysis (1998a).

It was the high and increasing level of unemployment in particular, combined with a government budget deficit, that forced policy makers to address the serious imbalances threatening to undermine the Dutch welfare state in the early 1980s (Wagner 1990, p. 170). Slowly, policy makers started to realise that the government should aim to improve the supply side of the economy (van Sinderen, 1990). The basis for economic policy shifted from the Keynesian to the Neo-classical paradigm. Ultimately, according to classical economists, the welfare of nations depends on the supply side of the economy and not on demand management. To stimulate investments in both physical and human capital, reconstruction and strengthening of the incentive structure should be given priority. The means to accomplish this were reform of public finances, the tax regime and the labour market, privatisation of government companies, deregulation and competition policy.

After 1981, when the commission on the restructuring of Dutch industry (the 'Wagner' Commission) published its report, things started to change. The Commission made three primary recommendations. First, moderation and differentiation of wages were considered necessary to ensure better functioning of the labour market. Second, a role for technology policy combined with attention for education was explicitly formulated as a goal of government policy. Third, industrial policy should be offensive ('picking the winners') rather than defensive ('helping the losers'), in order to stimulate the supply side in the long term.

In the first instance, there was considerable opposition from various sides against this proposed supply-side policy. After all, among Dutch academics the ruling paradigm was Keynesian (Wellink, 1987). For instance, in the early 1980s, a group of economists published an open letter in the national newspapers in which they criticised the supply-side oriented policy programme, because it would harm the demand side of the economy. The OECD, which was Keynes-oriented until the mid-1980s (Wellink, 1987), was not very helpful in preparing structural reform either. Not until 1983 did it pay any attention to structural adjustment in its *Economic Survey of the Netherlands*.

STRUCTURAL REFORM IN THE NETHERLANDS

In this section, we cover the specific design of the structural reform policy in the Netherlands over the last 15 years. Broadly speaking, the policy consisted of three successive steps:

- Reorganising public finances and social security
- Wage moderation
- Deregulation of product and labour markets

Reorganising Public Finance

Reorganising public finance was the cornerstone of Dutch structural reform. It started with government spending cuts to balance the budget and was followed by cuts in taxes and social security contributions. Tax cuts were not popular among mainstream policy makers in the Netherlands in the early

1980s (van Duijn, 1982). Most policy makers saw a reduction of government spending as the best policy device to restructure the Dutch economy and not tax cuts, because of the high budget deficit (van Bergeijk and van Sinderen, 1997, p. 6).

Table 3.1 Cuts in government spending (billions of NLG, 1983-1998)

Administration	Lubbers I (1983-86)	Lubbers II (1987-90)	Lubbers III (1991-94)	Kok I (1995-98)
Gross cuts	29	16	29	22
Extra expenditure	14	17	20	11
Net cuts	15	-1	9	11

The Lubbers I and Kok I administrations were relatively most successful in cutting back government expenditure (see Table 3.1). Painful measures were cuts in salaries of civil servants and social security benefits in 1983 84. Both the Lubbers II and III administrations had good intentions when they started, but in the end the net cuts turned out to be relatively small or even negative. However, the Labour-Christian Democrat Lubbers III government achieved much more than the Liberal-Christian Democrat Lubbers II administration. The second Lubbers government's bad record for public sector reform is the more striking in view of the improving economic climate in the second half of the 1980s. Economic growth and world trade were much higher than in the beginning of the 1980s and the interest rates were low.

In the early 1990s, GDP and employment growth slowed down (see Figure 3.1). Rising labour costs faced the Dutch economy with a minor crisis. To prevent a larger budget deficit, the Lubbers III administration decided to increase taxes (see Figure 3.5). Despite the economic downturn in the first half of the 1990s, the government managed to cut back spending still further. Paradoxically, it cut spending and increased taxes in a downswing, whereas Lubbers II cut taxes and increased expenditure in an upswing. Both policies were therefore pro-cyclical. Nevertheless, the economy recovered rather well in the following years.

After focusing on cutting spending in the 1983-86 period, the administration then switched the emphasis to reducing taxes and social security contributions. Although the Lubbers II administration was less successful in cutting back expenditure, it managed to restructure the Dutch tax system and to reduce the effective tax rates. One external difficulty for this administration was the decline in the price of natural gas, which reduced government revenues by about NLG 15 billion, or some 4 per cent, between 1985 and 1988. The drop in gas revenues was compensated rather smoothly and did not lead to a sharp increase in the budget deficit. As already mentioned, the Lubbers III administration (1991-94) increased taxes to balance the budget. Given the favourable international climate, the Kok I administration (1995-98) was able to cut taxes and social security contributions significantly. However, despite the favourable economic climate, net government spending cuts were substantially lower than planned (NLG 11 billion rather than NLG 22 billion).

Figure 3.5 Budget deficit and taxation (percentage of GDP)

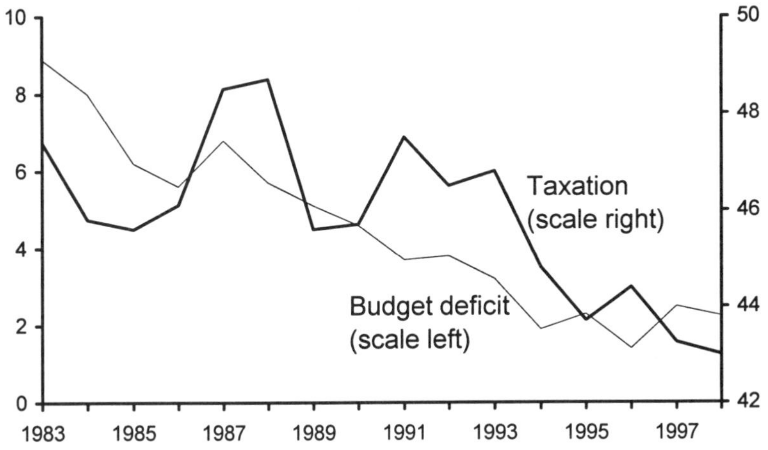

Source: Netherlands Bureau for Economic Policy Analysis (1998a).

Through the reorganisation of public finances, government spending as a percentage of GDP fell from 58 per cent in 1982 to an expected 45 per cent in 1998 (see Table 3.2). The reform of Dutch public finances was so successful because it was pursued more or less independently of the business cycle. The policy of further cutbacks in the early 1990s was particularly courageous. During these years, nearly all OECD countries tried to stimulate the economy by ways of demand management, whereas the Dutch government continued a deflationary policy. The transfers to households as a percentage of GDP also dropped between 1983 and 1998. However, income transfers to households still account for 56 per cent of total net government outlays. This implies that the restructuring of public finances in a more growth-induced direction has only been realised to a marginal degree. Public investments diminished as a percentage of GDP from 3.1 per cent in 1982 to 2.8 per cent in 1997. As a percentage of the total government expenditure they increased only slightly, from 5 to 6 per cent.

The Dutch policy of reorganising public finance differed from the American and British policies (van Sinderen, 1990). The US started by cutting taxes, in the hope that government outlays would follow, but produced a high budget deficit, whereas the UK increased taxes in order to balance the budget, which led to a recession and distorted incentives in the early 1980s.

Table 3.2   Composition of government expenditure (billions of NLG, percentages of total government spending)

	1982	1986	1990	1994	1997
Wages	12.6 (22)	10.8 (19)	9.7 (19)	9.7 (20)	9.3 (20)
Investments	3.1 (5)	2.6 (5)	2.8 (6)	2.8 (6)	2.8 (6)
Transfers	31.1 (53)	29.8 (54)	28.5 (57)	28.3 (58)	26.1 (56)
Other	11.6 (20)	12.4 (22)	9.2 (18)	7.5 (16)	8.3 (18)
Expenditure	58.4 (100)	55.6 (100)	50.2 (100)	48.3 (100)	46.5 (100)

Source: Netherlands Bureau for Policy Analysis (1998a).

Restructuring Social Security

The restructuring of social security took a considerable amount time in the Netherlands. Major reforms had to wait until 1987 and 1996. A striking example of the reform of social security was the cutback of sickness, disability and unemployment benefits (from 80 per cent to 70 per cent of last earned income). The Kok I administration (1995-98) focused on reducing the employers' social security contributions. Again, further reforms of the social security system were announced and are being implemented. The cornerstones of the restructuring operation are the privatisation of the health insurance system and restructuring of the disability insurance system. The unemployment benefit system has also been changed. The link between benefits and the claimant's employment record has been strengthened.

Wage Moderation

The labour market situation worsened quickly in the second half of the 1970s. Important reasons included the power of the trade unions, the government's tax policy and the indexation of wages, social benefits and subsidies to inflation. Repeatedly, the trade unions demanded real wage increases that outstripped the increase in labour productivity. Between 1977 and 1981, the government pushed wage costs up by increasing income tax by 2 per cent of GDP (Knoester, 1989). Indexation mechanisms led to an increase in government spending. A vicious circle resulted. Higher civil service pay led to higher taxation, which led to even higher wage claims, which led to extra government spending, etc. By 1980, automatic indexation mechanisms determined 75 per cent of annual wage increases (Visser and Hemerijck, 1997, p. 96). With small real wage gains and special allowances for low-paid workers, indexation mechanisms - often paid in flat rates - compressed wage differentials across skills and made it very difficult for unions and employers to respond adequately to changes in the labour market. This practice, combined with declining world trade, led to such a gloomy economic picture that economic policy had to change radically (van Sinderen, 1981).

In the early 1980s, many economic analysts and policy makers became convinced that wage growth would have to be moderated. The Wagner Commission, which advised the Lubbers I administration on structural reform, also advocated a policy of wage moderation. Advocates of wage moderation can be traced back to the mid-1970s. A study by den Hartog and Tjan (1976) was very influential. They showed that an increase in real wages above the increase in productivity implies that older vintages of machinery will become obsolete sooner. Because newer vintages are more capital-intensive, the production process will become less labour-intensive, even when the investment ratio remains the same. Whether machines will be replaced depends on the expected development of profitability. An increase in per unit labour costs will lead to an increase in the output price. In the end, this will lead to a loss of competitiveness and diminution of profits. A decline in profitability will have a negative impact on the incentive to invest. So high labour costs have two important effects. First, they make the production process less labour-intensive. Second, they have a negative impact on profitability, which leads to lower investments. As a result, employment growth slows down. Figures 3.6 and 3.7 show the relationship between wage costs, investment ratios and employment growth.[1]

Figure 3.6 Employment and GDP (1983-1998)

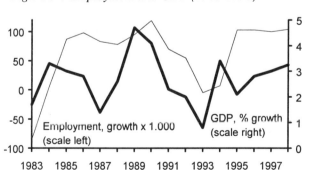

Source: Netherlands Bureau for Economic Policy Analysis (1998a).

Figure 3.7 Labour income share and investment ratio (1983-1998)

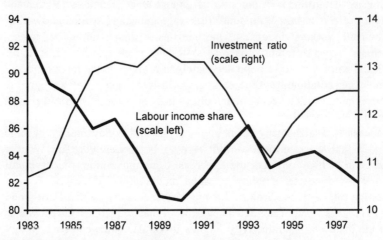

Source: Based on de Vries (1995).

The bad economic situation forced trade unions and employers' organisations to confer. Eventually, on November 24, 1982, the two sides signed the 'Wassenaar Agreement'. This agreement comprised the freezing of real wages for a number of years, abolition of the wage indexation mechanisms and a reduction in working hours. The government abolished automatic wage indexation mechanisms and announced the re-negotiation of existing wage agreements. Social security benefits and civil service salaries were frozen.

To emphasise the importance of wage moderation, the government made government spending cuts partly conditional on the growth rate of real wages. For instance, in 1983, cuts in government expenditure of NLG 10 billion were planned. However, the government promised to limit these cuts to NLG 7 billion if wage increases could be kept down by an extra 2 percentage points (Wellink, 1987). Actually, the wage increase was lower than projected and consequently the cuts in government spending were also limited. These agreements between government, employers and trade unions are seen as the foundations of the Dutch model of structural reform.

Because of the improving economic climate in the mid-1980s, the policy of wage moderation became increasingly difficult. To maintain this policy, the government promised to cut taxes and simplify the tax system. After 1990, the link between tax cuts and wage moderation was incorporated as a standard part of Dutch economic policy (de Jong, 1992). Earlier, in 1982, such a proposal failed.[2] At that time, the economic climate was far worse and the risk of an unsustainable high budget deficit as a result of tax cuts was much higher than in the 1990s.

However, to date, the changes in the institutional settings of the labour market have been relatively limited. Five institutional arrangements largely determine the wage formation process:

- The law on wage policy
- The statutory minimum wage
- The Extension of Collective Agreements Act (ECAA)
- Unemployment benefits
- The collective bargaining process

The wage policy reforms of 1987 abolished direct government intervention in wage formation. Only in crisis situations is the government allowed intervene. This change has increased the confidence of the social partners in the Dutch government. Since 1987, a Minister has only once threatened to intervene.[3]

The minimum wage has been, and still is, a subject of many political debates. Although the minimum wage as a percentage of average wages has decreased from about 77 per cent at the start of the 1980s to about 67 per cent in the 1990s, the law has never been abolished (Visser and Hemerijck 1997, p. 135). The net minimum wage is linked to net social security benefits. Therefore, it is very difficult to cut the minimum wage, which might then fall below subsistence benefit levels. In such cases, the already weak incentives to accept low paid jobs would disappear completely. The government has therefore chosen another way to stimulate the creation of low-paid jobs. A special reduction in labour costs for employers who hire low-skilled workers, and an 'artificial' public sector job scheme were introduced in 1994.

The ECAA, dating from 1937 - which imposes centrally negotiated wage rates on entire sectors (including for non-union members) - limits wage dispersion in the Netherlands significantly. In 1994, attempts were made to abolish this law, but both employers and trade unions successfully contested this move.

Although employment growth has been impressive in the 1994-98 period and labour agreements have become more flexible (for example, easier firing regulations and easier temporary employment terms), the participation rate remains low (see Figure 3.8), especially for lower qualified and older workers. Early retirement schemes combined with high tax rates encourage those older than 55 to retire early. The participation rate of this group is only 30 per cent. Further reforms are needed to address this problem.

Figure 3.8 Participation rates (Full Time Equivalents, 1994/95)[*]

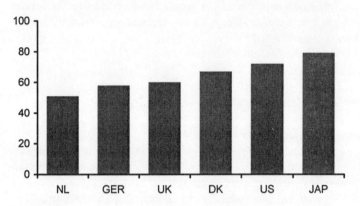

Note: * NL: the Netherlands; GER: Germany; UK: United Kingdom; DK: Denmark; US: United States; JAP: Japan.

Source: Netherlands Ministry of Economic Affairs (1997).

More Market, Less Government

Changing the composition of government expenditure from consumption to investment is one of the preconditions for better functioning of the economy. However, deregulation and privatisation are no less important. As Table 3.3 shows, the economic costs of regulation are high.

Table 3.3   Estimation of the costs of regulation (percentage of GDP, 1990)

Compliance costs social security	2.0 - 3.1
Net environmental costs	3.3
Road transport	0.1
Monopoly and cartels in notaries, banking, energy, public transportation (taxis) and pharmacy	0.2 - 0.5
Shop hours regulation	0.0 - 0.3
Costs of ECCA[*]	0.3 - 1.4
Segmentation of Europe before 1992	3.5
Common agricultural policy	1.8
Total	11.3 - 12.7

Note: * ECCA; Extension of Collective Agreements Act.

Source: van Bergeijk and Keuzenkamp (1997).

The dead-weight loss of taxes is widely known to economists, in contrast with the costs of regulation. The dead-weight loss of regulation should, however, be added to that of taxation. The welfare loss of the latter will increase exponentially when regulation increases (Browning, 1994). Regulation is often intended to address public needs (e.g. a cleaner environment). Therefore, the costs of regulation should be compared with the social benefits. From a political perspective, the distribution of the benefits is also important: much regulation favours special interest groups.

Since the early 1990s, deregulation of product and labour markets has been high on the political agenda in the Netherlands. The aims of this policy are to align Dutch and EU competition law and increase economic dynamism by creating a more healthy and competitive domestic business environment.

In 1993, the government overhauled Dutch competition policy and intensified the enforcement of competition rules. Horizontal price agreements were prohibited, as well as market sharing and collusive tendering. A new Competition Act came into force on January 1, 1998, prohibiting collusion unless there are proven public benefits.

Utilities are being reformed (including the liberalisation of the electricity sector) and state-owned companies are being privatised. There never has been large-scale nationalisation in the Netherlands, so that state holding in individual companies is relatively small. The ones that were owned by the Dutch government - the Netherlands Railway Company (NS), Schiphol Airport, DSM, government publisher SDU, the State Lottery and the Post, Telephone and Telegraph Company (PTT) - have either been privatised (PTT, DSM, SDU and the Lottery) or will be sold in the near future.

Alongside these measures, shop opening hours have been extended, the law on price regulation has been abolished and business-licensing law has been liberalised.

ASSESSING STRUCTURAL REFORM

In this section, we assess the general equilibrium effects of the structural adjustment of the Dutch economy, using the semi-general equilibrium model MESEM. We deal with the first two steps of structural adjustment (reorganising public finance and the policy of wage moderation) and the third step (competition policy and deregulation) separately. The first two steps will be assessed on the basis of realised results. We will try to draw some conclusions about the effectiveness of the policy pursued since the early 1980s on the basis of the model simulations. Because the Dutch economy is still in the process of deregulation, it is too early to assess the impact of this aspect of structural reform. Therefore, we determine the potential macro-economic benefits of future deregulation in a number of key sectors. The results that we give are highly tentative and should be seen as best 'guesstimates'.

The Model

MESEM is an applied semi-general equilibrium model that was built at the Dutch Ministry of Economic Affairs (van Sinderen, 1993). The model has been re-calibrated on a 1992 data set for the Netherlands. It is well suited to deal with aggregate shocks. MESEM has many properties of a general equilibrium model, but in the short term, disequilibria on the labour market may occur due to sticky real wages and other market imperfections, which have the effect that initial shocks may result in a disequilibrium in the labour market. In MESEM, the supply side of the economy is an important determinant of long-term economic performance. Four types of taxes on labour and capital are distinguished, as well as four types of government expenditure. The influence of taxes and social contributions on investments, labour supply and technological progress is modelled, as well as the wedge between total labour costs and net earnings. A wedge between interest receipts and payments is also modelled. In the model, a link is assumed between the investment ratio and export growth. Finally, it is assumed that capital is internationally mobile, whereas labour is assumed to be immobile.

The Reorganisation of Public Finance and Wage Moderation

To assess the macro-economic effects of the structural reform policies described above, we make a distinction between supply and demand effects of government policy. Switching off supply-side responses in the model isolates demand effects. Supply effects are determined by calculating the difference between the total effects and the demand effect. In the Appendix, the method is described in more detail. Table 3.4 shows supply and demand effects of government policy. We also include supply and demand effects that can be attributed to factors other than government policy, such as world trade. The first column shows the total simulation results of the MESEM model (e.g. average GDP growth of 3.2 per cent in 1983-97). The second and fifth columns show the total demand and supply effects. Columns (3), (4), (6) and (7) show the average change in a variable that can be attributed to either government policy or other factors.

Table 3.4 Demand and supply effects (1983-1997)

	TOTAL	DEMAND EFFECTS			SUPPLY EFFECTS		
		Total	Policy	Other factors	Total	Policy	Other factors
	(1)=(2+5)	(2)=(3+4)	(3)	(4)	(5)=(6+7)	(6)	(7)
GDP	3.2	2.4	0.2	2.2	0.8	0.4	0.4
X	5.5	3.7	-0.8	4.5	1.8	1.0	0.8
C	2.3	1.9	1.0	0.9	0.4	0.2	0.2
I	3.3	2.6	0.6	2.0	0.7	0.3	0.4
L	2.0	1.3	0.1	1.2	0.7	0.3	0.4

Note: * X: export; C: consumption; I: investment; L: employment.

The results suggest that 25 per cent of GDP growth in the 1983-97 period can be attributed to supply effects, i.e. 0.8 percentage points out of 3.2 percentage points GDP growth. The role of government policy in the economic recovery seems to be based mainly on supply-side measures (0.4 percentage points GDP growth through supply-side government policy versus 0.2 percentage points through demand-side policy). More than 15 per cent of the average GDP growth rate can be attributed directly to the supply-side policy pursued.

Both investment growth (*I*) and employment growth (*L*) have clearly been stimulated by government policy. A quarter of the growth of employment can be attributed to government policy. The policy of lowering marginal tax rates stimulates extra efforts. The marginal income tax rates have been lowered by approximately 1 percentage point per year and the marginal corporation tax rate by 2 percentage points (see the Appendix). In the 1984-1997 period, the collective burden declined by 1 percentage point a year. However, despite these lower tax rates, tax revenues have not declined but increased. So lower taxes 'can pay themselves back'.

Other factors dominate the demand effects. This is not surprising, because of the dependence of the Dutch economy on the growth of world trade. However, strong world trade growth alone is not sufficient for good export performance: Table 3.4 shows that more than 30 per cent of the export growth can be attributed to supply factors. Government policy, often said to be demand-unfriendly, has had a small but positive demand effect on the economy.

To conclude, the model simulations suggest that supply-side oriented government policy in the 1980s and the first half of the 1990s has had a positive influence on the economic development in the Netherlands.

Deregulation

The MESEM model can also be used to tentatively assess the potential benefits of deregulation.[4] This is an important and useful task, because of the existing lack of evidence of significant macro-economic effects that can be linked directly to the state of competition (OECD, 1993). The OECD's 1997 *Regulatory Reform* study analysed the benefits of deregulation in the key sectors of electricity, commercial airlines, road transport, telecommunications and distribution. The various sectoral changes in productivity, capital costs, profits, wages and technical progress are aggregated using the sectoral shares in business sector GDP as weights. This results in the following aggregate shocks which are used as exogenous variables in the MESEM model: pre-tax profits -1.6 percentage points, labour saving technological progress + 1.3, nominal pre-tax rate of return on domestic investment -2.9, and productive capacity + 1.1 percentage points.

Table 3.5 shows the general equilibrium effects of regulatory reform in the five sectors.[5] The first column shows that deregulation results in a substantial improvement of the budget balance of 0.8 percentage points of GDP. In the second column, the ex-post budget neutral policy option is shown. In this case, the budget surplus is applied to lower labour taxes in such a way that the budget deficit remains unchanged in the long run compared to the base scenario. The simulations suggest significant beneficial economic effects when deregulation is combined with lower taxes. The general equilibrium effects are substantial, both in terms of GDP (+ 4 per cent) and in terms of employment (+ 1 per cent, equal to 60,000 jobs). To conclude, deregulation can have substantial positive results.

Table 3.5   Long-run effects of deregulation in five key sectors (percentage deviation from baseline)

	Base variant	Ex post budget neutral
GDP	2.1	3.8
Employment	0.1	1.1
Labour productivity	2.0	2.7
Real pre-tax wage	2.1	2.5
Consumer prices	-1.8	-1.6
Budget balance*	0.8	0.0

Note: * Percentage points of GDP.

Source: van Bergeijk et al. (1997), p. 45.

WHAT HAVE WE LEARNED?

Structural reform in the Netherlands started in 1982 with the achievement of a broad consensus between the government, the trade unions and employers. This resulted in a gentlemen's agreement between government, trade unions and employers which combined a policy of reducing the budget deficit, wage moderation and restructuring of public finance. In the second half of the 1980s, the tax rate was decreased, and the tax system was simplified. During this period, the broad consensus weakened. The reductions in government spending stagnated. In the 1990s, taxes were increased again because of the threat of a rising budget deficit. As a result of high wage increases, job growth stagnated. Still, the cuts in government expenditure continued. In this period, the debate on the functioning and flexibility of product markets and the labour market began. After 1993, GDP started to grow very fast, and employment growth increased significantly. We conclude the Chapter with some lessons that can be learned from the Dutch experience of structural reform:

- A small open economy can clearly perform better (or worse) than its neighbouring countries. Our calculations show for example that a quarter of the increase in the employment rate in the Netherlands can be attributed to the typical Dutch approach of structural adjustment.
- The sequence of the structural reform policy is important for its success. The Dutch started by reorganising public finances and changing the wage formation process. Subsequently, taxes were cut, the social security system was reorganised and a start was made on the deregulation of labour and product markets. Structural reform takes many years. It is important to keep policy on track throughout these years - independent of the business cycle - to prevent benefits from disappearing.
- For the successful implementation of structural reform, responsibilities should be clearly distributed. Given the government policies, the employment situation is primarily the responsibility of the social partners. Therefore, the Netherlands has abolished its policy of active intervention in the wage formation process. Of course, the government still can influence the economic climate by its own means. The conditionality of wage moderation and public finance mentioned above had good results.

APPENDIX - DETERMINING DEMAND AND SUPPLY EFFECTS WITH THE MESEM MODEL

Table 3.6 shows the exogenous variables used for simulations with MESEM.

Table 3.6   *Exogenous variables (annual average percentage change, 1983-1997)*

Policy variables	
Government consumption	2.4
Government investment	2.3
Employment, government	-0.5
Basic allowances	0.1
Difference government and market wages	-0.8
Marginal income tax rate	-1.0
Marginal corporation tax rate	-2.0
Other variables	
World trade	5.1
Labour force	0.9
Foreign interest rates	-3.1
Labour productivity	1.2
Prices of competitors	0.2

Sources: Netherlands Bureau for Economic Policy Analysis (1998a, 1998b).

Table 3.7 provides an overview of the realisations and simulations based on the exogenous variables in Table 3.6 for a number of key variables.

Table 3.7   *Realisations compared to simulations with MESEM (annual average percentage change, 1983-1997)*

	Realisation	Simulation
GDP	2.7	3.2
Export	5.5	5.5
Consumption	2.3	2.3
Investment	4.2	3.3
Employment	1.6	2.0

Comparing realisations and simulations, we can conclude that the model forecasts relatively well over this period. Growth of GDP and employment is slightly over-estimated and growth of investment under-estimated. The over-estimation of economic growth and employment growth can be attributed to the fact that MESEM - being a general equilibrium model which supposes a perfectly functioning product market in the short term and a perfectly functioning labour market in the long term - is apparently too optimistic about the functioning of the Dutch economy. Further simulations show that MESEM performs better over the 1990s than over the 1980s, which can be explained as a success of structural reform.

We were able to make a distinction between supply and demand effects and policy and other factors by running two types of simulations. First, we made simulations including all exogenous variables (policy and other factors), but switching off the supply-side responses (including adjustments in labour supply, technological development and export performance). We assess what the result of government policy would have been if no responses had occurred in the supply side of the economy. Thus only the demand effects are determined.

Second, we made similar simulations but used the complete model, thus with the 'supply-side response switch' on. Subtracting demand effects from total effects gives the 'pure' supply-side effects on the economy. However, demand and supply effects cannot be separated easily. For instance, an increase in world trade is primarily seen as a demand impulse, but whether an economy can take advantage of this growth depends heavily on domestic production capacity. There is a similar problem for wage moderation. Wage moderation is partly induced by institutional arrangements and can be stimulated by tax cuts. As modelling institutional arrangements is very difficult, only the latter factor is included in our simulation. Therefore, the results should be interpreted with caution.

NOTES

1. Kleinknecht (1994) opposes this analysis. In his opinion, wage moderation will lead to lower technological development and thus a relatively obsolete production process and old fashioned products. However, besides the logic of the den Hartog and Tjan (1976) analysis, he implicitly assumes an unproved connection between new products and high labour costs.
2. This concerns the so-called 'Plan Schouten', launched by Schouten, a prominent member of the Social Economic Council, in January 1982. The plan was only published as one of three alternatives in the 1982 medium term policy advice of the Council. At that time the employers opposed the 'Plan Schouten', because they preferred a cut in government expenditures on its own and were not convinced that a cut in taxation would be effective, while the trade unions preferred a policy of redistribution of labour.
3. In 1994 Minister of Employment De Vries threatened to intervene in the wage negotiations, because he thought the desired increase in wages was excessive. In his opinion a crisis might emerge. This threat was enough to stimulate the social partners to lower their wage claims.
4. This section draws upon a report prepared by the Ocfeb Research Centre for Economic Policy for the OECD 'Regulatory Reform' study (van Bergeijk et al., 1997)
5. See van Bergeijk et al. (1997) for an analysis of the adjustment path.

4. Structural Reform in the Netherlands and New Zealand: Two Roads to Success?

Willem Adema and Dirk Pilat

INTRODUCTION

Over the past decades, the economic landscape of OECD economies has changed rapidly. Trade barriers have come down, some areas (notably the European Union) have seen an integration of trade and economic policies, there has been a shift to new exchange rate regimes, and domestic and international financial markets have been liberalised substantially. At the same time, OECD economies experienced a slowdown of real output and productivity growth, an increase in unemployment rates in many countries, widening income distributions in others, as well as rising public debt burdens (OECD, 1996b).

Poor labour market performance, in particular, has been a growing source of concern for OECD countries. The most visible symptom of poor performance has been high and persistent unemployment, but several countries also experienced weak employment growth and a low employment rate. In addition, rising income inequalities in some countries have combined with low productivity growth to exacerbate problems of poverty and social exclusion at the bottom of the income scale (OECD, 1997c). At the same time, social transfers have put upward pressure on government expenditure while weak employment growth has eroded the tax base.

In many OECD countries, the growing problems in labour markets have been aggravated by rigidities in product markets. Excessive regulation and a high degree of public ownership in some sectors was increasingly recognised as being obsolete, and possibly even harmful to economic growth (OECD, 1997i). In addition, there was recognition that government failure may be as capable of creating inefficiencies as is market failure.

Thus, it has become increasingly clear that many of the underlying problems - notably high unemployment and slow growth - are partly of a structural nature, and require the implementation of structural policies, including the reform of labour and product markets.[1] The policy response to inflexible labour and product markets has, however, been insufficient in many OECD countries. Although structural reforms have been significant in some areas - notably the financial sector and international trade, they have lagged in others, notably labour markets.

We discuss the experience with the implementation of the OECD Jobs Strategy in OECD Member countries, and particularly focus on the experience of the Netherlands and New Zealand in implementing structural reforms.[2] These countries are particularly interesting, as their roads to improved performance differ substantially in some respects. Whereas New Zealand has implemented wide-ranging and deep structural reforms since the mid-1980s, the Netherlands has taken a much more gradualist approach. This suggests that there are several roads to improved performance, and that country-specific conditions are an important determinant of the design of reforms to labour and product markets.

The Chapter is structured as follows. The following section provides a concise overview of the OECD Jobs Strategy and some lessons deriving from its implementation in OECD Member countries. The next section briefly discusses OECD economic performance over the past decades, and labour market performance in particular. It also compares the labour market performance of the Netherlands and New Zealand to that of a range of other OECD countries, both large and small. The fourth section looks in some detail at the policy response in the Netherlands and New Zealand to the slowdown in growth and deteriorating employment performance, while the fifth section comments on the effectiveness of these policies. The final section draws some broad conclusions and discusses some of the differences and similarities in reform between the two countries.

THE OECD JOBS STRATEGY: SOME LESSONS[3]

The OECD Jobs Strategy

The *OECD Jobs Study* of 1994 set out a broad programme of action designed to improve labour market performance in Member countries, in particular by lowering the unacceptably high rates of structural unemployment (OECD, 1994f). Subsequently, work has been undertaken to further develop and refine the appropriate policy response. The policy recommendations arising from this process can be grouped under ten headings (see below). Most of these recommendations have been followed up on a country-by-country basis in the work of the OECD Economic and Development Review Committee (EDRC), which has sought to derive specific recommendations for implementing the OECD Jobs Strategy in individual countries. Two recommendations of the OECD Jobs Strategy – policies to enhance the creation and diffusion of technical know-how and policies to nurture an entrepreneurial climate – have only recently been covered in thematic studies (OECD, 1998g, 1998j) and have therefore only partially been covered in the work by the EDRC.[4] These two recommendations are therefore not covered in detail in this Chapter.

Recommendations to enhance product market competition form an important element of the OECD Jobs Strategy, but policy action in this area also has its own momentum. Starting with comprehensive regulatory reform efforts in the United Kingdom and the United States, policies to strengthen product markets have moved beyond these countries to reform programmes in Australia, Japan and New Zealand. Within Europe, regulatory reform has gained momentum through the process of European integration, and many countries are now opening up markets that were, until recently, reserved for public monopolies. The OECD has recently proposed an integrated package of policy recommendations to further regulatory reform in OECD economies (OECD, 1997i), which is currently being followed up with a range of detailed country reviews.

The OECD Jobs Strategy

1. Set macro-economic policy such that it will both encourage growth and, in conjunction with good structural policies, make it sustainable, i.e. non-inflationary.
2. Enhance the creation and diffusion of technological know-how by improving frameworks for its development.
3. Increase flexibility of working-time (both short-term and lifetime) voluntarily sought by workers and employers.
4. Nurture an entrepreneurial climate by eliminating impediments to, and restrictions on, the creation and expansion of enterprises.
5. Make wage and labour costs more flexible by removing restrictions that prevent wages from reflecting local conditions and individual skill levels, in particular of younger workers.
6. Reform employment security provisions that inhibit the expansion of employment in the private sector.
7. Strengthen the emphasis on active labour market policies and reinforce their effectiveness.

8. Improve labour force skills and competencies through wide-ranging changes in education and training systems.
9. Reform unemployment and related benefit systems - and their interactions with the tax system - such that societies' fundamental equity goals are achieved in ways that impinge far less on the efficient functioning of the labour markets.
10. Enhance product market competition so as to reduce monopolistic tendencies and weaken insider-outsider mechanisms while also contributing to a more innovative and dynamic economy.

Progress in Implementing the Jobs Strategy

Progress in the 1990s in implementing the *Jobs Study* recommendations within specific structural policy areas differed considerably from country to country, in part because of the widely different starting positions of countries (OECD, 1997d, 1998i). In purely numerical terms, OECD countries took some action on almost two-thirds of the individual recommendations for reform. Action varied across policy areas, however. Most progress was made in strengthening the business climate by enhancing competition and improving conditions for start-ups and small firms. Much less action was taken in areas that might lead to a wider dispersion of incomes or that might antagonise insider groups in the labour market. Since structural unemployment remains high in a significant number of OECD Member countries and many recommendations have seen only a limited policy response, much remains to be done, however.

Given the great variety in policy responses, it has proved difficult to draw strong, area-wide conclusions at the EDRC reviews about reforms in specific areas in the 1990s. However, among the few general tendencies, a characteristic difference of approach can be identified between the countries pursuing comprehensive reforms and those adopting a more piece-meal approach. This relates to the impact of reforms on core constituencies in the labour market:

• Reforms in Australia, Canada, the Netherlands, New Zealand and the United Kingdom have typically affected very broad groups in the labour market, including those that may be characterised as 'insiders'.
• In contrast, reforms in some continental European countries have often affected persons at the margin of the labour market but with very little impact on core groups: for example, instead of relaxing general employment protection provisions, some governments have preferred to introduce short-term contracts and liberalise employment protection for part-timers or workers in small firms (e.g., Belgium, France and

Germany). Similarly, few countries have made large cuts to central parameters of unemployment benefit systems, such as replacement rates or the maximum duration of benefits, but many have tightened rules governing eligibility for benefits and controls on job-search behaviour.

Concerns about Social Cohesion

A key reason for slow and sporadic implementation of the OECD Jobs Strategy is the perception that undertaking reform involves trade-offs with policy objectives concerning equity and social cohesion. In particular, concern has been expressed in some quarters that the Jobs Strategy recommendations to enhance wage flexibility and to reform social transfer systems would conflict with the policy objectives of ensuring some degree of equity across members of the labour force or the population at large. The EDRC reviews did not provide conclusive evidence as to the nature and magnitudes of the potential trade-offs, though in some cases it was suggested that these objectives do not necessarily conflict when seen in a dynamic perspective. For example, increased employment as a result of policy reform will tend to at least partly offset the impact of increased wage-rate dispersion and restricted social transfers on income distribution.

In addition to the traditional arguments stressing market failure as a reason for government involvement in education, training and active labour market policies, many countries see these policies as a way of supporting horizontal equity. Some, most notably France, Belgium and the Nordic countries, resist a wider distribution of wage rates as a means to reduce unemployment and instead rely on these policies to bring the dispersion of individual productivity levels into line with the prevailing wage distribution. However, a compressed wage structure and generous social transfers limit the financial returns to private investment in human capital, and it is not clear to what extent public expenditure can compensate for weaker incentives for private investment in this area. There is also a question mark over the effectiveness of much public spending on active labour market policies (Fay, 1996), suggesting a need for further efforts to raise their efficiency if they are to play a substantial role in affecting the distribution of individual earnings capacities. Thus, it remains an open question whether a policy approach that sees public intervention in post-compulsory education, training and active labour market policies as a substitute for relative wage flexibility is effective, let alone cost-effective, particularly in a world of rapid structural change where shifts in demand for particular skills are likely to exceed the pace at which skill supplies can be adjusted through education and training.

Delegates to the EDRC from some countries, including France, Austria and Belgium, have also expressed reluctance to embark on broad and deep reform for fear of negative repercussions on social cohesion. Such repercussions are both undesirable in their own right and may also entail high economic costs. At the same time, however, high and persistent unemployment is itself likely to seriously impair social cohesion.

Concern for social cohesion need not imply a lack of policy action, however. At their meeting in Paris in 1998, OECD Ministers responsible for social policy agreed that social policies can best respond to relevant challenges by helping to maximise paid employment (OECD, 1998h, 1999). Under such an employment-oriented strategy, a high priority is attached to reducing the number of households with no adult in paid employment. Favourable economic and employment conditions as well as effective active labour market policies can help in achieving this goal. This strategy also requires minimising work disincentives arising from the interaction of tax and social security systems, especially as they impact on those with low incomes. Some countries have experimented with in-work benefits (particularly for families), improved incentives for social security recipients to take up part-time work, and continued entitlement to selected social benefits for a limited time once a person enters work. An employment-oriented social policy also means trying to limit any adverse impact that the financing of social programmes has on job creation. In recognition, a number of countries have recently reduced social security contributions and other non-wage labour costs, particularly for the low paid. Ministers indicated that more information is required on the effectiveness and consequences of these alternative approaches to implementing an employment-oriented social policy and called upon the OECD to devote a high priority to this task.

The process of policy design may also mitigate the impact on social cohesion. The Netherlands and, to some extent, Ireland, are examples of countries where significant structural reform programmes and macro-economic stabilisation policies have been introduced through a consensual process, involving the social partners and clearly not threatening social cohesion. Also, while the reform programmes in New Zealand and the United Kingdom were not implemented through a formal process of consensus, they have in fact met with considerable acceptance by the general public, as indicated by the fact that there is little political support for wholesale reversal of these reforms. A crucial common feature facilitating the reform processes both in the Netherlands, and, to some extent, Ireland, on the one hand, and in New Zealand and the United Kingdom, on the other hand, may have been the notion that individual reforms were part of a wider programme or strategy. Hence, specific reforms that affected particular groups met with less resistance because they were seen as part of an overall strategy affecting much wider groups and thereby possessing an element of fairness, which is an essential factor working for social cohesion.

Synergies and the Overall Strategy of Reform

Seeing structural reforms as part of an overall strategy is also important because reforms in one area produce better results if other areas are also reformed. The EDRC review process has confirmed the importance of one of the *OECD Jobs Study* conclusions that broad-based reform is likely to be more effective than reform focused in particular areas. A few prominent examples of such interactions include:

- Increasing incentives for seeking and accepting jobs is likely to be more effective when, on the one hand, product market reforms have ensured that labour demand will react swiftly and significantly to changes in wages and, on the other hand, regulations governing industrial relations, minimum wages and employment protection are reformed in ways which ensure that such a wage response will be forthcoming swiftly.
- The full benefits of increased product market competition will be reaped only if sufficiently flexible labour markets allow a swift reallocation of labour.
- Employment-conditional transfers are a means of simultaneously promoting employment and equity objectives, but if introduced in conditions of an artificially compressed wage structure they will either involve high budgetary costs because many workers will benefit or, if they are being phased out at a rapid rate to avoid this, will confront a large group of workers with very high marginal effective tax rates.

Synergies also exist between structural reforms and an appropriate setting of macro-economic policies. For example, progress in structural reform leading to lower unemployment rates may increase the credibility of macro-economic policies, with the end-result of reducing risk premia in interest rates and diminishing speculative pressures against currencies. Conversely, structural reform will be more effective when introduced in stable macro-economic conditions. For example, policies to increase work incentives through curbs on welfare provisions work best when the economy is generating a reasonable number of job vacancies. Similarly, relaxation of employment protection legislation is more likely to be followed by labour shedding when undertaken in a weak business climate (as seems to have been the case recently in Italy), whereas when activity is higher such deregulation may predominantly act to remove a disincentive for hiring. More generally, structural reform is usually aimed at giving greater scope for market forces. Where this leads to the destruction of economic rents - in the shape of excessive prices, wages or job security, or low work intensity - confidence could suffer. Macro-economic policy setting should, as far as possible, take this into account. It is noticeable that the countries where structural unemployment has fallen have all had rapid enough growth for actual unemployment to fall. However, at the same time there is a risk, which judged by past policy developments is non-negligible, that when economic conditions are relatively buoyant, the motivation could be weakened for undertaking necessary reform. Getting the balance right is obviously difficult but commitment to a long-term strategy of reform, with individual reforms implemented as appropriate, seems helpful.

Macro-economic Conditions

Macro-economic conditions are important in their own right. In the past, fiscal imbalances and uncertainty about medium-term inflation prospects led to high real interest rates. These, together with the general climate of uncertainty created by unsustainable policies, increased the cost of capital and reduced incentives for engaging in productivity-enhancing innovation activity. The result was reduced scope for real wage increases. Where real wages did not adjust flexibly, unemployment increased. This effect, highlighted at the EDRC review of France, underlines the importance of undertaking fiscal consolidation and maintaining price stability. It has been argued that moderate inflation may allow more rapid changes in relative wages and prices than in conditions of price stability, when reluctance to lower nominal prices and wages may retard adjustment, and also may enhance aggregate real wage flexibility in those countries where multi-layered wage bargaining puts a floor under wage increases. However, the counter-argument, presented at the EDRC review of Canada, is that once confidence in price stability has been established, wage floors should disappear and relative wage and price adjustment should be as quick as under moderate inflation, and with less uncertainty as to whether changes represent relative or generalised wage and price movements. As well, interest-rate premia will be lower.

Excessive macro-economic fluctuations can affect labour market outcomes in several ways. Countries with relatively large fluctuations in unemployment have usually also seen stronger rises in structural unemployment because increases in unemployment which were initially cyclical in origin have often tended, over time, to become structural. Indeed, the countries where structural unemployment rose the most in the 1990s were largely the ones where the cyclical volatility of unemployment increased significantly (Finland, Spain, Sweden, Switzerland). Some members of the EDRC have expressed the view that, correspondingly, New Zealand and the United Kingdom may not have reaped the full benefits of their structural reforms because fluctuations in unemployment became more pronounced in the past decade. Spain is a somewhat similar case where a further increase in already high cyclical volatility since the mid-1980s led to a rise in structural unemployment despite a number of important structural reform initiatives over the past decade. In contrast, the Netherlands succeeded in both reducing the extent of cyclical fluctuations and undertaking wide-ranging structural reform (OECD, 1997d).

The extent to which cyclical unemployment increases are transformed into higher structural unemployment depends on structural policy settings. Therefore, structural policy setting consistent with the recommendations of the Jobs Strategy is likely not only to reduce unemployment directly but also to reduce the risk that unemployment persists following a cyclical weakness in activity. It is noticeable that the United States, with a highly flexible labour market, has experienced considerable fluctuations in activity in recent decades with little or no upward drift in structural unemployment.

Making the Strategy Work

Improved labour market outcomes in the countries that have gone the furthest in implementing the Jobs Strategy, including Australia, Denmark, the Netherlands, New Zealand, the United Kingdom and, to some extent, Ireland, and deteriorating conditions in some of those that have not, is an indication that the Strategy works. At the same time, it has become clear how important the strategic aspect of reform is. First, pursuing a comprehensive approach to reform is likely to bring greater benefits than concentrating efforts in a few areas, even though the experience of the countries pursuing comprehensive reform suggests that the benefits of reform may still take a considerable time to show up. Second, comprehensive policy reform may ease some of the inherent policy trade-offs. By exposing wider segments of the population to structural reform, the process may be perceived as fairer, reducing strains on social cohesion. And reforms, which negatively affect the real incomes of labour market outsiders, will be perceived as less unfair if they are accompanied by other reforms aimed at getting the outsiders back into regular jobs.

The detailed recommendations by the EDRC reflected labour market conditions and existing policy stances that differed strongly across countries and policy areas. Nevertheless, there was some tendency for recommendations for high-unemployment, continental European countries to put greater weight on measures to increase labour and product market flexibility so as to enhance the economy's ability to adjust and adapt. For countries where flexibility was seen to be higher and unemployment lower, such recommendations played a less prominent role. However, where rising income inequality, poverty and slow real income growth were important problems, recommendations emphasised the need to upgrade skills and competencies and increase the effectiveness of active labour market policies, as well as to enhance the innovative capacity of the economy.

The fact that country-specific recommendations for implementing the Jobs Strategy have now been developed for most policy areas and the first cycle of EDRC reviews on its implementation in individual Member countries has been completed evidently does not mean that nothing more can be learnt. The process of deriving these recommendations and the EDRC reviews on their implementation in Member countries have themselves given rise to new insights. At the same time, the EDRC reviews have brought out more clearly areas where knowledge is weak. The linkages and trade-offs between reforms to enhance economic efficiency and the policy concerns for equity and social cohesion are a prominent example. Further country-specific work on the roles for labour market performance of entrepreneurship and technology could also provide new lessons. Continued monitoring of the effectiveness of the country-specific recommendations as they are being implemented is also likely to generate further insights, as is related work on labour market issues in other OECD Committees.

ECONOMIC PERFORMANCE AND THE LABOUR MARKET

Macro-economic Performance

From the mid-1970s onwards, macro-economic performance in OECD countries deteriorated rapidly. Initially, the concern focused on the combination of high inflation and relatively low output growth, that was disappointing by earlier post-war standards (OECD, 1994a). In fact, GDP growth in most OECD economies fell from around 4 to 5 per cent on an annual basis in the 1960s, to around 2 to 3 per cent - or even less - in the 1970s and 1980s (Table 4.1).

More recently, policy concerns have shifted to high rates of unemployment and the deterioration of public finances. Employment growth, which was already poor in most European countries during the 1960s, deteriorated further in the 1970s and 1980s, and employment actually fell in some OECD economies. In Europe, employment growth was particularly poor in the private sector, and most employment growth during the 1970s and early 1980s was in the public sector (OECD, 1994a). Unemployment increased rapidly across the OECD area, particularly in European countries. At the same time, labour productivity growth fell substantially in the United

States. European countries continued to catch up with the United States in labour productivity levels, although at a lower rate.

Table 4.1 Output, employment and labour productivity growth (annual percentage change, 1960-1997)[a]

	GDP growth			Employment growth			Labour productivity growth[b]		
	60-73	73-79	79-97	60-73	73-79	79-97	60-73	73-79	79-97
Netherlands	4.5	2.6	2.2	0.2	0.4	1.2	4.3	2.2	1.0
New Zealand	3.6	0.4	2.3	2.2	1.7	0.9	1.5	-1.3	1.5
United States	4.3	2.9	2.5	2.0	2.5	1.5	2.2	0.3	1.0
Germany	4.4	2.4	2.5	0.3	-0.3	1.4	4.1	2.7	1.1
France	5.2	2.8	1.9	0.8	0.4	0.1	4.3	2.4	1.8
United Kingdom	3.2	1.5	2.0	0.3	0.3	0.3	2.9	1.2	1.7
Australia	5.1	2.9	3.1	2.4	0.9	1.8	2.6	2.0	1.3
Belgium	4.9	2.3	1.9	0.6	0.1	0.0	4.3	2.2	1.9
Denmark	4.2	1.9	2.0	0.9	0.3	0.5	3.3	1.6	1.6
Ireland	4.4	4.9	4.6	0.1	1.2	0.9	4.3	3.7	3.7
Sweden	4.1	1.8	1.5	0.5	1.3	-0.4	3.6	0.5	1.9

Notes:
a Earliest available years are 1969 for the Netherlands and 1965 for France.
b GDP per person employed.

Source: Based on the OECD analytical database.

Table 4.2 Budget deficits and public debt (percentage of nominal GDP, 1981-1998)

	General government gross financial liabilities					General government financial balances				
	1981	1985	1990	1995	1998[a]	1981	1985[c]	1990	1995	1998[a]
Netherlands	50.9	71.5	78.8	78.5	69.5	-5.4	-3.6	-5.1	-3.7	-1.7
New Zealand	..	..	..	..	..	..	-6.8	-5.4	3.1	1.0
United States	36.2	49.5	55.5	63.1	60.3	-1.1	-3.2	-2.7	-1.9	0.4
Germany	35.0	42.8	45.5	62.2	64.5	-3.7	-1.2	-2.1	-3.3	-2.3
France	30.1	38.6	40.2	60.1	65.7	-1.9	-2.9	-1.6	-5.0	-3.0
United Kingdom	54.5	58.9	39.3	59.7	59.1	-2.6	-2.8	-1.2	-5.6	-0.8
Australia	..	31.0[b]	21.2	43.0	36.5	-0.6	-2.8	0.6	-2.0	0.2

Table 4.2   Budget deficits and public debt (continued)

	General government gross financial liabilities					General government financial balances				
	1981	1985	1990	1995	1998[a]	1981	1985[c]	1990	1995	1998[a]
Belgium	91.2	120.7	125.7	131.3	118.4	-12.7	-8.8	-5.5	-3.9	-1.7
Denmark	53.7	74.9	65.8	73.5	62.7	..	1.5	-1.0	-2.2	1.1
Ireland	77.4	104.6	97.2	85.7	59.6	-13.0	-10.9	-2.3	-1.9	1.5
Sweden	52.1	66.7	44.3	79.8	74.8	-5.3	-3.8	4.2	-7.0	0.8

Source: OECD (1998c).

Notes:
a Projections.
b Figure for 1987.
c For New Zealand: 1986, for Denmark: 1988.

Table 4.3 Public social expenditure (percentage of GDP, 1980-1996)[a]

	1980	1982	1984	1986	1988	1990	1992	1994	1996
Netherlands	28.5	31.0	29.9	28.6	28.5	29.7	30.2	28.7	26.7
New Zealand	16.5	18.2	17.0	17.5	19.9	22.2	22.5	18.9	19.2
United States	13.4	13.8	13.2	13.1	13.1	13.5	15.4	15.6	15.8[b]
Germany	23.7	25.0	24.0	24.5	24.9	23.2	26.7	27.5	28.0[b]
France	23.5	26.1	26.9	26.7	26.5	26.7	28.2	29.7	30.1[b]
United Kingdom	18.3	20.2	21.2	21.3	19.1	19.5	22.8	22.8	22.5[b]
Australia	11.7	13.0	13.8	13.8	13.0	14.5	16.5	16.1	15.7[b]
Belgium	24.6	27.0	26.7	27.5	26.4	25.6	26.6	26.8	27.1[b]
Denmark	27.5	28.0	27.3	25.6	27.7	28.1	29.7	32.6	31.4
Ireland	17.6	18.4	17.9	23.1	20.8	19.2	20.4	20.0	18.4
Sweden	29.8	30.9	30.0	31.2	32.0	32.2	36.4	35.9	33.0[b]

Notes:
a Excluding mandatory and voluntary social benefits provided through the private sector. The indicators here also abstract from the impact of the tax system, see Adema and Einerhand (1998).
b Data for 1995.

Source: OECD (1998f).

The deterioration in public finances and the rising burden of public debt reflect both the slowdown of growth and the increase in public spending during this period (Table 4.2). Public social expenditure makes up about 40 per cent of total government outlays in most European countries (OECD, 1995b), and the Netherlands, among several European countries, devotes close to 30 per cent of GDP to public social spending (Table 4.3 and OECD, 1998h).[5] At the same time, the tax burden on labour rose substantially in most countries. Over the past decade, most OECD countries have made progress towards fiscal consolidation, primarily by focusing their spending on areas that involve the provision of classic 'public' goods and on areas where market failures or social policy goals require government intervention, and by improving the efficiency of government expenditures, i.e. by 'doing more with less' (OECD, 1997h).

Labour Market Performance

Unemployment and employment developments over the 1990s have been very diverse across Member countries. In part, this reflects different cyclical positions. But estimates of structural unemployment rates have also shown diverse trends, often moving in the same direction as actual unemployment rates. In some countries, including Spain, Italy and, to a smaller extent, France, structural unemployment rose from already high levels. In others, most notably Finland and Sweden, structural unemployment has risen abruptly from previous low levels. The big non-European Member countries, including Canada, Japan and the United States, have had broadly stable structural unemployment rates, as have some European countries.

The most encouraging developments were registered in Australia, Denmark, Ireland, Netherlands, New Zealand and the United Kingdom where falls in structural unemployment rates either began or continued in the course of the 1990s. Changes in structural unemployment rates have generally gone together with sympathetic movements in a range of other labour market indicators. This suggests that changes in structural unemployment in most cases represented real changes in labour market conditions, not just substitution between different support programmes or statistical re-classifications. At present, some countries, including Japan, Norway and the United States, combine low unemployment with high rates of labour force participation. By contrast, Belgium, France, Italy, Spain and, despite strong recent improvements, Ireland combine high structural unemployment with relatively low labour force participation. Other countries are in intermediate positions between these extremes.

The Experience of the Netherlands and New Zealand

Labour market performance in the Netherlands deteriorated rapidly at the beginning of the 1980s, with the unemployment rate reaching its peak at 14.2

per cent in 1983 (OECD, 1996d). An adverse demand shock (the 'second oil shock'), the rapid increase of real and minimum wages in the 1970s (Hesemans and van Rijn, 1986), and relatively fast growing male and female labour supply (OECD, 1996c) contributed to unfavourable labour market outcomes at the beginning of the reform era.

In New Zealand, unemployment remained at a relatively low level until 1987, to increase sharply from 1987 to 1992. The deterioration in performance can partly be attributed to the structural reform of product markets from 1984 onwards, that preceded labour market reforms. Product market reforms contributed to high wage growth - as pre-reform price and wage freezes were lifted - and led to an employment shake-out in manufacturing and the government, as trade barriers came down and the government sector was liberalised (Evans et al., 1996).

Over the past five years, labour market performance of both the Netherlands and New Zealand has improved markedly and their current performance compares favourably to that of many other OECD countries (Table 4.4). The following indicators highlight the improvement in labour market performance:

- In both countries, structural unemployment has fallen during the 1990s. At about 6 per cent of the labour force in 1996, it is below the OECD average of 7.1 per cent.[6]
- Austria, Japan, Switzerland, Norway and the United States are the only OECD countries with standardised unemployment rates below 5 per cent of the labour force in 1997 (OECD, 1998b). At 5.2 and 6.7 per cent of the labour force in 1997 respectively, standardised unemployment rates in the Netherlands and New Zealand are below the OECD average.
- Employment/population ratios (around 67 per cent) and labour force participation rates (around 71 per cent) in both the Netherlands and New Zealand are above the OECD average. For the Netherlands, this indicates a major improvement, as participation rates were very low prior to 1980, mainly due to low female participation rates.
- The increased participation of women is reflected in the rising incidence of part-time employment in the Netherlands. In 1997, 55 per cent of female employment in the Netherlands was part-time (OECD, 1998b). Part-time employment is also more prevalent in New Zealand than in most OECD countries.
- Youth unemployment rates in Denmark and the Netherlands are now below levels in Germany (10 per cent), a country with traditionally low youth unemployment rates due to the success of its apprenticeship system.

Although the labour market performance of both the Netherlands and New Zealand has improved markedly in the above areas over the 1990s, certain structural problems remain. Unemployment for low-skilled workers remains a problem in both countries, although relevant unemployment rates are below the OECD average. In addition, the incidence of long-term unemployment (LTU) – which stands at 49 per cent – remains a structural problem in the Netherlands. In New Zealand, the incidence of LTU (almost 20 per cent) is well below the OECD average, but the number of persons claiming invalidity and sickness benefits has grown sharply over the past years. Another important concern in New Zealand is high unemployment and low labour participation among certain ethnic groups, notably Maoris and Pacific Islanders (OECD, 1996c).

Table 4.4 Labour market indicators

	Structural unemployment rates[a]			Standardised unemployment rates		
	1986	1990	1996	1983	1990	1997
Netherlands	8.0	7.0	6.3	9.7	6.2	5.2
New Zealand	4.7	7.3	6.0	..	7.8	6.7
United States	6.2	5.8	5.6	9.6	5.6	4.9
Germany[b]	7.3	6.9	9.6	7.7	4.8	9.7
France	8.9	9.3	9.7	8.1	9.0	12.4
United Kingdom	10.2	8.4	7.0	11.1	7.1	7.1
Australia	8.1	8.2	8.5	9.9	7.0	8.7
Belgium	11.7	10.8	10.6	11.1	6.7	9.2
Denmark	8.6	9.6	9.0	..	7.7	6.1
Ireland	15.3	16.0	12.8	14.0	13.4	10.2
Sweden	2.1	3.2	6.7	3.9	1.8	10.2
OECD[c]	7.0	6.8	7.1	8.4	6.1	7.3
	Employment-population ratio[d]			Labour force participation rate		
	1986	1990	1997	1983	1990	1997
Netherlands	52.0	61.1	67.5	59.0	66.2	71.5
New Zealand	61.6	67.3	65.4	65.3	73.0	70.5
United States	68.0	72.2	73.5	75.2	76.5	77.4
Germany[b]	62.2	64.1	63.5	67.5	68.4	70.4
France	62.0	59.9	58.8	67.4	66.0	67.1
United Kingdom	67.0	72.4	70.8	75.9	77.8	76.2
Australia	62.1	67.9	66.3	68.8	73.0	72.5
Belgium	53.5	54.4	57.0	60.5	58.7	62.6
Denmark	71.8	75.4	75.4	79.6	82.4	79.8
Ireland	54.0	52.3	56.1	62.8	60.2	62.7
Sweden	80.2	83.1	70.7	83.0	84.5	76.8
OECD	64.8	65.2	64.8	70.8	69.3	69.7

Table 4.4 Labour market indicators (continued)

	Youth unemployment (persons aged 15-24)			Unemployment by educational attainment (persons aged 25-64), 1995		
	1983	1990	1997	Less than upper secondary education	Upper secondary education	Tertiary level education
Netherlands	21.1	11.1	9.7	7.9	4.8	4.1
New Zealand	..	14.1	15.0	6.7	3.3	3.2
United States	17.2	11.2	11.3	10.0	5.0	2.7
Germany[b]	11.0	5.6	10.0	13.3	7.9	4.9
France	19.7	19.1	28.1	14.0	8.9	6.5
United Kingdom	19.7	10.1	13.5	12.2	7.4	3.7
Australia	17.9	13.2	15.9	8.5	6.2	4.0
Belgium	23.9	14.5	21.3	13.4	7.5	3.6
Denmark	18.9	11.5	8.1	14.6	8.3	4.6
Ireland	20.1	17.6	16.1	16.4	7.6	4.2
Sweden	8.0	3.7	15.4	10.1	8.7	4.5

	Long-term unemployment[e]			Part-time employment[f]		
	1983	1990	1997	1983	1990	1997
Netherlands	48.0	49.3	49.1	18.5	28.2	29.1
New Zealand	..	15.5	19.5	..	20.0	22.7
United States[g]	13.3	5.5	8.7	15.4	13.8	13.2
Germany [b, g]	41.6	46.8	44.3	..	..	14.2
France	42.2	38.0	41.2	8.9	10.4	15.5
United Kingdom	45.6	34.4	38.6	18.4	20.1	23.1
Australia[g]	27.5	21.6	30.8	27.1	29.1	31.8
Belgium	64.8	68.7	60.5	9.7	13.5	17.4
Denmark	44.3	30.0	27.2	19.2	18.8	17.9
Ireland	36.7	66.0	57.0	7.1	9.0	16.7
Sweden	10.3	4.7	29.6	..	14.5	14.2

Notes:

a Based on national definitions.

b Data for 1983, 1986 and 1990 concern western Germany.

c For structural unemployment: 11 countries mentioned and Austria, Canada, Finland, Greece, Iceland, Italy, Japan, Norway, Portugal, Spain, Switzerland, and Turkey. For standardised unemployment: idem, excluding Greece, Iceland and Turkey but including Luxembourg.

d Defined as total employment divided by the working age population (15-64).

e Defined as long-term unemployment as a percentage of total unemployment.

f Defined as part-time employment as proportion of total employment.

g For Australia, Germany and the United States the observations grouped under 1997 concern 1996. German part-time employment figure for 1997 concerns 1995.

Source: OECD (1997a, 1997b, 1997e, 1998b and 1998c).

These indicators do not capture some items that are specific to the labour markets of individual countries. For example, the low employment-population ratio in the Netherlands is partly the result of the high number of claimants of invalidity benefit (IVB). The number of IVB claimants skyrocketed from 194,000 in 1969 to 882,000 in 1990, while in 1996 the number of benefit recipients was 853,000 (Statistics Netherlands, 1997b). Adjusting for the available work-capacity within the stock of IVB claimants suggests that the 1990 structural unemployment rate understated the 'real' unemployment rate by about 3.3 percentage points (Adema, 1993).

THE POLICY RESPONSE IN THE NETHERLANDS AND NEW ZEALAND

The reform processes in both countries were initiated by the emergence of structural economic disequilibria in the early 1980s. New Zealand was an early starter among OECD countries in the introduction of structural reforms, together with the United Kingdom. The reform processes took place within a macro-economic framework giving precedence to stability oriented policy objectives, such as sound public finances and disinflationary measures. Apart from 'timing considerations' the policy response varied with the different starting positions of the two countries. Therefore, the policy responses are treated within the national context of the two countries concerned.

Labour Market and Social Security Reforms

The Netherlands
The trigger to labour market reforms was the growing realisation that economic policies pursued until the beginning of the 1980s were becoming unsustainable in view of competitiveness, a deterioration of public finances and labour market outcomes and growing concern about the feasibility of maintaining a workable welfare state.[7] Dutch social security reforms were inspired by strong growth in public social expenditures, resulting from increased take-up and increased generosity. Spending on disability increased steadily throughout the 1970s and 1980s, while unemployment rose sharply in the early 1980s. The generosity of insurance benefits increased to 80 per cent of last earnings. Hence, taxes on labour were on a very high level.

From the mid-1980s, benefit levels were reduced, as insurance benefits (covering unemployment benefits and IVB) were cut from 80 to 70 per cent of previous earnings. Nominal benefits were subsequently frozen by disentangling benefit levels and wage indexation. Measures were also taken to reduce the numbers of beneficiaries, by tightening entry conditions

(OECD, 1996d). Most important in this context was the introduction of stricter medical assessments to entrance and permanence in the disability programme. Hassink et al. (1997) find that only 10 per cent of recent entries into disability (after the tightening of procedures) were related to redundancies, which compares favourably to earlier estimates of work-capacity in the stock of disability claimants (Aarts and de Jong, 1992). The introduction of policies targeted at volume reduction was enabled by a growing acceptance in the Netherlands that the degree of labour market slack was unacceptably high.

Table 4.5   Business sector labour costs (annual percentage change)

	Compensation per employee			Unit labour costs		
	average 1985-1995	1997	projection 1999	average 1985-1995	1997	projection 1999
Netherlands	2.5	2.5	3.6	1.3	1.4	2.3
New Zealand	6.0	2.9	2.9	4.7	0.9	0.9
United States	3.8	4.2	3.9	3.1	2.3	2.7
Germany[a]	4.3	2.2	1.9	1.9	-1.5	-0.3
France	3.7	3.3	2.4	1.5	0.8	0.8
United Kingdom	6.1	4.9	4.8	4.6	3.4	2.8
Australia	4.8	4.3	4.4	3.8	1.7	3.0
Belgium	4.3	2.0	2.7	2.6	0.1	0.6
Denmark	5.0	4.0	4.7	3.2	2.5	1.8
Ireland	4.8	4.9	5.9	0.9	-1.3	2.8
Sweden	6.8	3.6	4.0	4.4	0.5	2.1
OECD[b]	4.1	3.6	3.0	2.6	1.8	1.4

Notes:
a Including former Eastern Germany.
b Excluding Czech Republic, Greece, Hungary and Poland.

Source: OECD (1998b and 1998c).

Another issue of major concern in the Netherlands was the relatively high labour costs, and especially high payroll taxes. The response to this particular problem has been persistent wage moderation and the scaling back of payroll taxes, particularly for low-wage groups. As early as the mid-1980s, the awareness among social partners of relatively high wage costs led to a sequence of collective agreements that induced persistent wage moderation.[8] In effect, the Netherlands is performing well in terms of wage moderation: from 1985 to 1995 compensation of employees (2.5 per cent) and unit labour costs (1.3 per cent) in the business sector grew at a pace well below the OECD averages, contributing to improved competitiveness of the

Netherlands (Table 4.5, and OECD, 1998c). In real terms the Netherlands is doing better than its European trading partners, while New Zealand is the only OECD country with negative real wage growth between 1989 and 1994 (OECD, 1997b).

Non-wage labour costs have declined in the Netherlands. The total tax wedge decreased from 46.8 per cent in 1991, to 42.5 per cent of gross labour costs in 1994, but the average tax wedge on labour remains high among OECD countries (OECD, 1996g). In order to improve the employment prospects of low-paid workers, payroll taxes were reduced in 1996 for workers earning up to 115 per cent of the minimum wage. This led to an effective reduction of payroll taxes by 25 per cent at the minimum wage level. The minimum wage for young people is a proportion of the statutory minimum wage for adults and increases with age.[9] The low costs of employment for this category of workers have contributed to the relatively low youth unemployment rate in the Netherlands.

Policy makers in the Netherlands are acutely aware of the disequilibrium between supply and demand of low-skilled labour. The creation of the so-called 'Melkert' jobs has expanded the range of publicly provided services in a number of areas, and improved individual labour market outcome for some unskilled workers.[10] Wages in this programme are limited to around 120 per cent of the statutory minimum wage. Other programmes to increase the employment prospects of the low skilled and the long-term unemployed help to reduce social security contributions for employers who hire these workers.

The *OECD Jobs Study* demonstrated that the increase in the OECD's summary measure of *gross* benefit generosity - which accounts for gross replacement rates and benefit duration for different types of households and levels of earnings - has been associated with the rise in unemployment (Figure 4.2).[11] In the Netherlands, benefit levels are linked to the statutory minimum wage, which in turn followed wage levels stipulated in collective agreements. At the beginning of the 1980s, this link was suspended. Hence, the gap between benefit levels and growth of average earnings widened. This development helped to improve the incentive structure in the Netherlands, which was further enhanced by entitlement restrictions.

Nonetheless, *net* replacement rates remain at a high level compared to most other OECD countries (OECD, 1998a). Immediate financial incentives to work vary with family composition, but also with age (Table 4.6). Social assistance benefits equal the net minimum wage for two-adult households with children, which limits the financial incentives for relevant beneficiaries. In contrast, net replacement rates for young people are significantly lower, as generous benefits are not available to them and social assistance benefits are only about 50 per cent of the basic social assistance rate for adults (VSV, 1997).

The social security reform process is ongoing, and recently resulted in an overhaul of administrative and social insurance institutions in order to contain abuses, introduce contestability in service delivery and improve efficiency of benefit delivery. Four executive insurance bodies (UVIs) under a supervisory tripartite body (LISV) now operate social insurance benefits. The reform process has culminated in the 'mandatory privatisation' of sickness benefits. For the first year of sickness, employers are now responsible for sickness payments, although these remain subject to public regulation. The introduction of employer-provided sickness benefits has also contributed to a decline in the ratio of public social expenditure to GDP after 1993 (Table 4.3). New disability insurance reforms were implemented in January 1998. This reform allows for premium differentiation and private reinsurance of the disability risk for a period of 5 years (OECD, 1998g). The effect on labour market outcomes and IVB take-up of these recent reforms is yet to be determined.

Table 4.6 Net replacement rates for four family types at two earnings levels[a]

	APW level[b]				2/3 of APW level[b]			
	Single	Married Couple	Couple 2 children	Lone parent 2 children	Single	Married Couple	Couple 2 children	Single parent 2 children
Netherlands	75	81	82	75	86	90	86	86
New Zealand	37	41	64	59	52	71	77	74
United States	58	60	59	60	59	59	50	52
Germany	70	66	80	80	73	74	76	80
France	76	74	79	80	85	85	87	87
United Kingdom	52	63	67	56	75	88	80	63
Australia	37	50	72	57	50	67	82	60
Belgium	65	57	60	66	84	76	76	82
Denmark	65	68	77	77	90	94	95	95
Ireland	33	49	64	59	45	64	72	71
Sweden	75	75	85	87	78	78	85	87

Notes:

a After tax and including unemployment benefits, family, and housing benefits in the first month.

b APW reflects the earnings level of the average production worker, see OECD (1997j).

Source: OECD (1998a).

New Zealand

Before 1984, the international competitiveness of New Zealand's export industries was slowly deteriorating, and much of the economy was heavily sheltered from the rest of the world (OECD, 1994d). This situation eventually became unsustainable. A range of structural reforms was implemented in response to an exchange rate and constitutional crisis in 1984. The reforms were wide-ranging but their pace was uneven, with financial and trade reforms leading the way, reforms of the product market coming somewhat later, and labour market reforms trailing behind.

Although labour market reforms in New Zealand have been far ranging, the most important reforms are relatively recent (Evans et al., 1996 and OECD, 1994d, 1996e). Prior to 1991, the government implemented some new policies, including a ban on unions of less than 1,000 members, some union contestability for groups of members and the introduction of the 1987 *Labour Relations Act*. This law was intended to achieve greater flexibility in bargaining structures, while still allowing for national awards. These reforms were quite limited, however, and there was no major increase in enterprise bargaining.

The crucial labour market reform was the implementation of the 1991 *Employment Contracts Act* (ECA). This act provides a legal framework for a highly decentralised wage-bargaining system, and replaced a rigid and complex system of industry-wide occupational awards (OECD, 1996e). Prior to the introduction of the ECA, New Zealand's system of wage bargaining was multi-tiered. It included an award system, which set minimum wages for various jobs at the national level; registered collective agreements which set minimum wage rates for various jobs at the enterprise level; informal house agreements, setting paid rates for particular jobs at the enterprise level; the national minimum wage; and general wage adjustments made by the government or the arbitration court.

The ECA aimed to encourage decentralised enterprise bargaining. Its main provision is to allow employers and employees to choose with whom, and within what structures, they associate. The Act made it illegal to give union members any preference in contracts, or to unduly influence an employee to belong (or not to belong) to an employees organisation or to negotiate a closed shop. The right to strike was somewhat limited as well. The Act preserved a statutory code of employment rights, including a minimum wage, holidays, sick leave, and protection against unjustified dismissal and occupational safety standards. The ECA also includes provisions for the settlement of personal grievances and disputes.

Apart from the reform of the ECA, there have been several other changes to labour market policies (Evans et al.,1996; OECD, 1996e, 1998e). The tax/benefit system was transformed, with major cuts and a tightening in the eligibility of unemployment-related benefits, a shift from direct to indirect taxation and a flattening of the schedule of income tax rates. Family benefit was abolished and substantial user charges were introduced for health and other services, although low-income earners were excluded. Social benefit rates were reduced by approximately 9 per cent, reducing government expenditure on these programmes and aiming to encourage work search by those on these benefits. As a result of these measures, the OECD's summary measure of benefit entitlements has come down considerably since 1987 (Figure 4.2). These reforms left high marginal tax rates in place, however. Relative to the average wage level, minimum wages have fallen considerably since 1987 (Figure 4.1).

Figure 4.1 Minimum wage relative to average earnings (1975 – 1995)

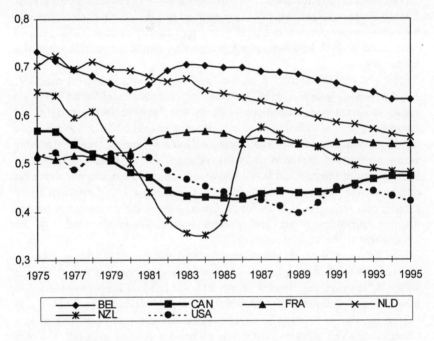

Source: OECD (1997b).

Figure 4.2 Summary measure of benefit entitlements (1975 – 1995)[*]

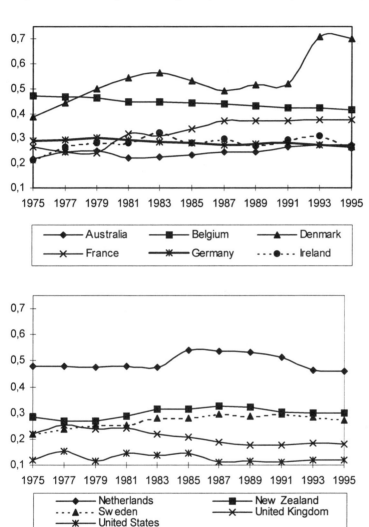

Note: * Average unemployment benefit replacement rates for two earnings levels, three family situations and three durations of unemployment, see OECD (1994e, Chapter 8).

Source: OECD Database on Unemployment Benefit Entitlements and Replacement Rates.

To address high marginal tax rates, and further improve labour market performance, a new range of reforms was introduced over the past few years, including the extension of active labour market programmes, a reform to benefit abatement, the strengthening of obligations to beneficiaries, income tax reductions and reforms to family assistance. The new government, formed in December 1996, also raised the minimum wage level somewhat in March 1997, from NZ$ 6.38 to NZ$ 7.00 for adults, and from NZ$ 3.83 to NZ$ 4.20 for teenagers (OECD, 1998e).

Product Market Reforms

Product market reforms can contribute to improved macro-economic performance and - over the longer run - to improved labour market performance. Regulatory barriers and lack of competition in product markets may result in poor sectoral performance - low productivity and technological backwardness, lack of innovation, and high and distorted pricing schemes - but may also have substantial negative systemic effects and distortions (OECD, 1997i). While structural reforms necessary to enhance product market competition may entail short-term dislocation of labour, over the longer run these policies could reduce monopolistic tendencies and weaken insider-outsider mechanisms, thus ensuring that labour demand reacts swiftly to changes in wages, and thereby contributing to higher levels of overall employment (OECD, 1994a and 1997d). Both the Netherlands and New Zealand have implemented far-ranging product market reforms over the past decade.

The Netherlands
Product market reforms in the Netherlands are relatively recent (OECD, 1996d). Horizontal price agreements, market sharing agreements and collusive tendering were prohibited in 1993 and 1994, while a new Establishment Act was introduced in 1996, substantially liberalising licensing rules. A new Competition Act came into force at the beginning of 1998. The Act is based on EU competition principles and is much stricter on anti-competitive conduct than the previous competition legislation. A new competition authority has also been established. Several sectors have been liberalised over the past years. Shop opening hours were substantially relaxed in 1996, the public telecommunications operator was privatised in 1994, and several other sectors are in the process of being liberalised over the next few years, partly in response to EU policies.

New Zealand

Product market reforms in New Zealand have been more comprehensive, which partly reflects the protectionist stance of the economy in the early 1980s. The New Zealand product market reforms entailed various measures, including the elimination of agricultural subsidies, import licensing and many tariffs, the privatisation and corporatisation of many state-owned enterprises, including the public communications operator, as well as the contracting out of many government services to the private sector.

The trade reforms, in particular, have had wide-ranging impacts. The reforms shifted from import licensing to a declining tariff schedule, removed export subsidies, reduced tax and industry assistance, liberalised financial markets and restrictions on foreign direct investment, and floated the exchange rate (OECD, 1994d). In addition, a free market in goods and most services was established between Australia and New Zealand. As a result, estimates of the rate of protection indicate a marked decline in assistance, although mainly for exporting industries. The New Zealand government has unilaterally committed itself to reduce tariffs to zero well ahead of the year 2010 (OECD, 1998e).

Reforms of the public sector, including the privatisation and corporatisation of public enterprises, have been more gradual (OECD, 1996e). The 1986 *State-Owned Enterprises (SOE) Act* established a framework for the operation of government-owned enterprises and provided for the corporatisation of nine departments in SOEs. The Act stated that the SOEs' primary goal is to operate as a successful business. If the government wants the SOEs to pursue non-commercial objectives, it can explicitly contract them to do so, while compensating them financially for the loss of profit. Although practice does not always conform to this framework, the SOE Act has radically changed government policies towards these enterprises. Furthermore, many public enterprises have been privatised over the past decade, Telecom Corporation being the most notable example. Recent government efforts focus on, amongst other things, improving the state of competition in the electricity industry (OECD, 1998e).

HAS STRUCTURAL REFORM BEEN EFFECTIVE?

The Netherlands

Most product market reforms in the Netherlands have been too recent to judge their effectiveness. However, Dutch labour market performance has improved considerably; unemployment has been falling in recent years, while employment/population ratios have risen and are currently above the average level for OECD countries. The main reason for improved performance lies in consistent wage moderation, particularly in comparison to the European trading partners (Table 4.5).[12] In addition, the flexibility of the labour market has been enhanced by the continuous increase in part-time employment. The role of 'temporary employment' agencies has expanded, helping to provide Dutch employers with a flexible supply of labour. Employment creation has predominantly been in the form of part-time jobs, and has been concentrated in the service sector (Netherlands Ministry of Social Affairs and Employment, 1996). Employment creation has favoured middle- and high-skilled labour, and the growth of job opportunities for the low skilled in the private sector has lagged behind.

Overall labour market outcomes were also favoured by a relatively modest growth of labour supply, particularly of male workers. In comparison with other OECD countries, productivity growth has been moderate over the past years. Past gains were to some extent 'artificial' as they also reflected the shake-out of older workers into disability programmes. The existing stock of disability beneficiaries remains one of the main structural problems of the Dutch labour market. Tighter access and stricter medical procedures have stabilised the inflow into the disability stock. Such measures should be maintained and supplemented with policies that effectively stimulate the reintegration of beneficiaries in the labour force.

The introduction of the so-called 'Melkert' jobs (see note 10) has improved employment possibilities for low-skilled workers. However, the incidence of long-term unemployment remains high and a further policy effort may be required. The effectiveness of these active labour market programmes should be closely monitored to ensure that undesirable crowding out effects do not dominate labour market outcomes.

Despite the fact that a substantial number of people still depend on benefit income, there has been a noticeable fundamental change among policy makers (benefit income is now typically dependent on job-search activity) and large parts of the population: living off the State is 'out', while work is 'in'. The challenge is therefore to maintain and improve the present structure of employment opportunities for all and particularly those benefit claimants who are physically able to return to the labour market. Persistent wage moderation and a significant improvement of the incentive structure have played an important role in improving labour market outcomes in the Netherlands. The continuation of such policies will contribute to a lasting improvement of labour market outcomes in the Netherlands.

New Zealand

Although the evidence does not all point in the same direction, most indicators suggest that New Zealand's macro-economic and labour market performance has improved substantially over the past decade.[13] At the macro-economic level, the complete reform package has resulted in a sharp break with New Zealand's pre-reform history of heavy regulation, import protection, high fiscal deficits and high inflation. Inflation has come down sharply and the state of public finances has improved markedly.

Furthermore, product market reforms have helped to markedly improve the competitiveness of New Zealand's industries, whereas the corporatisation and privatisation of SOEs are estimated to have resulted in large increases in productivity, real price cuts and quality increases (in many cases) and higher profitability of these enterprises. Employment in SOEs fell sharply, however, and this has probably contributed to the increase in unemployment over the period 1985-91.

The implementation of the 1991 ECA appears to have had wide-ranging effects on labour market performance (OECD, 1996e). The direct effects were manifold. First, the coverage of collective bargaining fell by about half from 1991 to 1994. Second, union density fell sharply. Third, there was a sharp decline in labour unrest. Fourth, during the first two years following the Act's implementation, there was an increased dispersion in the size of wage settlements, leading to a marked readjustment of relative wages. Fifth, there is some evidence at the disaggregated level that the ECA has led to increased flexibility and improvements in productivity.

The overall impact of the ECA is more difficult to assess (OECD, 1996e). It could be expected that the ECA would allow the labour market to function more flexibly by allowing relative wages to respond to skill shortages; would shift bargaining power towards employers, thus potentially lowering the non-accelerating wage rate of unemployment (NAWRU); and might allow more responsiveness to the different labour needs of firms, thus improving resource allocation, lowering the NAWRU and increasing productivity.

Given the relatively recent introduction of the ECA, it is difficult to estimate its overall impact. The Act appears clearly to have affected the seasonal pattern of wages and earnings, as negotiation is no longer concentrated on an annual wage round. Furthermore, the link between changes in real producer wages and a measure of skill shortages now appears to have broken down. This could imply that whereas a skill shortage in a particular industry in the past was likely to lead to general wage inflation, it is now more likely to lead to a change in relative wages. A recent OECD study (OECD, 1997h) found that actual wage growth in New Zealand was substantially below 'predicted' wage growth over the period 1990-96.

Finally, more disaggregated work on employment and wages suggests that the ECA, by reducing trade union membership, has led to an increase in employment and downward pressure on wages.

At the economy-wide level, labour market performance improved sharply after the implementation of the ECA. Estimates of the structural unemployment rate suggest a considerable fall, overall labour force participation has improved substantially, and business sector employment rates have improved as well (Table 4.4). Long-term unemployment has increased somewhat, however, although it remains at a very low level compared with most other OECD countries. Academic research attributes some of the fall in unemployment explicitly to the ECA - apart from the improvement in macro-economic conditions during the same period (Evans et al., 1996).

CONCLUDING REMARKS AND SOME LESSONS

Summing up, developments in recent years have provided evidence that high and persistent unemployment can be cut on a durable basis by adopting the right policies. The task is not an easy one, and undertaking it requires political will. However, there is no reason for countries to become resigned to high and persistent unemployment: a comprehensive approach along the lines of the Jobs Strategy holds out promise of improved labour market performance. Pursuing this approach should also help generate the necessary political momentum for reform - both because the Strategy has been seen to work, and because its comprehensive character means that both the benefits and the inevitable costs of adjustment will be widely shared. General policy recommendations for implementing the Jobs Strategy have been available for some time, but so far they have been acted upon only partially and insufficiently in most countries. Country-specific recommendations in line with the strategy have now been derived for most policy areas. What remains is to proceed with the practical implementation of these recommendations.

The experience of the Netherlands and New Zealand - and that of Australia, Denmark, Ireland and the United Kingdom - suggests that structural reforms can help to improve macro-economic and labour market performance. There are common lessons from the experience of these countries, but also some important differences in the ways policies were implemented. It should be noted, however, that labour market reforms in both countries occurred in a framework of stability-oriented macro-economic policies, i.e. a focus on achieving sound public finances and an effective control of inflation (OECD, 1997d). This reinforces the view that such a framework is very important to ensure improved labour market outcomes.

In some ways, the experiences of the two countries are quite different. Whereas the Netherlands used its consensus model - and close co-operation with the unions - to moderate wage growth at the centralised level, New Zealand moved towards enterprise level bargaining and largely broke the power of unions in the country. Partly, these differences reflect the starting position of the two countries (OECD, 1997d). The Netherlands, with high labour costs and payroll taxes, focused its efforts on achieving general wage moderation through centralised bargaining and tax reductions, a lowering of minimum wages relative to the average wage level, and the scaling back of payroll taxes. New Zealand, which was possibly the most protectionist OECD country in the early 1980s, focused much of its efforts on trade liberalisation and a reduced role for government. Consequently, product market and other structural reforms have been of much greater importance in New Zealand, in improving performance, than they have been in the Netherlands. Reform of the social security system has also been more important than in the Netherlands, which also reflects a different starting point.

There are also important similarities in experience, however. Both countries have sustained their efforts at structural reform over a long period, with improved performance - as far as labour markets are concerned - only emerging over the past five years. Reforms in both countries have also affected very broad groups in the labour market, including 'insider' groups (OECD, 1997d). The reforms were thus seen as part of a broad strategy. Specific reforms affecting particular groups were seen as part of a strategy affecting much wider groups, which implied an element of fairness. Although reforms in the Netherlands were more consensus-driven than in New Zealand, reforms in New Zealand have in fact met with considerable acceptance, and there is little support for reversal of the reforms. In addition, the experience of the two countries suggests some important interactions - and possible synergies - between reforms in different markets. For example, the full benefits of greater competition in New Zealand only emerged when labour markets were reformed, allowing a more rapid reallocation of labour.

The experience of the two countries, and their distinct roads to improved performance, suggests that there are several roads to success, and that the specificity of each country needs to be considered carefully when designing structural reforms.

NOTES

This Chapter draws on a large body of work at OECD, mainly that in the context of the OECD Jobs Study and the OECD programme on Regulatory Reform. The views expressed in this Chapter are those of the authors and cannot be attributed to the OECD or its Member governments.

1. OECD studies in the 1980s and early 1990s (for example, OECD, 1987a, 1990 and 1994f) already called attention to the structural aspects of poor economic performance in the OECD area.
2. This Chapter does not discuss structural reforms in financial markets, although these have often preceded reforms in labour and product markets.
3. This section is based on OECD (1997c, 1997d and 1998i).
4. Policy recommendations on entrepreneurship have been developed by the EDRC for five countries, namely Australia, the Netherlands, Spain, Sweden and the United States. Country-specific policy recommendations to enhance the creation and diffusion of technology will be developed for the 1998 EDRC report of France.
5. The high level of budgetary allocations to social spending in the Netherlands deserves some qualification. The Netherlands taxes its benefits rather heavily, clawing back about 5.9 per cent of GDP (at market prices) through direct taxes and social security contributions in 1993. Adjusting also for tax breaks for social purposes, government revenue from indirect taxation on consumption from benefit income, and mandatory private social expenditure, leaves the Netherlands - and Denmark - with a net public social spending level below that of Germany and close to the United Kingdom (Adema et al., 1996). The increase in gross public social spending recorded for Denmark from 1993 to 1994 is also related to changes in the tax system (Adema, 1998). Similar estimates concerning 1995 for a wider group of OECD countries will become available in the course of 1998.
6. In contrast to the standardised unemployment rate, the structural unemployment rate has been calculated using national definitions. The national unemployment definition that is 'en vogue' in the Netherlands differs from the standardised unemployment definition as based on ILO guidelines. According to the national unemployment definition in the Netherlands, a person is unemployed if he or she wishes to work for more than 12 hours per week. For standardised unemployment, the relevant threshold is only one hour per week. This difference in definitions is particularly important for the calculation of employment/population ratios and labour force participation rates.
7. Given the wide variety of opinions and characters in the Netherlands, the Dutch have long since realised that consensus is a prerequisite in maintaining a working society. Policy reforms therefore hardly ever take the form of 'quick fixes'. Although Dutch reform processes may develop slowly, they have the benefit of being accepted across a broad spectrum of the population, thus enhancing the effectiveness of reforms once they occur.
8. Although the 'Dutch model' is often used to advocate co-operation between the government and the social partners, social partners do not always operate in line with government policies. Government policies to reduce effective replacement rates took some time to materialise, as in the early stages of the generosity reforms, employers and workers topped up public benefits - often to 100 per cent. Only when this practice became unsustainable did unions and employers start to moderate relative increases. Furthermore, effective minimum wages - as stipulated in collective agreements - have increased in line with collective wage levels, while government policies reduced statutory minimum wages.
9. For persons who are 15 years of age the relevant minimum wage is 30 per cent of the minimum wage for 23-year-olds.

10. The Melkert-1 programme entails the creation of 40,000 jobs for long-term unemployed on a permanent basis. Employment is often related to the provision of security services (e.g. surveillance of buildings, car parks, etc.) and the provision of residential care (washing of patients and other nursing tasks that do not require a nursing certificate). Three other programmes, Melkert-2, 3 and 4, have been introduced in co-operation with local authorities and institutions, and aim to create temporary jobs on an experimental basis (OECD, 1998g).

11. These gross replacement rates do not adjust for the impact of taxation. Net replacement rates are generally higher than gross rates, as benefits are exempt from deduction of employee social security contributions in most OECD countries, and because the progressivity of tax systems ensures that the average tax rate on benefits is less than the average tax rate on earnings. Also, the summary measure does not account for housing benefits or allowances for child related benefits. Net replacement rates are normally more relevant than gross rates. Nonetheless, the summary measure is a useful indicator for developments in generosity over time. Martin (1996) provides a detailed discussion on these issues.

12. Van Sinderen and Vollaard in Chapter 3 and OECD (1998g) discuss the role of wage moderation in the Netherlands in more detail.

13. For an assessment of the effectiveness of New Zealand's structural reforms to date see OECD (1998i) and Hall in Chapter 2.

PART TWO

Modelling Structural Reform

5. Gains from Improved Sectoral Efficiency in Norway

Erling Holmøy

INTRODUCTION

The development of Computable General Equilibrium (CGE) models over the last decades has resulted in a large literature which estimates welfare effects of various structural policy reforms affecting the incentives facing producers and consumers in a market economy. Foremost, CGE models have been used to evaluate the welfare effects of reforms of the tax system and protective trade policies. However, as noted by e.g. Vennemo (1992), and Krugman (1992), the estimated welfare gains from both actual and more hypothetical reform proposals are typically rather low, ranging between 0 and 5 per cent of the initial consumption possibilities. These results suggest that the welfare potential from structural reform policies is of the same order of magnitude as normal economic growth over one or two years. Provided that the estimates are unbiased, such policies should of course still be implemented, but policy advisers should be careful not to create too optimistic expectations about the welfare gains.

However, one might suspect that these estimates include a negative bias because CGE models are in general not able to capture distortions creating inefficiency at the micro level. There is a lot of anecdotal evidence of waste of resources and X-efficiency at the micro level. In particular, there are lots of 'horror stories' about what is going on in government-controlled sectors.[1] On the other hand, in order to be operational, even the largest CGE models are confined to analysing reallocations of resources between relatively aggregated sectors of the economy. Thus, the hypothesis emerges that a major source for welfare improvement lies in inefficiency at a much more detailed level of aggregation than the ones that can be described in operational CGE models. Information about such inefficiency problems can only be obtained by detailed sector studies, and one might argue that a partial equilibrium analysis is the most relevant approach for assessing the potential welfare loss associated with the inefficiency.

Compared with CGE assessments however, the partial equilibrium approach has two well-known shortcomings. First, partial equilibrium assessments assume that the shadow prices can be measured by observable market prices, but the equality between these price concepts is violated by distortive taxes and market imperfections. With such distortions correct shadow prices cannot in general be calculated analytically. Thus, shadow prices are more realistically evaluated by a CGE model than by a partial equilibrium approach. Second, if the potential efficiency improvements are substantial rather than marginal, the assumption of constant shadow prices is unlikely to hold as an acceptable approximation. Such endogenous adjustments of shadow prices may be due to large efficiency improvements in a single industry or a result of simultaneous improvements in several industries. A consistent account of the endogeneity of the shadow prices requires a CGE model.

Against this background the most fruitful approach may therefore be to assess the potential aggregate welfare gain from efficiency improvements within different sectors by combining detailed sector studies of inefficiency with a CGE analysis of the aggregate welfare effects. I will discuss the methodology and the results from a project following such a strategy when assessing the scope for improved efficiency in the Norwegian economy. The report from this project, see Norman et al. (1991), concluded that the order of magnitude of the welfare potential was as large as 29-31 per cent of the GDP level in 1987.[2] This Chapter will not discuss the realism of the sectoral inefficiency estimates, which of course are the basic determinants of the aggregate welfare effect. The primary aim of the Chapter is rather to use the results to demonstrate and explain that the CGE analysis may improve on the estimate of the aggregate welfare gain significantly compared to the partial equilibrium approach. As a matter of fact, the Chapter shows that a partial equilibrium approach overestimates the welfare gain by more than 30 per cent compared to the general equilibrium estimate. On the methodological side, the Chapter discusses how one should design and interpret the CGE model simulations of the particular kind of information offered by the sector studies. Special attention is given to the problem of how estimates derived from a static framework should be interpreted and used in a dynamic model.

The Chapter is organised as follows. First, I present the estimates of potential efficiency improvements reported in the sector studies. Then, I describe how these are converted into appropriate shifts in exogenous variables in a Multi Sectoral Growth Model (MSG-5). In addition, I present a non-technical overview of MSG-5, as well as an explanation of the particular way in which the model has been simulated. Next, I present the MSG-5 estimate of the welfare gain and discuss the main reasons why this estimate is considerably lower than the sum of partial equilibrium estimates over sectors. The final section draws conclusions.

EFFICIENCY GAINS IDENTIFIED IN PARTIAL SECTOR STUDIES

In 1989-90 a commission was set up by the Norwegian government with the task of identifying and quantifying the welfare loss generated by inefficiency in government sectors and private sectors heavily controlled by the government authorities. The commission interpreted its mandate in a rather broad way, so the measure of total inefficiency included:

- Inefficiency within sectors producing public services (Education, Health services and Government administration)
- Inefficiency within private production sectors directly controlled by the Government (Domestic transport, Electricity supply)
- Inefficiency within private production sectors heavily regulated through Government Assistance (Agriculture, Fishery)
- Inefficiency caused by Government transfers (the Social security system, Foreign aid)
- Dead-weight losses due to excessive tax distortions of the price system
- Inefficiency caused by unemployment

For each of these 'sectors' selected experts wrote a report. Each report contained three key elements: first, a description of the underlying reasons for the existing inefficiency, second, a quantitative assessment of the potential for efficiency improvement, and third, recommendations of policy reforms that, if implemented, would bring about realisation of the estimated potential for efficiency improvement. These sector studies were critically examined and extensively utilised in the final commission report, see Norman et al. (1991). As noted before, this Chapter will not question or repeat the rationalisations provided in these reports of the assessments of the potential sectoral efficiency gains. Therefore I borrow the relevant conclusions drawn by Norman et al. (1991) concerning the magnitude of these gains (see Table 5.1). A brief account of the sources underlying these efficiency improvements is given in the Appendix.[3]

Table 5.1 Summary of the partial sector estimates of potential efficiency gains

Sectors	Sector studies	Waste of resources			Estimated welfare gain[c]	
		1,000 Man-years	Real capital[a]	Material input[a]	Released resources[a]	Total gain[b]
Public services						
Education	Robertsen and Friestad (1990), Øvereng (1990), Andersen (1990)	93.3	15.0	0.7	19.3	3.3
Health	Grund (1990)	21.0			3.9	0.7
Administration	Johnsen (1990)	12.4		2.0	4.3	0.7
Regulated sectors						
Transport	Hiorth (1990)	16.0	8.5	3.2	6.9	1.2
Transfers						
Fishery	Hanneson (1990)	23.0	5.5		4.7	0.8
Agriculture	Aanesland (1990)	70.0	15.0		14.2	2.4
Social security	Rødseth (1990)	138.0			25.7	4.4
Foreign aid	Pedersen (1990)				4.6	0.8
Unemployment	Norman et al. (1991)	140.0			26.0	4.5
Total		513.7	44.0	5.9	109.6	19.7

Notes:
a NOK billion.
b Percentage of GDP.
c Fixed 1987 factor prices.

The following two general remarks apply to the interpretation of all sector studies. First, most of the estimates found in the sector studies were substantially reduced before they were used as inputs in Norman et al. (1991). This was due to a risk averse attitude to the large degree of uncertainty associated with most of these estimates. Second, in order to transform the estimates of wasted labour, capital and other material inputs into corresponding estimates of potential welfare gains, explicit shadow prices have to be associated with the resources. In the partial equilibrium assessments, the fixed shadow prices reflected average market prices in 1987.

The shadow price of labour was set equal to the average wage cost per man-year.[4] If producers behave rationally, this wage cost reflects the average marginal productivity of a man-year in the Norwegian economy. The shadow price of real capital was set to 8 per cent, which reflects several estimates of the average real rate of net return to capital in the Norwegian business sector. The shadow value of released material inputs was assumed to be equal to the market value actually paid by the sectors releasing these goods and services. The total welfare gain from eliminating inefficiency in a sector is computed by the equation:

Value of released resources (1987 prices) =
(released man-years * NOK 186,000 / man-year)
+ market value of released real capital * 0.08
+ market value of released material inputs.

The first three columns in Table 5.1 report the estimated waste of the labour, real capital and material inputs respectively. The fourth column includes the partial equilibrium evaluation of the potential welfare gain from use of these resources. The fifth column presents the gains as a percentage of GDP in 1987. The figures are substantial, especially when compared to the 0-5 per cent gain typically found in the CGE literature on structural policy reforms, see e.g. Krugman (1992) and Vennemo (1992). The next sections discuss whether and to what extent this large partial equilibrium estimate includes a positive bias due to neglecting general equilibrium effects.

A CGE ASSESSMENT OF THE WELFARE GAIN OF ALL REFORM PROPOSALS

A Brief Overview of the MSG-5 Model

Relevance
The numerical model MSG-5 was used to estimate the total welfare gain of a simultaneous elimination of the inefficiency identified by the sector studies. Being a CGE model, MSG-5 has two general properties that makes it relevant for such an analysis. First, contrary to macro-econometric models in the Keynesian tradition, the model treats resources as scarce in the sense that each one has a positive shadow price. The idea that resources can be wasted and that *gains* can be obtained from efficiency improvements depends fundamentally on the conception that resources are *scarce* in the economy. Second, the model has a consistent micro theoretical foundation. In particular this applies to the determination of marginal utilities and productivities,

which are the basic determinants of the shadow prices of the specified resources. An important point in this respect is that the model describes explicitly how taxes and market imperfections cause shadow prices to deviate from the corresponding market prices. Welfare gains are measured by the growth in the real value of consumption. Hence, the shadow price of a resource equals the increase in consumption caused by a marginal increase in the supply of the resource.

A final point is that MSG-5 is operational for this project because the sectors covered by the sector studies are specified individually in the model. However, although quite disaggregated with respect to industry and commodity classification, MSG-5 could not be used to check the primary estimates of waste reported in the sector studies. As stated above, the role of the model was confined to improving the evaluation of the welfare gains from reallocation of wasted resources.[5]

Structure of the model
The following paragraphs present some key features of the MSG-5 model. The first version of the model is described in Johansen (1960). A complete description of the equation structure and parameter estimates of the model is given in Holmøy et al. (1995).

The model specifies 41 commodities and 28 private production sectors. For most manufactures and for some services, which jointly cover about 50 per cent of total exports, each commodity is an Armington composite of a domestic and a foreign variety, which are regarded as imperfect substitutes. Thus, for these tradeables import shares are price dependent. Import prices are exogenous, and the exchange rate is normalised to unity. Since the Armington assumption is supposed to hold also for foreigners, Norwegian manufacturing firms face export demand functions that are decreasing in the ratio between the domestic price and the exogenous world market price. Production of resource based commodities like primary industry products, crude oil and natural gas, is determined by exogenous supply-side conditions, and the prices of these products are assumed to be equal to the corresponding exogenous world prices. The model specifies five input factors including labour, capital, electricity, fuels and other material inputs, which are optimally combined.

Competition ensures that domestic producer prices equal total unit costs that are independent of production levels due to the general assumption of constant returns to scale. Domestic prices will in general deviate from the corresponding world market prices for tradeables, because domestic products are considered to be imperfect substitutes for corresponding foreign products. The model includes a detailed description of how indirect taxes and subsidies create wedges between producer and purchaser prices, and the user cost of each capital good is augmented to include a detailed description of capital income taxation. The assumption of constant returns to scale, combined with exogenous output determination in those sectors where economies to scale are regarded as essential, make prices independent of the demand side of the economy.

Household demand is derived from utility maximising behaviour. A separable structure of Stone-Geary and CES utility functions imposes strong restrictions on the Slutsky matrix and gives a recursive demand system. However, important features of the household's ability to substitute between specific activities are retained.

Labour supply is exogenous in MSG-5. Assuming the aggregate stock of real capital and the current account exogenous, imposes two additional resource restraints. The capital market and the exogenous current account are balanced by endogenous adjustments of the shadow price of capital and the wage rate. The resource restraints imply that the aggregate private consumption level is determined basically from the supply side.

Model Application and Interpretation of the Results

Implementing efficiency improvements from sector studies in MSG-5
The sector studies estimate the reductions of inputs that would follow from efficiency improvements while implicitly assuming the industry specific output levels to be fixed. The released resources are employed in a hypothetical sector where their social values are constant and equal to their average market prices. In MSG-5 the relevant implementation is to shift factor specific productivity coefficients in the model. Since the sector studies focused on the inefficient use of labour, the following explanation of the transformation of sector study estimates into relevant exogenous shifts in the MSG-5 simulations is confined to labour only. To the extent that real capital and material inputs have been changed, the same lines of reasoning apply to these factors.

In the government sectors Education, Health Services and Administration, no independent measures of output exist. The MSG-5 model follows the practice in the National Accounts where the output value is set equal to costs. Moreover, the activity levels and the input composition in these sectors are exogenous in MSG-5 due to well-known problems of modelling the behaviour in government sectors. The labour productivity improvements in these sectors have been implemented by keeping the levels of government consumption equal to the exogenous initial reference level, whereas the input coefficients have been adjusted in order to bring about input reductions in accordance with the sector estimates. In this way, the effect of these shifts is equivalent to an increase in the total labour supply without reducing government consumption. In education the main part of the efficiency potential was found to be due to not allowing children to start school at six rather than at the age of seven, as well as waste of schoolchildren's and students' time during the years within the education system. Elimination of both kinds of excess time consumption, as well as the potential employment from reforming the social security system, has been implemented in the MSG-5 simulations as a further expansion of the total labour supply.

Elimination of excessive employment in Agriculture, Fishery and the domestic transport sector has been implemented in MSG-5 as exogenous reductions of the input coefficient for labour so that the base year output levels can be produced by the employment estimated in the sector studies. The consumption growth from reducing foreign aid is captured in the MSG-5 simulations through an increase in the value of net imports within the constraint of a fixed current account surplus.

Design of the policy experiments and interpretation of estimated gains
In practice, implementation of the proposed reforms and the completion of their effects are likely to take considerable time. In principle, the dynamics associated with the policy reforms call for a comparison between time paths rather than comparative statics. The reference, or pre-reform, path should be a 'neutral' projection with no efficiency improvements. The alternative post-reform path should have the same exogenous input as the reference path except that the productivity in, for example, agriculture is increased. The gain from the reforms should be calculated as the present value of changes in the instantaneous welfare measure, which is real private consumption per year in MSG-5 analyses.

However, there are several reasons why this ideal approach is impossible to follow. First, the sector studies made no assessments of either the time profile of the implementation of the reform, or of the dynamic effects of the reforms. Instead their approach was completely static, and the efficiency gain estimates were interpreted as long-run effects feasible within an unknown time horizon. Accordingly, these studies provide no guidelines for specifying a realistic dynamic development for the changes in the relevant exogenous variables in MSG-5. Second, although MSG-5 generates dynamic paths due to capital accumulation, which is described in terms of year-to-year development of the variables, the model is not able to calculate comparative dynamics in a realistic way. Being a CGE model, it is not formulated with the ambition of giving a realistic description of the speed of adjustment and tatonnement processes. Rather, the standard interpretation of these models is that they are confined to providing a relevant suggestive description of different long-run equilibria. Consequently, even in the hypothetical case where the sector studies provided information about the dynamics of the productivity effects of the reforms, the unrealistic equilibrium dynamics in MSG-5 makes it hard to utilise this information to improve the gain estimates compared to the case of only static information about the productivity effects. In particular, the fact that MSG-5 neglects all kinds of disequilibrium problems during the transition period implies that the simulated welfare gains in these years are likely to have a positive bias. The bias of the present value of the welfare effects is strengthened through the discounting by an *annual* discount rate. Operational equilibrium models describing the true dynamics of an economy have not been developed yet. The focus in both the sector studies and in Norman et al. (1991) is on the potential gains provided that the market mechanism brings about new employment opportunities of the released resources. Such a focus implies that the analysis emphasises the long-run effects. One may say that this view has been taken to its extreme since both the partial and the general equilibrium analyses are confined to the stationary long-run effects only.

One might argue that the model would be improved if individual inter-temporal behaviour based on perfect foresight were built into the model.[6] I would not agree with this view. Although, such inter-temporal models facilitate the interpretation of the model results, the distinction between *short-run* and *long-run* effects in inter-temporal models is relevant only as a characterisation of the dynamics within the model itself. It does not follow that the simulated dynamics, in particular the short-run effects, represent a good description of what will actually happen in the short run measured by true calendar time.

The reference point
When the analysis is restricted to focus on the stationary long-run effects, it is not obvious how a relevant reference situation describing the pre-reform economy should be specified. In the partial sector studies, the situation in 1987 was taken as the reference point. But assessment of the long-run effects rather warrants that the reference situation is chosen as a long-run equilibrium point on the simulated pre-reform scenario. The case of efficiency improvements in agriculture serves as a good example of how the choice of reference situation may generate misleading results. It is widely expected that technology improvements will contribute to a further gradual reduction of the use of resources in this sector even if no explicit policy reform takes place. If exit of firms is motivated by profitability considerations, it is likely that such a development will have a positive effect on the average productivity of the sector.[7] Then the basis for potential efficiency gains will be reduced along a realistic reference scenario compared to the hypothetical potential in 1987.

In spite of this argument, the general equilibrium assessment of the potential gains has been made relative to a reference point which was constructed on the basis of the situation in 1987. One reason for this choice was to make the general equilibrium results comparable to the results in the sector studies. More fundamentally, it is indeed not easy to see how the information in the sector studies can be exploited unless the reference point is the same in the two approaches. In order to justify the estimates as long-run gains, the choice of reference situation has, however, been supported by a more abstract and counterfactual interpretation of both the partial and the general equilibrium estimates. We interpret the results as a measure of the potential efficiency gains to be exhausted in 1987 if an alternative policy had been followed over a sufficiently long period prior to this year. The normative character of our study motivates this approach. All kinds of welfare measurements imply a choice of how the benefits are exhausted. Our approach implies a hypothetical assessment of how much it would have been possible to raise current private consumption if the sector reforms had been implemented a sufficiently long time ago.

To make the results from simulating MSG-5 consistent with such an interpretation, the model simulations were designed in a particular way, which is quite different from the approach typically followed when tracing out 'realistic' long-term projections for the Norwegian economy. In short, the design aimed at producing results that could be given a comparative statics interpretation applying to two hypothetical descriptions of the Norwegian economy in 1987. First, we constructed a reference scenario describing a hypothetical base year (1987) situation for all simulation periods, in which no efficiency improvements had taken place. This was done by fixing all exogenous variables at their 1987 level.[8] Such a pre-reform scenario eventually becomes stationary after a transition period, in which resources are reallocated from production of capital goods. This reallocation of national income from savings, i.e. future consumption, to current consumption accounts for the main differences between the simulated hypothetical stationary base year situation and the observed 1987 situation. The alternative post-reform equilibria were simulated after perturbation of the exogenous variables mentioned above by the constant long-run shifts, while keeping other exogenous variables at the same level as in the reference simulation. After some simulation periods the alternative scenarios also become stationary. Each one of these is interpreted as the hypothetical post-reform equilibrium in 1987 if the reform policy had been followed historically. Thus, when comparing the post- and pre-reform levels of private consumption, both figures should be interpreted as measures of a hypothetical maximal sustainable consumption level in 1987.

Note that our approach ensures that the hypothetical 1987 situation in the pre-reform scenario does not include any effects of the reform proposals suggested in the sector studies. If a more realistic projection had been chosen as a reference scenario, it is likely that such a scenario would incorporate parts of the potential efficiency improvements found in the sector studies. The general equilibrium estimate of the efficiency gain would then include some degree of double counting.

THE GENERAL EQUILIBRIUM ASSESSMENT OF THE POTENTIAL FOR EFFICIENCY IMPROVEMENTS

Interpretation of Macro-economic Equilibrium Effects

As explained in the previous section, the consumption effects are basically due to simultaneous positive shifts in labour supply and factor productivities. In order to interpret the numerical results, it is useful to provide an intuitive explanation of the key macro-economic effects of partial changes in these exogenous variables.

Increased labour supply
To see why relative prices must change when the labour supply increases, consider the hypothetical case where all prices are constant. Then exports, import shares and the input composition in each industry would also stay constant. The increase in labour demand necessary to balance the labour market would be followed by a roughly proportional increase in the demand for real capital.[9] However, the MSG-5 simulations do not allow the capital stock to increase relative to the pre-reform scenario, and equilibrium in the capital market commands an increase in the shadow price of capital. In the product markets the supplies produced by the additional labour supply are absorbed by an increase in private consumption as long as exports, investment and government consumption remains constant.

Turning to the impacts on the current account, the increase in private consumption and intermediate inputs would cause imports to grow, thus violating the fixed current account constraint. Restoring the external balance requirement calls for a decrease in the Norwegian price level relative to the exogenous world prices through a fall in the wage rate. Notice that the adjustment of the wage rate must also compensate for the endogenous rise in equilibrium costs of capital. The economy becomes more labour intensive due to the reduction of the real wage rate for two different reasons. First, factor substitution takes place within the individual industries. Second, the price sensitivity on the demand side causes expansion of the relatively most labour-intensive industries and contraction of the most capital-intensive industries. Holmøy (1992) provides a more comprehensive analytical description of the various substitution effects in MSG-5.

In the new equilibrium the increase in production capacity has been absorbed by higher private consumption. Imports have increased since, empirically, the decline in the price sensitive import shares represents a weaker effect than the income effect on import demand. The import growth has been financed by a rise in exports made possible by a depreciation of the real exchange rate, i.e. the ratio between Norwegian and international price levels. However, this effect, which follows from the Armington specification of foreign trade, implies that the benefits from the growth in the labour endowment cannot be enjoyed without a loss in terms of trade. Accordingly, the consumption possibilities increase by less than GDP.

Positive productivity shifts

Improved labour productivity implies an increase of the effective labour supply. There is also an additional effect working through the reduction of unit costs in domestic production. Competition forces prices to follow the reductions of unit costs. These price effects are spread through the economy by the input-output structure that links domestic prices to each other. Thus, prices of produced factors of production, including real capital, are reduced relative to the wage rate. Moreover, the international competitiveness of Norwegian industries improves, which causes export growth and lower import shares.

Since the capital stock is not allowed to adjust, the positive shift in the demand for capital must be neutralised through a rise in the equilibrium rate of return. The impact on the equilibrium wage rate is ambiguous. The negative price effect of the productivity calls for a higher wage rate in order to re-establish the necessary international competitiveness. On the other hand, the positive income effect on net imports, as well as the price effect of the rise in capital, implies a downward pressure on the wage rate.

Simulation Results

The results from the MSG-5 simulations are presented in Table 5.2 below. The simulated welfare gain in terms of consumption growth equals NOK 94.0 billion when measured in 1987 prices. A small fraction of the consumption growth is due to reduced gross investment. This is due to a negative covariance between the reallocations of the fixed aggregate stock of capital and the industry and asset specific rates of capital depreciation. The negative covariance implies that the aggregate capital stock is reallocated in a way that reduces the average rate of depreciation.

The corresponding partial equilibrium estimate - obtained by adding gain estimates from the partial sector studies - equals NOK 109.6 billion. In other words the latter estimate includes a positive bias equal to 100 * (109.6 - 94.0) / 94.0 = 16.6 per cent. The subsequent paragraphs discuss the main reasons behind the discrepancy between the two estimates.

Table 5.2   Macro-economic effects of all sector reform proposals (volumes in billions of NOK, 1987 prices)

Consumption	94.0
Net exports	0.9
Exports	18.4
Imports	17.5
Gross investment	- 3.3
GDP	91.6

Choice of shadow prices
First it is principally and empirically important to make clear that the price concepts underlying the evaluation of the welfare gains are not the same in the partial and the general equilibrium approach. The subsequent discussion explains why a consistent evaluation based on a common set of shadow prices increases considerably the upward bias of the partial equilibrium estimate.

The partial equilibrium estimate uses average factor prices paid by the producers as shadow prices. Assuming competitive behaviour, these factor prices equal the value of the marginal product of the factor when employed in a sector paying average factor prices. However, the precise value concept in this context is production evaluated at *producer prices*. Consequently, the partial equilibrium estimate of the total welfare gain measures the *producer value* of the output produced by re-employment of wasted resources.

On the other hand, the estimate of the total welfare gain obtained by simulating MSG-5 equals the growth in consumption, which is measured in fixed *consumer* prices. Indirect taxation makes the aggregate consumption evaluated at consumer or market prices substantially higher than the corresponding volume evaluated at producer prices. A rough estimate of this difference can be obtained by comparing GDP evaluated at the two sets of prices. For 1987, the producer value of GDP equals 88 per cent of the consumer value of GDP.[10] Since both the reference and the alternative scenarios in our calculations differ from the observed situation in 1987 with respect to the composition of GDP, this ratio will take on a somewhat different value in the simulations. However, it is suggestive for the order of magnitude. If anything, the average tax wedge between consumer and producer prices in our computations is likely to be even higher because the GDP share of consumption, which is taxed higher than other final delivery components in GDP, is larger in our simulations than the observed share. The sum of partial gain estimates can be approximately evaluated at consumer rather than producer prices by multiplying the reported estimate by the factor $1/0.88 = 1.14$. The resulting sum of partial gain estimates then becomes $109.6 * 1.14 = $ NOK 124.5 billion in 1987 consumer prices. Consequently the reduction of this estimate due to general equilibrium effects increases to $124.5 - 94.0 = 30.5$ billion. Alternatively, compared to the MSG-5 calculations the sum of partial gain estimates includes a positive bias equal to $100 * 30.5/94.0 = 32.4$ per cent when both estimates are measured in consumer prices. This bias is substantial.

Endogenous prices and marginal productivities
There are two main reasons why the general equilibrium effects contribute to a reduction in the estimated total welfare gain. First, there are diminishing returns to partial increases in the production factors. The strong increase in labour supply relative to the increase in the supply of other factors cannot be absorbed without reducing the marginal productivity of labour. Second, the negative income effect on the trade balance cannot be neutralised by increasing Norwegian market shares in foreign and domestic demand unless the prices of Norwegian tradeables are reduced relative to the fixed world prices. The empirical importance of both effects are, however, crucially dependent on the degree of openness of the Norwegian economy. This point justifies a more careful examination of the implications of the modelling of foreign trade in small open economies.

For the sake of reference, a small and completely open economy (SOE) can be defined as an economy that produces tradeables only, and all product prices are fixed world prices. The reason why the SOE represents an interesting reference case is that the factor prices will be independent of changes in factor endowments under some restrictions on production functions and the changes in endowments. The SOE will absorb the changes in labour supply by reallocating resources from the least to the most labour intensive sectors (the Rybczynski effect). Accordingly, the closer a CGE model is to the SOE model, the less sensitive will the marginal factor productivities and the factor prices be to changes in factor supplies. It follows that the accuracy of the partial equilibrium approach will be improved the more equal the actual economy is to the SOE.

Compared to the SOE the degree of openness of the Norwegian economy, as described by MSG-5, is restricted in several respects. Most importantly, industries producing either non-tradeables or tradeables subject to protective trade policies employ a much larger share of the production factors than industries exposed to international competition. In addition, MSG-5 like several other CGE models adopts the Armington hypothesis, according to which tradeables produced in the Norwegian exposed industries are close but imperfect substitutes for corresponding products from other countries. Thus, export growth and lower import shares require a reduction in Norwegian prices relative to the corresponding world prices.

However, although MSG-5 is widely different from the stylised SOE model, modified Rybczynski effects still play a role in the model. For example, when the increase in labour supply brings about a reduction in the wage rate, the price of labour intensive products will decline relative to other products.[11] As long as the price elasticities of the demand for these products are not particularly low relative to other products, labour intensive industries will crowd out production in other industries. Although the Armington specification excludes infinite price elasticities, tradeables are much more price sensitive than sheltered commodities. The resulting contribution in favour of a more labour intensive industry structure modifies the need for downward adjustment of the wage rate and the marginal productivity of labour. In MSG-5, however, the Rybczynski effects are modified and often dominated by several other equilibrium adjustments.[12]

The modification of the total efficiency gain caused by lower export prices can be approximated by the change in the fixed prices value of net exports.[13] That is, exports evaluated to NOK 0.9 billion 1987 prices could have been consumed if export prices were constant. This figure accounts for 5.6 per cent of the discrepancy between the general equilibrium estimate and the added partial estimates of the total efficiency gain. This figure is not an exact measure of the negative terms-of-trade effect on welfare. The primary reason is that if commodities are consumed rather than exported, they are evaluated at consumer prices, which exceed export prices by the effective indirect tax rate on consumption. Consequently, export prices under-estimate consumers' willingness to pay for the exported products.

One might expect that the endogenous adjustments of marginal productivities and prices would have been less significant if the capital stock were allowed to increase in order to equate the marginal return to capital to the world market interest rate. However, simulations on MSG-5 with the appropriate closure rule show that this is not the case as far as the stationary long-run results are concerned. Under this alternative closure rule the capital stock would have grown by roughly the same proportion as employment as long as the wage rate was constant. The capital accumulation crowds out private consumption during the first periods and yields a return in terms of a stronger long-run growth in private consumption compared to the case where the capital stock is kept constant. The expansion of the economy implies a positive income effect on imports compared to the simulations based on a fixed capital stock. Consequently, the equilibrium reduction of the wage rate must be stronger under this closure rule in order to raise exports by a sufficient amount, and there is a stronger modification of the welfare gain through the terms of trade effect.

As to the impact on the estimate of the welfare gain, endogenous capital formation requires that the changes in consumption in the different periods be weighted together in a dynamic welfare measure. As MSG-5 has not incorporated inter-temporal behaviour such an evaluation can only be done by additional ad hoc calculations. As shown in Norman et al., a first order approximation of the welfare gain indicates that allowing the capital stock to adjust has minor influence on the estimated welfare gain. The same conclusion is derived in Vennemo (1992).

CONCLUSIONS

This Chapter has made a case for the use of CGE models in the evaluation of welfare effects of structural policy that targets inefficiency problems at the micro level, even if this level cannot be described in an operational CGE model. The CGE approach solves the problems that correct shadow prices are unobservable in practice. The effect on the welfare estimate due to endogenous shadow prices is more significant the more serious are the initial inefficiencies. On the other hand, if elimination of inefficiency basically generates an increase in factor supplies, the CGE modifications of the partial equilibrium estimates will be smaller the more equal the economy is to the textbook model of a small open economy. The approach taken in this Chapter suggests that general equilibrium effects have substantial influence on the estimated welfare gain, at least when the initial waste of resources is as large as reported in the sector studies for Norway.

The Chapter has also discussed how static measures of inefficiency, derived from detailed sector studies, can be implemented in a CGE model that recognises at least parts of the real world dynamics. The discussion reveals that it is not straightforward to design the model simulations appropriately. The solution that is suggested in this Chapter implies a much higher degree of abstract interpretation of the simulation experiment than is usually required when CGE models are employed for long-run projections of economic growth. Neither is it obvious how partial sector assessments of efficiency improvements should be interpreted.

APPENDIX - POTENTIAL EFFICIENCY IMPROVEMENTS IN PARTIAL SECTOR STUDIES

Public Services

Education
Three sector studies, covering respectively primary and secondary schools, junior colleges and universities and colleges, estimated to what extent it was possible to reduce the input of time spent by pupils, students and teachers without reducing the quality of the educational system.

Primary and secondary schools Robertsen and Friestad (1990) applied a micro simulation model of the cost structure in the primary and secondary schools teaching children aged from 7 to 15 years. This model can be used to estimate how input of resources is affected by different assumptions about how these schools are being operated. The calculations used in Norman et al. (1991) are based on an alternative where neither the working time for teachers nor the average size of schools is in conflict with any official standard requirements in Norway. The increased efficiency implies that the pupil/teacher ratio rises from the 1989 level of 10.7 to 15.8, which is equal to the Norwegian average in the mid 1970s. The corresponding ratio was 17 in both Netherlands and West Germany, which equals the ratio for Norway in 1970. Robertsen and Friestad point out that only half of the decline in the Norwegian pupils/teacher ratio can be attributed to various reforms in the Norwegian schools system during 1970-1989. Furthermore, there is no evidence indicating that Norway has 'better' schools than these countries.

A far more significant source of potential efficiency improvements is to let children start school at the age of six rather than at seven. Such a reform would bring Norway in line with most other countries with respect to the age when children start school.[14] Ceteris paribus the long-run effect would be an increase in the labour force by one cohort, i.e. about 2.5 per cent or 60,000 man years. Norman et al. (1991) judged the historical reasons for starting school at seven rather than at the age of six not to be valid anymore. The final assessment took into account that the reduction in the average age of children in the primary school requires an increase in the teacher/pupil ratio. On the other hand, such a reform will reduce the amounts of resources used on nursery.

Junior colleges Øvereng (1990) identifies the following possibilities for cost reductions: First, an increase of the size of classes, where this is not in conflict with pedagogical principles, would reduce the number of teachers by 6 per cent. Second, reducing the number of optional subjects to be chosen by the students would save 1 per cent of the teachers. Accordingly, the total number of man-years used for teaching in junior colleges could be reduced by 7 per cent. This was considered to be a very cautious estimate since it did not include the effects of capacity problems, especially pronounced within vocational training, causing junior college students to waste time on irrelevant courses and/or relatively unproductive work.

Universities and high schools According to Andersen (1990), the main problems in higher education appear to be that too many students leave before finishing their education, and that the average student uses too much time in order to obtain his final exam. Resources could therefore be saved if the academic institutions promote exits at an earlier stage or if they could increase the share of students who finished their studies through positive efforts. The report mentions three major reasons for excessive time consumption at universities. First, waiting in queues as a way of allocating the limited capacity within different branches of study to students. Second, students finance part of their consumption by taking irrelevant work due to borrowing constraints. The third reason is insufficient pedagogical support from the institutions.[15] The report points out some measures that could be used to provoke earlier desertions and reduce the students' time consumption. In order to assess the net benefit from such changes, one should in principle subtract the utility of just being a student. Such information is not available. On the other hand, it has not been taken into account that the social value of time is higher after graduation than before.

Health services
Grund (1990) points out that the institutions within the health system probably have managed to increase their cost efficiency during the last years. However, he still calculates a substantial potential for further cost efficiency improvements, see Table 5.1. This potential is related to very significant differences in efficiency, measured by unit costs, between relatively similar institutions. In short, Grund estimates that 12.5 per cent of the labour input in health services can be saved if the best practice technology is implemented everywhere. However the implementation of the best practice technologies is not costless. On the other hand Grund has not considered the possibilities of a better utilisation of the capital stock within the institutions. No quantitative information is available about these two effects. As a 'neutral' assumption Grund's estimate was chosen.

Administration in the government sectors

Johnsen (1990) examined the potential for efficiency gains within internal administration in the government sector. From comparative studies of Sweden and Denmark, and of different public institutions in Norway, Johnsen estimates that 12.5 per cent of government employment is occupied with unnecessary internal administration of zero social value. In health care and education the share of the employed occupied with internal administration is lower, and we assume a potential equal to 10 per cent of the man-years for these two sectors. The potential for reduction in material inputs was assumed to be of the same relative order.

Sectors Strongly Regulated by the Government[16]

Domestic transport

The composition of transport services in Norway reflects partially the topological characteristics of the country and the location of the population. The relative importance of transportation by sea, air and car is greater than in other countries. However, Hiorth (1990) argues that Norway could benefit from further adjustments to these characteristics. Based on Hiorth's study, Norman et al. (1991) recommend:

- a shift in long distance transport of passengers and goods from least profitable parts of the railroad system to road transport and aircraft,
- replacing parts of the existing ferries and ships used in coast traffic by more modern ones,
- a shift from the use of private cars to bus and train in and outside the large cities,
- deregulation of different transport markets (buses, ferries, ships, aircraft).

Hiorth calculates the yearly loss caused by too low investments in the road system to be about NOK 2.9 billion in 1987 prices. A major share of this figure can be attributed to sub-optimal financing of the road investments.

A comparison with the Swedish truck sector shows that the Swedish efficiency is 31 per cent higher than the Norwegian. Hiorth attributes most of this gap to unnecessary slack in capacity utilisation. Norman et al. (1991) considered a 10 per cent increase in efficiency to be a cautious estimate of the potential. In fixed 1987 prices the partial equilibrium estimate of the welfare gain from eliminating this slack would be NOK 2.6 billion.

It should be noted that the welfare estimate in Norman et al. (1991) did not include any benefits from changes in taxation from the present system which taxes car *investment* to a system taxing the *use* of cars. The present system makes it optimal to keep the cars too long causing excessive costs related to maintenance and repairs.

Efficiency Losses caused by the Transfer System

The transfer system includes transfers between urban and rural regions organised through assistance to the primary production sectors agriculture and fishery, transfers between domestic households through the social security system, and international transfers through foreign aid.

Fishery
The government transfers to fishery can be traced back to the mid 1950s. The support was initially intended to be limited to years with exceptional low catches and to be of transitory character. However, it became a permanent and important income source for the sector peaking in 1981 when it accounted for 90 per cent of its factor income. In the late 1980s the direct government transfers equalled about 20 per cent of the sector's value added. This is really a paradox since Norwegian fishery is based on some of the world's richest natural resources and fishermen and equipment of high quality. In other countries, e.g. Iceland, where the natural resources are quite equal to the Norwegian, the fisheries contribute a lot more to GDP. Hanneson (1990) explains the paradox as a result of a policy that has generated:

- permanent large excess capacity,
- maintenance of an inefficient industry structure,
- excessive exploitation of the fish resources,
- an administration giving first priority to a maximum of employees and security against bankruptcy.

Hanneson shows that the consequences of implementing the best practice techniques and structure in the various kinds of fishery would reduce the number of active fishermen by about 66 per cent (22,500 man years) and the number of employees in the processing industry by 50 per cent (7,000 man years). And this could be done without significant reduction in the sector's output. In addition, Hanneson estimates a reduction in the number of bureaucrats working in institutions administrating various supportive transfers to the fishery sector.

Efficiency improvement would also reduce the input of real capital and this effect is likely to dominate the need for new investment that is necessary when new technologies are to be implemented. Norman et al. (1991) considered a relative reduction in the capital equal to 50 per cent of the relative reduction of employment to be a cautious estimate.

In order to obtain these gains, Hanneson recommends a new policy based on the following principles. The role of the government is to find the optimal level of exploitation of the reproducible fish resources and to oversee that the stocks of fish are not subject to excessive exhaustion by the fishery sector. The role of the fishery sector is to maximise the pure rent of these resources. The simplest and most effective way to achieve this goal is to replace the existing system of detailed regulations by a system of marketable quotas.

Agriculture
Through negotiations with the government the farmers have obtained arrangements which guarantee an average income level among farmers equal to the average for wage earners in manufacturing industries. As a result the sector was subsidised to about 60 per cent or by NOK 15 billion per year at the end of the 1980s.

There are two main sources to efficiency gains in the agricultural sector. First, the historical and present output level of food products can be supplied by less input of factors.[17] Second, Norwegian consumers could benefit from trade liberalisation and free import of agricultural goods. Norman et al. (1991) confined the quantification of potential efficiency gains to the first source only. The reason for neglecting benefits from raising imports was not of course that it was considered to be empirically insignificant. Rather, it was a consequence of serious problems in measuring the relevant shadow prices. In principle, import prices should be used as shadow prices in a free trade regime. However, in practice a drastic reduction of the agricultural sector is not a flexible reversible process. Thus, the products should be evaluated by a set of import prices over a sufficiently long period. The actual observable world prices are unlikely to be representative indicators of their long-run levels because world markets for agricultural products are heavily distorted through various kinds of government assistance, causing observed world prices to lie well below unit costs. This limitation of the potential efficiency gains introduces a negative bias to the estimated figures.

The estimated waste of resources was based on Aanesland (1990), who calculates the resource savings from eliminating inefficient excess supply and implementation of best practice technologies that were already in use in Norway in 1989. This methodology results in an estimated annual labour requirement equal to 19,400 man-years. This figure should be compared to the actual number of farmers that are likely to have an alternative value as employees with normal productivity in other sectors. Based on official data (from 'Budsjettnemda'), this number was 78,000. Implementation of the productivity improvements would therefore imply that the number of farmers can be reduced by ca. 58,000 or 74 per cent. In addition, a reform giving first priority to efficiency would also reduce the administrative bureaucracy both within the government sector and within the farmer's own organisations. Aanesland estimated that this effect would imply that as many as 12,000 man-years could be re-employed in other sectors. Consequently, the total potential labour saving then becomes (58,000 + 12,000) = 70,000 man-years.

The capital stock can not be reduced by the same proportion as labour. First, the new operating units will be more capital intensive compared to the current average. Second, parts of the capital stock in agriculture are types of consumption capital. As a cautious estimate compared to Aanesland's assessments, the report suggested that 16 per cent of the capital stock could be allocated to alternative purposes. Measured in 1987 prices, the total value of resources released for alternative purposes exceeds NOK 14 billion.

The most important elements in a reform policy would be:

- A gradual, but significant increase in the official efficiency standard requirements that entitle farms to government transfers.
- Cancellation of the concession arrangements for greater and more efficient farms within the production of pork and poultry.
- Elimination of production limitations.
- Abolition of the income guarantee arrangements.

The social security system
Expenditure related to the social security system is the largest single category in the Norwegian government budget. Outlays increased much faster than the general income level, from 7.9 per cent of GDP in 1967 to 15.3 per cent in 1987. The expenditure growth is due to both growth in the real value of transfers per recipient, and the inclusion of new categories of legitimate recipients. As a matter of fact, the total number of recipients entitled to long-term benefits increased from 476,000 persons in 1967 to 879,000 in 1987, i.e. 44 per cent of the labour force.

A large international literature concludes that economic incentives, depending on the design of the social security system, affect unemployment, absence due to sickness, the number receiving disablement benefits and the choice of retirement date. This literature defines the concept 'equivalent social security benefit' as the level of the benefit which, combined with no paid work, gives the individual the same welfare as he or she has when working. Normally the level of equivalent benefits is lower than income from paid work. Only when the actual social security benefit is below the equivalent benefit will misuse of the system not occur. The Norwegian system includes several benefits that are likely to exceed the equivalent level. In particular, sickness benefit stands out in this respect.

Rødseth (1990) has estimated the loss of labour force that is likely to be generated by the design of the Norwegian social security system. He has done this separately for three kinds of social security benefits: unemployment, sickness and disability. The results will necessarily depend on what the alternatives to the present system are. The alternative considered by Rødseth is a privately funded system without public benefits.

Rødseth estimates that 25,000 man-years per year are 'lost' as a consequence of the present system of sickness benefit payments instead of the alternative. The corresponding estimate for the system of unemployment benefits is 30,000 lost man-years, and the amount of lost employment caused by the rules for disablement benefits lies in the interval 105,000-138,000. Norman et al. (1991) regarded the upper bound of this interval to be the most realistic point estimate.

Norman et al. (1991) included unemployment exceeding the NAIRU level as waste of resources. The report does not however point to any concrete policy reforms that can be used in order to achieve full employment. Any estimate of the NAIRU for Norway in the late 1980s will be uncertain. Based on an estimate of 1.5 per cent, elimination of inefficient unemployment would imply an additional labour supply equal to 140,000 man-years in 1989.

Foreign aid
The foreign aid offered through the public budgets amounted to 1.1 per cent of national income in 1987, and Norway is therefore among the nations that offer relatively most aid to the developing countries. Of this amount 10 per cent was spent on temporary expedients. The rest, NOK 5.8 billion, was given as development aid, distributed between bilateral aid (3.2 billion), multilateral aid (2.4 billion) and administration (0.2 billion).

Based on the arguments and documentation in Pedersen (1990), Norman et al. (1991) pronounce a very negative judgement on the effects of the part of the Norwegian foreign aid that is given for development purposes. Whereas there is no reason to suspect that the effects of temporary expedients offered to areas hit by catastrophes etc. can be improved, recipients would be equally well off without any of the bilateral aid and half of the multilateral aid. In this case the administration too is wasting resources. The total value of wasted resources then becomes NOK 4.6 billion. The relevant interpretation of 'resources' in this case is net imports; a cut in the foreign aid would improve the Norwegian current account by the same amount without reducing Norwegian net wealth.

NOTES

1. Every issue of the Norwegian financial magazine *Kapital* includes an article about how the government sectors waste money.
2. This estimate should not be interpreted as a measure of the *net* welfare effect. In several cases, as e.g. the question regarding the start of schooling, there may be good reasons for maintaining the present regime. Consequently, the welfare gains presented in this paper should rather be interpreted as a price tag on some existing conditions.
3. MSG-5 is not sufficiently detailed to capture the efficiency improvements due to reallocations of electricity from energy intensive industries to other consumers, deregulation of transport markets and additional investments in the road system. The gains associated with these improvements are therefore not calculated in the MSG-5 analysis, but the gain estimates made in the corresponding sector studies are included in Norman et al. (1991).
4. Average wage cost per man-year is equal to NOK 186,000. One man-year is defined as 1725 hours.
5. In addition, the systematic use of a CGE model turned out to be a useful disciplining framework for how to extract the most relevant information from the sector studies. For example, many of these studies did not originally have estimates for the increase in the productivity of other factors than labour.
6. See e.g. Turnovsky (1991) for an introduction to inter-temporal macro-economic modelling based on rational individual behaviour.
7. Strictly, this effect presupposes a positive correlation between profitability and productivity at the individual farm level, which may be violated if government assistance is too strongly directed to the least productive farms.
8. In some sectors the level of gross investment is exogenous. These levels were set equal to the level of real capital depreciation ensuring that the capital stocks in these sectors were constant along the simulated paths.
9. The deviation from exact proportionality would be due to different capital intensities in the different industries.
10. Strictly, in this comparison I used the National Accounts concept 'basic prices' rather than producer prices. However, the choice between these price concepts has no empirical significance.
11. Factor intensities should be measured after correction for the indirect use of primary factors through the input-output system.
12. A more elaborate discussion is given in Holmøy (1992).
13. In Norman et al. (1991) the estimated welfare loss due to reduced export prices is equal to NOK 5.9 billion, which is much larger than the figure used in the text.
14. In fact, the reform in 1997 implies that children start schooling at the age of six.
15. Andersen (1990) mentions that the representative student in the late 1980s was occupied with irrelevant paid work 10 hours a week, whereas the number of hours used on studies was only 26. The average age of graduates has increased since 1970 for all subjects in the universities. On average the increase has been from 26.5 to 28 years. For humanistic subjects the increase has been from 29 to 35 years.
16. Norman et al. (1991) includes the electricity sector in this group of sectors. Bye and Johnsen (1990) estimates inefficient allocation of hydropower between different consumer groups. It was not possible to describe such types of inefficiency in MSG-5 when the calculations were undertaken. Consequently, inefficiency in this sector has been omitted in the present paper.
17. In addition, the calculations include the efficiency gains from shutting down the (relatively small) part of production that is sold on the world market at strongly subsidised prices.

6. A Dynamic CGE Analysis of the Danish 1993 Tax Reform Act

Martin Knudsen, Lars Haagen Pedersen, Toke Ward Petersen, Peter Stephensen and Peter Trier

INTRODUCTION

Recent tax reforms in most European countries have aimed at reducing the tax burden and the progressivity of the labour income taxation. The Danish tax reform of June 1993 is in line with this development. Furthermore, the Danish tax reform may be seen as an attempt to introduce 'green' elements in the tax structure, as the reform introduced taxation of polluting consumption goods as a revenue raising instrument. The reform was initiated in 1994 and is phased in over a period of 5 years, such that the reform is fully implemented in 1998. In addition to the elements mentioned above, the reform contains a restructuring of taxing income from capital goods which implies a reduction in the capital income taxation and measures towards broadening the tax base of both corporate and personal taxation including taxation of capital gains on shares.

In this Chapter we aim at describing the effects of the reform on the incentives of consumers and producers. We quantify the effects by applying the benchmark version of DREAM - a model that is currently being developed at Statistics Denmark. DREAM (Danish Rational Economic Agents Model) is a dynamic computable general equilibrium (CGE) model of a small, open economy with overlapping generations, endogenous capital accumulation, a public and a private production sector and rational agents with perfect foresight. The presentation of the model is kept to a minimum and serves only as a remedy for analysing how changes in the tax structure are fed into the economy through changes in the individual behaviour. For a description including a complete derivation of the behavioural equations from first principles, see Knudsen et al. (1998a).[1]

DREAM is being designed with the specific aim of evaluating welfare state and labour market reforms, such as the 1993 tax reform. However, as the version used for this analysis is a benchmark version of the model, we abstract from any imperfections in the markets in the economy. In particular this implies that the labour market is assumed to be perfectly competitive and that the level of unemployment in the initial equilibrium is assumed to be voluntary. In the present version, the tax and transfer system and the Armington approach to modelling foreign trade cause the only 'distortions' from first best.

In the initial equilibrium the behaviours of the consumers are subject to the following major distortions: First, the labour supply is distorted by the labour income tax system and by the presence of unemployment benefits that in this perfectly competitive model are modelled as a subsidy to leisure. Ceteris paribus these distortions both tend to reduce the labour supply. Second, the savings decision is distorted by the presence of capital income taxation and age-dependent transfers such as pensions. The life cycle motive and a positive utility from leaving bequests drive savings. Again both distortions tend to imply, ceteris paribus, that the level of savings becomes too low. Third, the behaviour of firms is distorted by the presence of capital income taxation, accelerated depreciation for tax purposes and a difference in the taxation of equity and debt. These distortions imply that the private cost of capital in the stationary state is lower than the social cost of capital, which is equal to the world market rate of interest, such that the domestic stock of capital (ceteris paribus) is higher than the social optimum.

These distortions may be taken to imply that, in the initial equilibrium, the stock of assets held by the private sector is too low and the composition of the assets is biased towards a too high proportion of domestic capital stock. The final major distortion is caused by the modelling of foreign trade that follows the Armington approach (Armington, 1969). This implies that the domestic economy produces a tradeable good, which is differentiated from the tradeable goods produced abroad. The terms of trade are therefore endogenous. On the other hand domestic firms are price takers, and thus the domestic firms do not exploit the potential 'monopoly' gain from the finite elasticity of foreign demand. Economic policy actions that increase the domestic price level serve as 'beggar thy neighbour policies' through the resulting increase in the terms of trade, even if the Danish economy is considered 'small' in the world economy.

The Tax Reform Act

The evaluation of the tax reform is performed starting from a stationary state equilibrium where the model is calibrated to data for the Danish economy in

1995 given these initial distortions. The result of the evaluation therefore depends on whether the overall effect of the 'distortions' is increased or decreased by the reform and how this in turn affects welfare. When evaluating the reform we divide the reform into three sub-reforms: First, the reform of labour income taxation, second, the green taxes, and third, the capital income taxation. Finally, we simulate the total reform package. Even if the three sub-reforms do not add up to the total reform, due to the non-linear nature of the general equilibrium model, considerable insights can be gained from a decomposition of the reform as the three parts affect different parts of the economy.

The total reform package contains several aspects from which we abstract in the present Chapter. Our definition of the tax reform implies that the following taxes and transfers in the model are affected:

- A change in the personal income taxation scale which implies that the effective average tax rate for a fully employed person is reduced from 45.1 per cent in 1993 to 41.5 per cent in 1998. For a fully unemployed person receiving the maximum unemployment benefit level, the effective average tax rate is reduced from 35.7 per cent in 1993 to 28.1 per cent in 1998.
- A reduction in the pre-tax unemployment benefit level of 4.3 per cent (in fixed prices) in the period from 1993 to 1998. The resulting effect on the real unemployment benefit after tax is an increase of 7.0 per cent in the period from 1993 to 1998.
- Other taxable public transfers such as public pension are assumed to be regulated such that the after tax value of the transfers is not affected by the reform.
- A reduction in the effective marginal capital income tax rate from 51.5 per cent in 1993 to 46.7 per cent in 1998.
- A reduction in the effective tax rates on dividends from 36.1 per cent in 1993 to 31.6 per cent in 1998.
- An increase in the effective accrued equivalent marginal tax rate on real capital gains from 15.1 per cent in 1993 to 25.1 per cent in 1998.
- An increase in excise taxes ('green taxes') by 3.0 percentage points from 1993 to 1998.

Summary of Results

The main macro-economic results are summarised in Table 6.1.

*Table 6.1   Effects of the reform package (billions of DKR)**

	Initial stationary state	5 years	10 years	25 years	50 years	New stationary state
Private consumption	416	419	417	418	422	433
		(0.7)	(0.2)	(0.5)	(1.4)	(4.1)
Real GDP	830	834	832	820	813	812
		(0.6)	(0.3)	(-1.2)	(-2.0)	(-2.2)
Employment, index	100.0	100.1	100.1	100.0	100.0	100.0
		(0.1)	(0.1)	(0.0)	(0.0)	(0.0)
Capital stock	2664	2640	2612	2563	2533	2527
		(-0.9)	(-1.9)	(-3.8)	(-4.9)	(-5.2)
Value of firms	1489	1695	1714	1741	1763	1791
		(13.9)	(15.1)	(16.9)	(18.4)	(20.3)
Foreign assets	-259	-241	-211	-145	-82	45

Note: * The numbers in parentheses are the percentage change compared to the initial stationary state.

The main message from Table 6.1 is that the effects on the overall performance of the economy are very minor, especially if one focuses on the first 25 years. There are three main effects. First, there is a tendency toward higher savings in the economy. This tends to increase the stock of private non-human wealth in the economy over time. Gradually and very slowly the increased wealth tends to increase consumption. However in the first part of the period the main effect of the increased savings is an increase in the stock of foreign assets held by the private sector. This effect is sufficient to change the foreign asset position of the economy from a substantial debt to a positive net foreign position in the very long run.[2] Second, the reduction in the capital income taxation and the increase in the capital gains tax both tend to increase the cost of capital in the stationary state of the model. This gives the firms an incentive to reduce their stock of capital. Third, the reduction in the labour income taxation - ceteris paribus - tends to decrease the labour cost in the model. Total demand for labour remains however virtually unaffected since the reduction in the wage is counteracted by the reduction in the marginal productivity of labour, which is a consequence of the reduced capital stock in the economy.

Figure 6.1 Generational welfare effects of the reform package

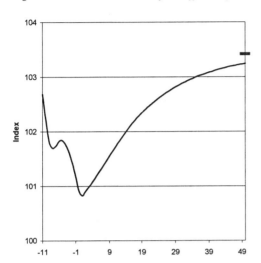

Concerning the welfare consequences of the reform, Figure 6.1 shows the relative increase in the utility for current and future generations. On the vertical axis the index value of utility is measured. The level 100 is the situation where the generation in question has the same utility as in the stationary equilibrium that prevails prior to the reform. A level above 100 implies an increase in utility as a consequence of the reform. The horizontal axis measures the generations according to birth year. The generation labelled -11 has lived for 11 5-year periods as adults prior to the reform. These persons are 73 years old and experience one 5-year period after the reform has been introduced. The generation labelled 0 is the generation that enters the economy as adults at the age of 18 at the time when the reform is implemented. Therefore generation 1 is the generation that enters the economy one 5-year period after the reform has been initiated.

Figure 6.1 reveals that the tax reform implies a Pareto-improvement, in the sense that all generations are better off after the reform. For those generations that enter the economy around the time of the reform, the welfare improvements are the smallest.[3]

The very small net effect of the tax reform covers up the fact that each of the components of the reform has a significant effect on the economy, but these gross effects tend to counteract one another. The remaining part of the Chapter discusses the incentive effects of the three parts of the total reform in some detail. The distinctive features of DREAM are described along with the presentation of the incentive effects. The rest of the Chapter has the following structure: first, we discuss the effect of the reduction in the labour income taxation. The next section contains a similar discussion of the introduction of green taxes on consumption, and the fourth section discusses the changes in the capital income taxation. This amounts to a discussion of the effect of a reduction in the taxation of interest income and in the dividend taxation complemented with an increase in the taxation of capital gains. Finally, the outcome of the total tax reform is described.

All parts of the tax reform are introduced as unforeseen changes implemented at the beginning of period 1. For period 0 the variables assume their value in the steady state baseline, except for the forward looking variables (such as the value of firms) which are allowed to jump on impact. It should be stressed that the public sector budget is assumed to be balanced in each period *via* lump sum transfers to households, so that for example tax rate cuts are counteracted by increased lump sum taxes (decreased lump sum transfers) of households. In this way the incentive effects of the tax reduction may be separated from the incentive effect of the financing rule.

REDUCTION IN THE TAXATION OF LABOUR INCOME

This section evaluates the effects of the reduction in the labour income tax rates only. The experiment consists of a gradual reduction in the tax rates applied to wages by 3.6 percentage points and to unemployment benefits by 7.6 percentage points, whereas pensions after tax are not affected by the reform. The nominal unemployment benefits before tax fall by 4.3 per cent as a direct consequence of regulations connected with the tax reform. The total effect on the marginal reward of working is a 3.8 percentage points increase. Finally, a relatively small increase of employers' payroll tax rate at 0.6 percentage points is also a part of the experiment.

There are two main channels through which the reduction in the labour income tax rate affects the economy: a supply effect and a demand effect. The supply effect appears because the reduction in the marginal tax rate generates a permanent outward shift in the labour supply curve. On impact this increases employment by 0.1 per cent. This feeds into the marginal product of capital, which leads to increased investments and gradually increased capital stock. In the final stationary state the capital stock has increased by 0.9 per cent (see Table 6.3). After 25 years, more than 50 per cent of the total increase in output has taken place.

The demand effect is the following: The experiment favours the younger generations (who are in the labour force) at the expense of the older generations, therefore the life cycle behaviour of the agents is affected. There are two effects that counteract each other. First, young agents increase their propensity to save so that they are able to smooth consumption over the life cycle. Second, the supply-side effect implies that the activity in the economy is increased which adds to the value of firms and gradually also to the level of human capital in the economy.[4] The two latter effects tend to increase consumption whereas the former tends to reduce consumption. The result of the simulation reveals that in the first 25 years the net effect on consumption is negative, whereas the expansive effects dominate in all following periods. Therefore expansion of consumption is fairly slow compared to the expansion of production.

We start the analysis by concentrating on the supply-side effects.

Supply-side Effects

Initial labour supply
The total labour supply is the sum of the labour supply of the households. Each adult below 61 years supplies labour, whereas older household members are retired from the labour market and receive pension. The labour supply of the household members is chosen such that the lifetime utility of the household is maximised. The present version of the model embodies the simplifying assumption that the instantaneous utility function is additively separable in utility of leisure.[5] This assumption implies that the amount of work is chosen such that, at each moment of time, the level of non-interest income net of disutility from work is maximised, since this expands the feasible value of the instantaneous utility index. Therefore the labour supply decision is not subject to inter-temporal speculation, but rather chosen as a sequence of a-temporal optimisation problems. Perhaps more importantly, this means that the labour supply is independent of the wealth of the household.

To be able to calibrate the model (with a perfect competitive labour market) to the actual level of unemployment in the Danish economy, we assume that persons who belong to the workforce and supply less labour than an institutionally fixed maximum supply, $\bar{l}$, are entitled to (supplementary) unemployment benefits. Thus the labour market equilibrium implies that agents voluntarily reduce their individual labour supply, $l_{i,t}$, such that underemployment and work sharing prevails. The calibrated level of unemployment in the model is thus by assumption entirely voluntary.

The non-interest income associated with activity in the labour market is the sum of the salary net of taxes, and the unemployment benefit net of taxes. This amounts to:

$$(1-T_t^{\omega})W_t \ell_{i,t} + (1-T_t^{b})b_t(\bar{\ell} - \ell_{i,t}) \tag{6.1}$$

where W_t is the wage rate at time t, b_t is the level of unemployment benefits measured per hour, T_t^w and T_t^b are the effective average tax rates of income from employment and unemployment benefits respectively.[6]

Given the specified utility function, the labour supply decision, identical for all generations and both genders, is given by:

$$\ell_t = \left(\frac{(1-T_t^\omega)W_t - (1-T_t^b)b_t}{\gamma_1 P_t} \right)^\gamma \qquad (6.2)$$

where γ is the labour supply elasticity, and γ_1 is a level parameter for the disutility of labour supply. In modelling the tax system, we assume that the income from employment and unemployment benefit are taxed by separate tax systems.

Observe that this very simple labour supply function has the property that if there is a fixed replacement level after tax (i.e. after tax unemployment benefits are increased by the same (absolute) amount as the real after tax wages), then complete real wage flexibility with respect to the labour tax rate prevails. On the other hand if unemployment benefits are indexed to for example the wage level (as in the present case), then real wage resistance is the outcome and a decrease in the tax rate of employed persons will increase employment. These effects are the typical outcome of models with imperfect competition in the labour market, irrespective of whether models of bargaining, search or efficiency wages are employed (see for example Pissarides (1998) for a survey of these models). Therefore one should not expect the qualitative effects from these kinds of models to differ.

On the other hand it is well established that in labour markets with imperfect competition a decrease in the progressivity of the tax system tends to increase the equilibrium wage whereas the opposite is true in labour markets with perfect competition. Hansen et al. (1995) show that if the bargaining model is extended to the case where both the wage and the length of the working day are negotiated then decreased progressivity may have both a decreasing and an increasing effect on the wage rate. The sign of the effect depends upon the elasticity of the labour supply and the bargaining power of the union. The present formulation of the tax system where no progressivity effect is present sidesteps this problem. This lack of progressivity effects is consistent with a recent analysis based on panel data for the Danish economy in Pedersen et al. (1998), where only very small progressivity effects (of both signs) are reported.

Given this simple labour supply function (6.2), the tax reform affects labour supply through the changes in the average tax rates (note that the average and marginal tax rates are equal). These are calculated using the structure of the Danish labour income taxation and the distribution of taxable incomes. The results are presented in Table 6.2 below.[7]

Table 6.2 Average taxation rates and the replacement ratio

	1993	1994	1995	1996	1997	1998	1994-98
Average taxation rate							
- employed worker	45.1	43.3	42.7	42.3	42.1	41.5	42.4
- unemployed worker	35.7	31.4	30.6	30.0	29.2	28.1	29.9
Replacement ratio after							
tax	79.9	79.9	79.6	79.3	79.8	80.0	79.7

Inserting actual numbers into the labour supply function (6.2) shows the quantitative effect of the shift in the labour supply function. Normalising the wage rate to 1, the numerator for 1993 (prior to the tax reform) amounts to $(1 - 0.451) - 0.680 * (1 - 0.357) = 0.549 - 0.437 = 0.112$. The reform changes the numerator for 1998 to $(1 - 0.415) - 0.680 * (1 - 0.043) * (1 - 0.281) = 0.585 - 0.468 = 0.117$.

As the denominator is not directly affected by the labour income tax changes, the direct initial effect is therefore an increase in the marginal reward of working of $0.122/0.112 = 4$ per cent. This initially expands the labour supply by around 0.4 per cent as the labour supply elasticity, γ, is equal to 0.1. In sum, increasing the marginal reward of work, in a standard competitive labour market with an upward sloping labour supply schedule, initially shifts the labour supply curve outwards (to the right), since at the optimum the marginal disutility of work must be equal to the marginal benefit from work.

Initial labour demand

The increase in the payroll tax rate from zero to 0.6 per cent shifts the firms' labour demand schedule inwards. The net outcome of the outward shift of the labour supply curve and the inward shift of the labour demand curve is that the real wage rate drops, while the impact on employment is theoretically undetermined. However, the payroll tax hike is so small that the impact on employment can safely be expected to be positive, dominated by the outward shift of the labour supply curve.

Capital accumulation

The firms in the private sector have convex cost of installation of capital, so that investments are a function of Tobin's *q*. This implies that the capital stock only gradually adjusts as a function of the increased marginal productivity of capital. Due to the solution in 5-year steps no overshooting of investments appears. However, as mentioned this does not prevent the supply side of the economy from reacting relatively fast to the change in the tax structure.

Demand-side Effects

Budgetary effects of the labour income tax reduction
The reduction in the tax rate implies that the tax revenue to the public sector is reduced. Even though the wage sum is increased and the level of unemployment is reduced the automatic stabilisers are not sufficiently strong to prevent a substantial loss in revenue of DKR 15 billion. As mentioned we assume that this revenue loss is financed through lump sum taxes. The lump sum transfer is identical for all adults - workers as well as pensioners. The net initial effect on current disposable income of the generations alive is that those generations that belong to the labour force experience a positive effect, whereas the current disposable income of each pensioner declines. The present value of future disposable income flows therefore initially declines for pensioner generations. It increases initially for generations who are young enough for their remaining periods in the labour force to generate additional disposable wage income sufficient to outweigh their discounted future loss as pensioners. This picture of gains and losses initially stimulates the savings of the younger generations to smooth consumption over the life cycle.

Consumption of households
The combined assumption of perfect capital markets and perfect foresight implies that the consumption of a household in DREAM is a function of the sum of the stock of financial assets, $a_{b-1,t-1}$ and the level of human capital, $H_{b-1,t-1}$. As we assume that the inter-temporal elasticity of substitution is less than one, the consumption function may be written as a standard CES function in current prices and an index of future prices, $\eta_{b,t}$, where b is the age of the household at time t. Future prices are age specific as the household faces a finite time horizon and therefore the vector of relevant future prices depends upon the remaining life time of the household.[8]

Consumption of household b at time t, $C_{b,t}$, is determined as

$$C_{b,t} = \xi_b^s \left(\frac{1+\theta}{(1+r_t^r (1-t_t^{EF}))N_{b-1,t-1}} \right)^{-S} \left(\frac{P_t}{\eta_{b-1,t-1}} \right)^{-S} \frac{a_{b-1,t-1} + H_{b-1,t-1}}{\eta_{b-1,t-1}} + Z_{b,t}$$

$18 \leq b \leq 78$ (6.3)

Where ξ_b is the bequest preference (differing from 1 for b=78 only), θ is the rate of time preference, r_t is the rate of interest, t_t' is the tax rate applied to interest income, $N_{b-1,\,t-1}^{\;EF}$ is the size of the generation in the previous period, S is the inter-temporal elasticity of substitution, $\eta_{b-1,t-1}$ is the index of future consumption prices for generation b and P_t is the current consumer price index. $Z_{b,t}$ is the disutility of work.

To determine the evolution of the consumption over time we analyse the impact of the reform on the two components of total wealth and on the development of consumer prices.

Human capital

Recall that human capital is defined as the discounted stream of future non-interest income. For the retired part of the population this amounts to the stream of future pensions after tax and other transfers from the government including the lump sum tax that is used to finance the public deficit. As pensions after tax are unaffected by the reform the public deficit implies that the level of human capital for pensioners is reduced on impact. Therefore this tends to reduce consumption for these age groups.

For younger generations the expected lower level of pensions also tends to reduce the human capital. On the other hand the increased wage after tax that follows from the reduction in the labour income taxation and the increased employment tends to increase the stock of human capital. If the age group in question has a sufficiently long remaining time as active on the labour market the positive effect will dominate the reduced expected pensions. The aggregate level of human capital is reduced on impact but gradually the increase in the wage sum becomes pronounced as new generations enter the economy in a phase with a higher production and therefore higher wage sum.

Non-human capital

The non-human capital consists of the net financial wealth of the private sector. The domestic private sector owns by assumption the domestic stock of shares.[9] In addition to this the domestic private sector holds a stock of bonds (either government bonds or foreign bonds).

The increased production described in the previous sub-section implies that the dividends of the domestic firms are increased from 5 years on. Forward looking markets foresee this and the value of firms increases on impact.

Consumer prices

Consumer prices initially fall by 0.3 per cent and gradually increase from this point on. After 50 years the prices have returned to the original level and continue to increase. The steady state price level is 1 per cent higher than the original level. This development tends to increase the initial level of consumption ceteris paribus as the consumers engage in inter-temporal price speculations. The price development follows from the fact that the increase in production is faster than the increase in consumption. Therefore excess domestic supply has to be sold in the foreign markets in the initial phase. This causes lower prices on domestic production that drives the reduction in the consumer prices. Gradually this is reversed such that excess domestic demand prevails relative to the initial equilibrium.

Consumption

Initially the negative effect on human capital for most generations alive when the reform is introduced dominates a positive stimulus to consumption from increased non-human wealth and temporarily low consumer prices. The resulting initial drop in aggregate private consumption is 0.8 per cent. The process of increasing consumption is very slow. Private consumption is back to the original level after approximately 25 years and after 50 years the increase is about 1 per cent. This slow adjustment is explained by the fact that with perfect foresight the gradual increase in the aggregate level of human capital which generates the increase in consumption is a consequence of the turnover of generations. Aggregate human capital only increases because the human capital of new generations is higher than that of their predecessors. This increase appears because activity in the economy in their life span is higher. Therefore the long horizon of each cohort determines the slow turnover.

The Total Effect of the Labour Income Tax Reduction

Table 6.3 shows the main macro-economic effects of the reduction in the labour income taxation. It is hardly surprising that reducing the distorting tax on labour income and replacing it with a non-distorting tax, one generates higher labour market participation and thereby higher activity in the economy. Perhaps more surprisingly is the fact that a very large part of the population alive at the introduction of the reform is actually better off without the reduction of the distorting tax.

Figure 6.2 shows that the generations that have not yet entered the labour market, all gain from the introduction of the reform. Among the existing generations, only the younger generations gain from the reform. This is caused by opposite effects: after-tax wages increase, whereas the value of lump sum transfers (that all individuals receive) falls. The reason that the middle-aged are worse off than the old is that they are subject to the new tax system for a longer period.

*Table 6.3   Effects of the labour income tax reduction (billions of DKR)**

	Initial stationary state	5 years	10 years	25 years	50 years	New stationary state
Private consumption	416	413	414	417	421	432
		(-0.8)	(-0.5)	(0.2)	(1.2)	(3.8)
Real GDP	830	830	831	833	834	835
		(0.0)	(0.2)	(0.4)	(0.5)	(0.7)
Employment, index	100.0	100.1	100.4	100.4	100.4	100.5
		(0.1)	(0.4)	(0.4)	(0.4)	(0.5)
Capital stock	2664	2667	2669	2675	2681	2690
		(0.1)	(0.2)	(0.4)	(0.6)	(0.9)
Value of firms	1489	1490	1492	1495	1501	1519
		(0.1)	(0.2)	(0.4)	(0.8)	(2.0)
Foreign assets	-259	-250	-241	-214	-176	-70

Note: * The numbers in parentheses are the percentage change compared to the initial stationary state.

Figure 6.2 Generational welfare effects of the labour income tax reduction

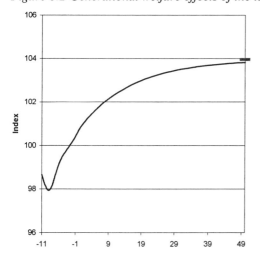

The most striking development presented in Table 6.3 is the effect on the foreign asset position that moves from a debt of DKR 259 billion to a debt of

DKR 70 billion from the initial to the final steady state. This effect is the accumulated result of the increased savings rate of each generation. Observe however that also this development is pretty slow as less than 50 per cent of the reduction has taken place after 50 years.

Observe that this improvement in long-run macro-economic measures comes at a cost. First, to generate the increased labour supply the difference between the net wage rate and the net unemployment benefit rate must rise, thereby generating higher intra-generational inequality on impact. Second, to increase the savings rate, the income after tax of the retired generations has to fall (at least relatively). This generates higher inter-generational income inequality on impact. Therefore one may conclude that the long-run efficiency gains appear at the cost of higher inequality on impact.

GREEN TAXES

The introduction of green taxes on the (household) consumption of energy and use of water is modelled as an increase in the general excise on the aggregate consumption good. This is obviously not a satisfactory way of introducing green taxes (especially from an environmental point of view) as it ignores the substitution effects within the consumption bundle - away from polluting goods. From a green perspective this is perhaps the most important effect and probably the main reason for the introduction. However, the high level of aggregation of the product market in the version of DREAM that is used in the present analysis leaves no alternative. This is especially worth noticing since the resulting long-run effect of the pure increase in the green duties is an increase in consumption and production and therefore probably also in (flow) pollution.

Green taxes are therefore consumption taxes. The revenue from green taxes is raised gradually from DKR 2.7 billion in 1994 to DKR 12 billion in 1998. The excise tax rates in the model are calibrated such that these revenues are generated.

Like the labour income taxation, the green taxes have both a supply and a demand effect. The supply effect appears because the increased indirect taxes reduce the net gain from being employed and therefore shift the labour supply curve inwards generating a contraction of the supply in the economy that works through the same mechanisms as the supply expansion described in the previous section. In addition the green taxes generate a demand effect, similar to the demand effect described in the previous section. It may seem paradoxical that introduction of a consumption tax gives rise to a shift in the demand over the life cycle, as it is a proportional tax on lifetime resources. However, as noted by Frederiksen (1997), the effect cannot be isolated from the impact of the recycling of revenue over generations. In the present simulation lump sum transfers that are identical for all adult individuals distribute the increase in net revenue. On the other hand the calibration of the model implies that consumption for a given adult is increasing through the life cycle, due to the fact that the interest rate after tax exceeds the rate of pure time preference. This consumption path implies that the net income loss from the green taxes is increasing with the age of the individual in question. Thus older generations become worse off on impact and younger generations foresee that this will also be the case for them and therefore increase their savings.

The Supply Effect

Following the procedure employed in the previous section, we may calculate the direct initial effect on the marginal reward from being employed as 2 per cent. This implies a contraction of the labour supply by 0.2 per cent. On impact this reduces the marginal product of capital leading to a lower level of investment and therefore also to a lower capital stock.

The Demand Effect

Initially the introduction of green taxes implies an increase in the consumer price index which, ceteris paribus, tends to reduce the real value of both the stock of human capital and the stock of non-human capital. For the retired persons and the older age groups on the labour market this effect is not neutralised by an increase in the stock of human capital. For pensioners this is because the increase in the lump sum transfer is not sufficiently large as argued above. For those generations that are active on the labour market the initial phase also implies a reduction in the real value of the stock of human capital since the disposable wage is almost constant the first 25 years, whereas employment is reduced.[10] These effects imply that total consumption drops by 0.5 per cent in the initial phase and only gradually recovers such that after 50 years the original level has been exceeded by 0.2 per cent. From this point on consumption continues to grow and in the steady state consumption is approximately 2 per cent higher than in the original equilibrium.

The slow gradual increase in consumption follows from the increased incentive to save. This gradually increases the stock of non-human assets held by the private sector, which again stimulates consumption. The relative increase in consumption gradually generates an excess demand for the domestically produced good relative to the initial phase. Through the Armington specification of the foreign trade this generates an increased price of the domestic product. The increased producer price increases the value of the marginal input factors, which increases factor demand. The effect is however slow and very small. After 50 years the capital stock recovers to the initial level after a minor redressing in the initial phase. In the new stationary state the capital stock has increased by 0.1 per cent. The employment remains virtually unaffected by the increased labour demand, which is due to the indexation of the unemployment benefits that keeps the replacement ratio constant and in this way keeps employment down. The macro-economic effects of the green taxes are shown in Table 6.4 below.

Table 6.4   Effects of green taxes (billions of DKR)[*]

	Initial stationary state	5 years	10 years	25 years	50 years	New stationary state
Private consumption	416	418	414	416	417	422
		(0.3)	(-0.5)	(-0.2)	(0.2)	(1.4)
Real GDP	830	830	828	829	829	830
		(0.0)	(-0.1)	(-0.1)	(-0.1)	(0.0)
Employment, index	100.0	100.0	99.8	99.9	99.9	99.9
		(0.0)	(-0.2)	(-0.1)	(-0.1)	(-0.1)
Capital stock	2664	2662	2662	2663	2665	2668
		(-0.1)	(-0.1)	(0.0)	(0.0)	(0.1)
Value of firms	1489	1485	1487	1489	1492	1500
		(-0.3)	(-0.1)	(0.0)	(0.2)	(0.7)
Foreign assets	-259	-261	-257	-246	-229	-181

Note: * The numbers in parentheses are the percentage change compared to the initial stationary state.

Figure 6.3 shows the inter-generational welfare effects. It shows the impact of the net income loss, which as previously mentioned is increasing with the age of the individual. Older generations become worse off, whereas younger generations foresee the change and increase their savings.

Figure 6.3 Generational welfare effects of the green taxes

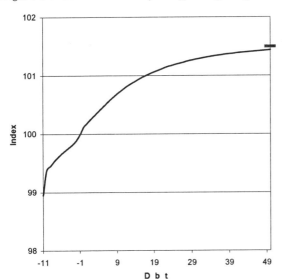

The Total Effect of the Green Taxes

As mentioned in the introduction to this section the evaluation of the green part of the reform cannot take into account the shift towards a more environmentally friendly composition of the private consumption bundle, as the production sector of DREAM is highly aggregated at a given point in time. Therefore no attempts has been made to model welfare effects of the reform's influence on the environment. The welfare measure is highly traditional and includes only utility from private consumption of consumer goods and utility from leisure. Utility from consuming the publicly produced good is also ignored.

For these reasons the effect described in this section comes down to an evaluation of a general consumption tax. As in the case of the labour income taxation this part of the reform implies that the stock of wealth of the private sector is increased in the long run. This increase generates higher consumption in the long run. Observe however that this asset accumulation effect depends on the generational distribution of the revenue from the taxes. Given the assumption of uniform age-independent transfers per individual one may also in this case argue that the positive long-run result has a short-run cost, as the elder part of the population alive at the introduction of the reform are better off before the introduction of the consumption tax. The negative effect on employment may also increase intra-generational inequality.

CAPITAL INCOME TAXATION

The tax reform affects three different capital income taxes in DREAM: the tax rate on interest income is reduced, the tax rate on dividends is reduced and the capital gains tax is increased. The calculated changes in these three different tax rates are shown in Table 6.5 below.[11]

Table 6.5   Capital income taxes (1993-1998)

	1993	1994	1995	1996	1997	1998	1994-98
Tax on interest income	51.5	49.3	48.7	48.2	48.0	46.7	48.2
Tax on dividends	36.2	35.7	35.0	32.7	32.6	31.6	33.5
Tax on capital gains	15.1	25.8	25.7	25.5	25.5	25.1	25.5

One should note that the capital gains tax of DREAM follows the mainstream formulation and assumes taxation of capital gains on accrual, whereas the capital gains tax in Denmark taxes the gain on realisation. The calculation of effective tax rate on accrual follows the procedure of King and Fullerton (1984).

Before evaluating the supply and demand effects of these taxes it will be useful to describe the modelling of firm behaviour in DREAM in some detail.

Behaviour of Firms

We assume all firms to be organised as joint stock companies. The value of firms is determined from an arbitrage condition (Equation (6.4) explained below), which states that the gains from investing in shares must be the same after tax as investing in bonds.

The assumption of perfect capital mobility and absence of uncertainty implies that domestic and foreign bonds are perfect substitutes. Therefore a tax-adjusted version of the uncovered interest parity (UIP) holds in the model. Absence of exchange rate movements implies that, in equilibrium, the domestic interest rate after tax equals the foreign interest rate after tax. With a residence-based taxation of personal capital income this implies that the domestic (pre-tax) interest rate is equal to the foreign (pre-tax) interest rate.

Since Danish personal capital income taxation is a residence-based tax, we assume as a starting point that the marginal Danish investor is a domestic citizen, who is subject to Danish domestic tax laws.[12] This assumption is not innocent for two reasons. First, foreign investors may be the marginal source of funds, if domestic tax laws give higher incentives to investment in bonds than do foreign tax laws (assuming all countries use a residence-based tax).

In this case foreign tax rates are the relevant ones. Second, a large part of Danish savings take place in pension funds, which are not subject to the same tax laws as citizens. The tax laws give pension funds an incentive to invest in shares.

The consequence of the domestic-private-investor assumption is that the model will exaggerate the effect of changes in personal capital income taxation on the market value of shares.

The assumption that the investor is subject to Danish tax laws for private agents and the fact that there is no risk in the model implies that the marginal investor will be indifferent between investing in bonds and in shares if:

$$r\,(1-t_t^r)V_{t-1} = (1-t_t^d)\,D_t + (1-t_t^g)\,(V_t - V_{t-1}) \qquad (6.4)$$

where r is the interest rate equal to the world interest rate, which in a world with perfect mobility of financial capital is given for the small open economy. For simplicity we assume that the interest rate is constant through time. V_t is the (end of period) value of the firm.[13] D_t are dividends. The tax rates are: t_t^r, tax rate on interest income, t_t^d, tax rate on dividend income, and, t_t^g, tax rate on capital gains.

The left-hand side is the opportunity cost of holding shares, whereas the right-hand side is the sum of dividends and capital gains after tax, which is equal to the total income from holding the value V_{t-1} in shares.

Observe that due to the possibility of different tax rates the investor is not indifferent between a unit increase in the (pre-tax) dividends and a unit increase in the (pre-tax) market value of shares. A unit decrease in the dividends may be compensated by $(1-t_t^d)\,/\,(1-t_t^g)$ units increase in the market value of shares. Similarly, a 1 percentage point increase in the (pre-tax) interest rate requires an increase in the market value of shares of $(1-t_s^r)/(1-t_s^g)$ per cent for the arbitrage condition (6.4) to hold. These tax adjustment factors will appear frequently in the expressions concerning the behaviour of the firm.

Solving the arbitrage condition (6.4) for V_t yields the result that the market value of firms is given as the tax adjusted stream of dividends:

$$V_s = \sum_{t-s+1}^{\infty} \frac{1-t_t^d}{1-t_t^g} D_t \prod_{v=s+1}^{t} \frac{1}{1+r_v\left(\dfrac{1-t_v^r}{1-t_v^g}\right)} \qquad (6.5)$$

Dividends are defined as:

$$D_t = (1 - t_t^c)\left(p_t Y_t - p_t^M M_t - (1 + t_t^a)W_t L_t - r_t B_{t-1}^c\right)$$
$$- p_t^I I_t + t_t^c \hat{\delta} \hat{K}_{t-1} + \left(B_t^c - B_{t-1}^c\right) \tag{6.6}$$

where p_t is the (producer) price of the domestically produced good, Y_t is the (net) production, p_t^M is the price index of materials, M_t is the input of materials, t_t^a is the payroll tax rate, W_t is the wage, L_t is employment, B_{t-1}^c is the stock of corporate debt at the beginning of period t, p_t^I is the price index of investments, I_t is investment, K_{t-1} is the book value of the capital stock given the tax system, $\hat{\delta}$ is the rate of depreciation allowed by the tax system and t_t^c is the corporate tax rate.

Concerning the financing decision of the firm we adopt the so-called 'new view on dividend taxation', and assume that the firm in question debt finances a fixed part of its current capital stock and abstains from issuing new shares. These assumptions imply that investments are financed through retained earnings plus debt, and that the residual cash flow is always distributed to the owners.

These assumptions imply that capital income tax rates will affect the investment decision of the firm. Due to the convex cost of installation of capital, the firm has a demand for investments and in general not a demand for capital. In the stationary state we may however write an implicit demand for the stock of capital using the cost of capital. Given the tax system of the model the required marginal product of capital is given by the following expression (time subscripts are eliminated to indicate that the expression is only valid in the stationary state of the model):

$$F_K' - \frac{p^I}{p}\delta = \frac{p^I}{p}\left[r\left(g + \frac{1 - t^r}{(1 - t^g)(1 - t^c)}(1 - g)\right) + \frac{\dfrac{1 - t^r}{(1 - t^g)(1 - t^c)}rt^c(\delta - \hat{\delta})}{\dfrac{1 - t^r}{1 - t^g}r + \hat{\delta}}\right]$$
$$+ \frac{\partial \Phi}{\partial K}(\delta, 1) + \left(\frac{1 - t^r}{1 - t^g}r + \delta\right)\frac{p^I(p, 1)}{p}\frac{\partial \Phi}{\partial I}(\delta, 1) \tag{6.7}$$

where δ is the physical rate of depreciation, g is the debt ratio of the firm and Φ is the cost of installation of capital. The left-hand side of Equation (6.7) is the required net marginal product of capital in the stationary state. The right-hand side is the cost of capital. Observe that the cost of capital may be decomposed into three components: financial costs, costs of depreciation, and costs of installation; these terms correspond to the three terms in Equation (6.7) (two terms in the first line, and the last term in the second line). If the capital income taxation is neutral, i.e. if $(1-t^i) = (1-t^s)(1-t^c)$, then the degree of debt financing does not affect the financial cost which remains equal to the rate of interest, r. Similarly, if the depreciation allowed by the tax system is identical to the true rate of depreciation, then the cost of depreciation vanishes.

Given the current calibration of the initial steady state, there is a minor advantageous tax treatment of financing through retained earnings, which implies that the financial costs are lower than the rate of interest. The cost of depreciation is negative, since the allowed rate of depreciation of the tax system exceeds the true rate of depreciation. Therefore the effect of the capital income taxation in the initial stationary state is - ceteris paribus - a distortion towards a too high level of the domestic capital stock.

Given this description of the behaviour of firms we are now in a position to evaluate the changes in the capital income taxation. We do this by focusing on each of the tax rates separately.

The Reduction in the Dividend Taxation

If the change in the dividend taxation is considered a once and for all change, then the dividend tax rate is a neutral tax rate, in the sense that the level of the tax rate does not affect the optimal level of investments and employment. Because of the fact that the value of the firm is the discounted stream of tax adjusted dividends, it follows that if the reduction in the dividend tax rate is a once and for all change, then the value of the firms increases by the discounted value of the sum of saved dividend taxes for the whole future. Thus the present shareholders reap the entire gain from the reduction in the tax rate.

The fact that the change in the dividend taxation is not a once and for all change but a gradual reduction over two periods in the model implies that the behaviour of firms in fact is affected as well. The effect is the following. With the introduction of the tax reform the phase-in of changes in the tax rates is announced with certainty. In period 1 the firm therefore knows that the dividend taxation is lower in period 2 and the following periods. To increase the after-tax stream of dividends the firm will want to postpone dividends until the low tax rate has been introduced. However given the fact that the financing rule is fixed in the model the only way to postpone dividends is to undertake physical investments.[14] Therefore investment peaks in period 1 and is reduced again in period 2.

Apart from this investment peak the reduction in dividend taxation only affects the economy through the shift of resources from future generations to current shareholders, since the lack of revenue is financed through lump sum taxes on future generations.

Reduction in the Taxation of Interest Income

The reduction in the taxation of interest income contains both a supply and a demand effect. The supply effect follows from the fact that the interest rate after tax has increased by the reduction. This implies that the user cost of capital in the stationary state has increased, see the right-hand side of Equation (6.7). The firm therefore reacts by reducing the level of investments. This gradually reduces the capital stock, which again reduces the marginal product of labour and therefore labour demand.

The demand effects are driven by the following changes. First, the current population experiences an initial capital loss on shares. This capital loss accrues due to both the reduced activities in the economy and the increased discounting of future dividends that follows from the increased interest rate after tax. Second, the increased interest rate after tax increases the excess of interest payments over the pure rate of time preference implying that each individual prefers a steeper consumption path over the life cycle than was the case prior to the reduction in the tax rate. This reduces the initial consumption and increases the savings ratio.

On impact the contraction in demand exceeds the contraction in supply, which generates an excess supply of the domestic production that has to be sold in the world market, generating a price reduction on the domestic product. However, accumulation of non-human capital, which to a large extent takes the form of reduced foreign debt gradually increases domestic demand so that consumption is 0.3 per cent higher than in the initial equilibrium after 25 years. The speed of growth remains relatively high and in the new stationary state consumption is 8.6 per cent higher than in the initial steady state. This is financed through a significant increase in the stock of assets of the private sector. Domestic activity remains fairly constant through time.

The Increase in the Capital Gains Tax

An increase in the capital gains tax shares some characteristics with both a reduction in the tax rate on interest income and a reduction in the dividend taxation. The capital gains tax works through both a supply and a demand effect.

The supply effect of an increase in this tax is similar to the supply effect of a reduction in the taxation of interest income. Both tax changes tend to increase the cost of capital in the stationary state, see the right-hand side of Equation (6.7). This generates a reduction in investment and gradually also in the stock of capital, which leads to the contraction of supply as explained earlier.

The reason why the capital gains tax appears in the user cost of capital is that the financing decision implies that investments are partly financed through retained earnings, i.e. through a reduction in current dividends.

The demand effect is initiated in much the same way as the supply effect. The increased capital gains tax gives the firm an incentive to avoid capital gains by increasing dividends to the owners. From the definition of dividends, see Equation (6.6), it follows that the only way that the firm can increase dividends is to reduce investments. The increase in current dividends increases the initial value of the firm since the present value of the sum of future dividends increases due to the increase in current dividends. Thus the current generation of shareholders experience a capital gain at the expense of future generations that will inherit an economy with a lower productive capacity.

Therefore consumption initially increases but as the aggregate human capital is reduced due to the lower activity in the economy gradually decreases. After approximately 25 years consumption is back to the original level. The slow reduction in demand implies a rather rapid accumulation of foreign debt. In the final steady state the foreign debt has doubled compared to the initial equilibrium and has reached a level of approximately DKR 500 billion.

The Total Effects of the Changes in the Capital Income Taxation

Combining the three elements discussed above raises the interesting question of whether this favours current or future generations (or both). The reduction in the interest income taxation generally favours future generations at the expense of those currently alive. On the other hand both the increase in the capital gains tax and the reduction in the dividend taxation tend to favour current generations at the expense of future generations. Table 6.6 below shows the macro-economic consequences of the change in the capital income taxation whereas Figure 6.4 shows the generational distribution of utility relative to the initial stationary state.

The macro-economic variables in Table 6.6 reveal that even if the lifetime consumption path becomes more steep for each individual, implying an increased propensity to save then this is not sufficient for the aggregate consumption to remain at the initial level. This is due to the decreased activity in the economy in the long run.

The utility diagram shows that the combined effect of the reduced dividend taxation and the increased capital gains tax dominates the effect from the reduced taxation of interest income. Consequently, the total capital income tax part of the reform redistributes utility from future generations to current generations and especially to the older part of the generations currently alive. This is so since most of the positive transfer to current generations takes the form of capital gains and the older generations are the wealthiest generations.

*Table 6.6 Effects of the changes in capital income taxation (billions of DKR)**

	Initial stationary state	5 years	10 years	25 years	50 years	New stationary state
Private consumption	416	421	421	418	416	411
		(1.1)	(1.2)	(0.5)	(0.0)	(-1.4)
Real GDP	830	834	831	818	810	805
		(0.5)	(0.2)	(-1.4)	(-2.4)	(-2.9)
Employment, index	100.0	100.0	99.9	99.8	99.7	99.6
		(0.0)	(-0.1)	(-0.2)	(-0.3)	(-0.4)
Capital stock	2664	2640	2610	2554	2517	2497
		(-0.9)	(-2.1)	(-4.1)	(-5.5)	(-6.3)
Value of firms	1489	1699	1713	1733	1744	1740
		(14.1)	(15.1)	(16.4)	(17.2)	(16.8)
Foreign assets	-259	-247	-231	-205	-199	-242

Note: * The numbers in parentheses are the percentage change compared to the initial stationary state.

Figure 6.4 Generational welfare effects of the changes in the capital income taxation

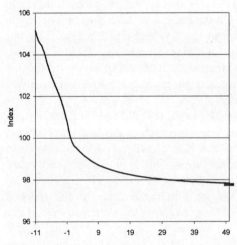

CONCLUSION

The Danish tax reform of 1993 involves all major parts of the tax system except the corporate tax rate and the VAT. The reform features a shift of the tax burden away from labour income taxation towards green taxes on consumption. At the same time it involves a change in the structure of both the labour income taxation and the capital income taxation.

We showed that the net effect of these changes on the macro-economic performance is modest if one considers a time horizon of 50 years. The only relatively large effect is the accumulated increase in the total stock of assets held by the private sector in the economy and the simultaneous reduction in the domestic stock of capital. However these two effects are important as the initial equilibrium was subject to distortions that created too low a level of asset accumulation and too high a domestic capital stock. Therefore the tax reform is a move in the right direction from an efficiency point of view. Furthermore, the analysis revealed that the reform generates a (strict) Pareto improvement, in the sense that all current and future generations are better off (in terms of welfare) than before the reform. To this one may add that to the extent that the reform succeeds in shifting consumption away from polluting goods there may be an additional positive utility effect from the cleaner environment.

The conclusion of the analysis is that the reform is well balanced when inter-generational distribution is considered. As the analysis revealed each of the elements of the reform do not strike this balance. The labour income tax part of the reform tends (when considered in isolation) to favour future generations at the expense of generations currently alive. The same is true for the green part of the tax reform in isolation. On the other hand, the capital income tax part of the reform tends to favour current generations at the expense of future generations. Given the relative sizes of the different parts the total reform becomes balanced.[15]

In the appendix presented below a sensitivity analysis is performed. This analysis may be taken to reveal that the economic effects of the reform - and therefore the conclusion presented above - seem fairly robust to changes in key parameters in the model.

APPENDIX - SENSITIVITY ANALYSIS

This section investigates the sensitivity of the evaluation of the total tax reform to the size of some of the parameters essential for the results, cf. the last remarks in the section above. Technically, changing one parameter necessitates changing at least one other parameter for the calibrated model to be able still to reproduce the benchmark data set exactly. In other words it implies a re-calibration of the model. In most cases the consequence is a change in a trivial parameter with little effect for the marginal properties of the model. For example changing the labour supply elasticity necessitates a corresponding change in the level parameter, γ_1, of the labour supply function and changing an elasticity of substitution involves changing the distribution parameters of the CES function in question. However, changing one parameter in households' inter-temporal utility function involves changing the other two non-trivial inter-temporal parameters because the inter-temporal utility parameters are calibrated simultaneously.

Table 6.7 summarises the outcome of the sensitivity analysis by listing the dynamic course in six key variables as a result of the total reform.[16] This is done both for the central calibration, referred to as the base case, and for three alternative parameter set-ups - namely, first, double labour supply elasticity, second, double foreign trade elasticities, and third, a 5 per cent higher bequest parameter. The first row for each of the six variables put together reproduces Table 6.1, whereas the following rows state the percentage change compared to the initial stationary state for the base case and the three other simulations, respectively.

Double Labour Supply Elasticity

In this simulation the labour supply elasticity is assumed to be equal to 0.2 instead of the central calibration value of 0.1. Looking at the labour supply Equation (6.2), this implies that the impact of a change in the real reward of working on the labour supply doubles. Table 6.7 shows accordingly that compared with the central calibration, the effect of the total tax reform on employment doubles right from the start as there is no inter-temporal speculation in the supply of labour. In the longer run, as the capital stock adjusts downwards, the effect on unemployment disappears, just as in the central case. However, the equilibrium capital stock declines slightly less than in the central case. It falls by 5.1 per cent compared with a fall of 5.2 per cent in the central calibration. The larger input of the factors of production means that production falls less (from -2.2 to -2.1 per cent), along with a larger increase in consumption (from 4.1 to 4.3 per cent) and wealth.

Double Foreign Trade Elasticities

In this experiment the elasticities of substitution in the Armington specification of import demands are doubled from the central calibration range of 1.1-1.5 to 2.2-3.0, and the numerical export price elasticity is doubled from 1.4 to 2.8. This implies that the increased net supply of the domestic good to the foreign market, which appears in the short run, leads to a lower reduction of the price of the domestic good. Therefore the initial effect is a more rapid accumulation of wealth in the private sector, which appears as a significant improvement in the current account. The gradual contraction in domestic output, which follows from the increased cost of capital, does not imply the same increase in the domestic price level as in the case of low foreign price elasticities. Therefore the contraction does not generate the increase in the consumer real wages that followed from the reform in the case of low price elasticities. This reduces the increase in domestic consumption and activity in the long run and almost offsets the effect on consumption from the increased stock of assets. The fact that the reduced domestic production does not to the same extent generate a price increase on domestic products implies that future generations benefit less from the reform than in the base case. In fact the result is that future generations gain less than those currently alive and for those generations that enter the economy in the distant future there is approximately no effect. Therefore the positive long-run effect of the reform depends to a large extent upon the Armington specification and the price elasticities of foreign trade. The price elasticities used in the base case are the long-run estimates of Statistic Denmark's Macro-econometric model ADAM.

Bequest Parameter 5 per cent Higher

When performing central calibration, the rate of time preference is set to 1.25 per cent (0.25 per cent on an annual frequency). Given this, the inter-temporal elasticity of substitution and the preference for bequests are calibrated endogenously to be 0.983 and 0.799 respectively (the calibration procedure is described in detail in Knudsen et al., 1998b). Equally one can fix the bequest parameter to 0.799 and calculate the rate of time preference and the inter-temporal elasticity of substitution to 0.0125 and 0.983 respectively. The interpretation of the bequest parameter value is that at the optimum, the utility of leaving DKR 0.799 of bequest equals the utility of DKR 1 worth of consumption in the last 5-year period of a household's life, i.e. the utility of bequest is equal to the utility of 3.995 units of the last year's consumption.[17]

Increasing the bequest parameter by 5 per cent of its central calibration value now equates DKR 1 of bequest with 4.195 units of end period consumption. The corresponding values of the two other inter-temporal utility parameters are 1.256 for the inter-temporal elasticity of substitution and 0.035 for the rate of time preference (0.007 on an annual frequency). Increasing the bequest parameter increases the end of life assets and therefore it must increase the inter-temporal elasticity of substitution to stimulate savings,

Table 6.7 Effects under alternative parameter values (billions of DKR)[*]

	Initial stationary state	5 years	10 years	25 years	50 years	New stationary state
Private consumption	416	419	417	418	422	433
Base case		(0.7)	(0.2)	(0.5)	(1.4)	(4.1)
Double elasticity L_s		(0.7)	(0.2)	(0.5)	(1.4)	(4.3)
Double elasticity P_f		(0.4)	(-0.1)	(0.4)	(1.0)	(0.8)
Bequest par. + 5%		(0.4)	(-0.1)	(0.4)	(1.8)	(7.1)
Real GDP	830	834	832	820	813	812
Base case		(0.6)	(0.3)	(-1.2)	(-2.0)	(-2.2)
Double elasticity L_s		(0.6)	(0.3)	(-1.2)	(-2.0)	(-2.1)
Double elasticity P_f		(0.7)	(0.3)	(-1.5)	(-2.5)	(-2.9)
Bequest par. + 5%		(0.6)	(0.3)	(-1.2)	(-1.9)	(-1.9)
Employment, index	100.0	100.1	100.1	100.0	100.0	100.0
Base case		(0.1)	(0.1)	(0.0)	(0.0)	(0.0)
Double elasticity L_s		(0.2)	(0.3)	(0.0)	(-0.1)	(0.0)
Double elasticity P_f		(0.1)	(0.1)	(-0.1)	(-0.2)	(-0.2)
Bequest par. + 5%		(0.1)	(0.1)	(0.0)	(0.0)	(0.1)
Capital stock	2664	2640	2612	2563	2533	2527
Base case		(-0.9)	(-1.9)	(-3.8)	(-4.9)	(-5.2)
Double elasticity L_s		(-0.9)	(-1.9)	(-3.8)	(-4.9)	(-5.1)
Double elasticity P_f		(-1.1)	(-2.3)	(-4.5)	(-5.9)	(-6.4)
Bequest par. + 5%		(-0.9)	(-1.9)	(-3.7)	(-4.8)	(-4.7)
Value of firms	1489	1695	1714	1741	1763	1791
Base case		(13.9)	(15.1)	(16.9)	(18.4)	(20.3)
Double elasticity L_s		(13.9)	(15.1)	(16.9)	(18.4)	(20.4)
Double elasticity P_f		(13.3)	(14.0)	(15.1)	(15.7)	(15.8)
Bequest par. + 5%		(13.8)	(15.1)	(17.1)	(18.9)	(22.2)
Foreign assets	-259	-241	-211	-145	-82	45
Double elasticity L_s		-241	-211	-143	-79	55
Double elasticity P_f		-225	-175	-81	-30	-30
Bequest par. + 5%		-237	-203	-121	-32	208

Note: * The numbers in parentheses are the percentage change compared to the initial stationary state; L_s: labour supply; P_f: foreign price.

so that total assets can reproduce the benchmark values (to which the model is calibrated).

The net effect of the increase in the inter-temporal elasticity and the rate of pure time preference is that the optimal consumption path over the life cycle becomes steeper. Therefore younger generations tend to increase their savings whereas older generations tend to reduce savings. However as the bequest parameter is also increased the generation in question dies with a higher stock of financial wealth. In the short run these shifts in the structure of the life cycle demand have little effect on the economic activity. Gradually the effect on aggregate consumption is increasing, first because younger generations receive a larger inheritance from their parents but also due to the increased tendency to save for younger persons which stimulates aggregate wealth and therefore also aggregate consumption. Future generations are therefore significantly better off after the tax reform with this new calibration than in the baseline case. However the difference does not appear in the macro-economic performance until after 50 years.

In conclusion, the long-run level of aggregate consumption seems to be the most volatile variable with respect to the parameter changes in the sensitivity analysis. This is so since consumption partly is determined by the accumulated stock of wealth, which is a consequence of a very long accumulation process in the present model. Changing parameters that affect the savings behaviour in the model therefore tend to have relatively large effects on long-run consumption. In the sensitivity analysis this effect appears in the case of the increase in the bequest parameter. In the case of the increase in the elasticity of foreign trade a reduction in consumption relative to the base case appears due to the lower stock of human capital, which is the second main determinant of aggregate consumption. On the other hand the sensitivity analysis revealed that parameters that work through the supply side of the economy do not generate these accumulation effects. Doubling labour supply elasticities hardly affects the outcome of the economy. One should however bear in mind that even in the case of doubled elasticity the absolute value remains relatively low. In all cases the reform entails a welfare improvement for both current and future generations. In that respect this sensitivity analysis shows that the results are somewhat robust to the values of the investigated parameters. On the other hand, the numbers also reveal that a more marked and still plausible change in some parameter values might produce a rather different outcome. For example, even in the alternative calibration with doubled foreign trade elasticities, they seem rather small numerically. Increasing them still further could change the results so that the welfare gain for future generations may turn to a welfare loss. Finally, changing several parameters simultaneously might produce more pronounced differences.

NOTES

We would like to thank Jesper Hansen and Morten Lobedanz Sørensen for skilful research assistance. We thank Katrine Lange, EPRU, for assistance in the interpretation of the Tax Reform Act.

1. Additional information about the DREAM model can be found on the Internet at www.dst.dk.
2. The government is assumed to run a balanced budget in each period. The entire change in the net foreign position is therefore due to changes in the behaviour of the private sector.
3. Lange et al. (forthcoming) also perform a dynamic CGE analysis of the Tax Reform Act of 1993. This is done using the EPRU model, which differs from the present model in several aspects. However, the qualitative structural effects reported in their paper do not differ distinctively from the present experiments. They too find the reform to be a Pareto improvement.
4. In this paper human capital is defined as the discounted stream of future non-interest income.
5. The instantaneous utility function is the utility function for each period in the lifetime. Utility is derived from consumption, and disutility is incurred from time spent working. An agent's lifetime utility function depends on these utilities as well as utility from leaving a bequest.
6. Observe that the wage is assumed to be identical across generations and gender, implying that labour productivity is the same for all generations and both genders.
7. A detailed description of the Danish tax system and the calculations that lead to these average tax rates are given in Knudsen et al. (1998b) which is an extended version of the present chapter.
8. The age of the household is by definition equal to the age of the female in the household. Households exist until the female reaches the age of 78 years. People who survive this limit are assumed to consume the value of their age-dependent transfers.
9. The value of shares is determined from an arbitrage condition that states that the after-tax yield from holding bonds must be identical to the after tax yield from holding domestic shares in equilibrium.
10. The gradual in-phasing of the reform implies that green taxes are known to increase rapidly from the first period to the next. This implies that consumers engage in inter-temporal speculation and in fact increase consumption in the first period.
11. For detailed descriptions of the calculation of these tax rates see Knudsen et al. (1998b), which is an extended version of the present analysis.
12. By personal capital income taxation we mean taxation of personal interest income, dividend taxation and taxation of capital gains. Observe that corporate income taxation is source based.
13. Note that the end-of-period dating rule is used. This means that stock variables active in period $t+1$ are denominated t. For instance the relationship between investment and capital stock in the model (with exponential delay) is written as $K_t = (1-\delta) K_{t-1} + I_t$.
14. This highly unreliable feature of the model appears because the financing decision is not a result of optimal behaviour but a fixed (arbitrary) rule, which is applied to avoid corner solutions to the financing problem. It highlights the danger of introducing ad hoc assumptions in CGE models. It should be noted that this is the only arbitrary rule that is applied in DREAM.
15. The question remains whether the same is true when the intra-generational distribution is concerned. The present analysis, which considers a representative household in each generation, is not suited for this type of analysis.

16. Since the model is in 5-year intervals, all flows in the model are five times their annual amounts, while stocks are the same. In the table however, all flows are converted into their corresponding 1-year value.
17. Namely 0.428 times an extra period of 5 years.

PART THREE

Measuring Structural Reform

7.   A Miracle or Not? Recent Trends in the Growth Performance of the Dutch Economy

Bart van Ark and Jakob de Haan

INTRODUCTION

Since the late 1980s, the Dutch economy has outperformed neighbouring countries in several respects. It has achieved higher employment and GDP growth in combination with low inflation, and it had the lowest long-term interest rates in the European Union (EU). Dutch per capita GDP growth, which had moved well below the Northwest European average during the first half of the 1980s, is now almost back to that average.[1] The economy of the Netherlands also suffered less than other European economies from the recessions in 1992-93 and 1995. This performance represents a marked turnaround from the early 1980s, when the country faced a deep recession, the profitability of firms was close to zero, unemployment had risen sharply, and the fiscal deficit amounted to 9.5 per cent of GDP.

The rapid growth performance of the Dutch economy in terms of growth in real GDP, employment and per capita income can be traced back to the mid-1980s (OECD, 1996d; van Ark and de Haan, 1996; van Ark and de Jong, 1996; van Ark et al., 1996). The acceleration in GDP growth and in particular in employment growth has been so rapid that this turnaround has been referred to as the 'Dutch miracle' by parts of the media and other popular press.

We argue that there has been no miracle. The recent growth performance of the Netherlands has primarily been the result of a correction of the below-average performance of earlier times (i.e. the 1970s and early 1980s). This correction was mainly brought about by a significant wage moderation since the early 1980s, probably strengthened by the creation of a more effective wage negotiation structure and measures to reduce the share of the public sector outlays in GDP.[2] We argue that there is no conclusive evidence that other aspects of structural reform, such as deregulation of labour and product markets, greatly enhanced economic performance in the Netherlands. Furthermore we show that the euphoria about the miracle is dampened by a slowdown in labour productivity performance which appears to be particularly serious in major parts of the services sector.

The remainder of this Chapter is structured as follows. We start with a comparison of growth and level estimates of GDP and GDP per capita in the Netherlands relative to Northwest Europe, the EU and the OECD since 1960. One of our aims here is to see whether the Netherlands really is a special case or whether there are more cases of below-average performance in Northwest European countries in one sub-period that lead to faster growth during the next. Then, we discuss two aspects of structural reform that are often put forward as the main causes of the Dutch 'growth miracle', namely wage moderation and deregulation. Next we turn to the issue that despite accelerated employment and output growth, labour productivity growth in the Netherlands has slowed down since the mid-1980s. In the fourth section we analyse a number of labour supply measures. Then, we investigate whether the overall slowdown in productivity growth can be related to an increased concentration of labour in low productivity sectors, or whether it is the result of a slowdown of productivity growth within the sectors. We also look at the intra-sectoral productivity slowdown itself and provide tentative estimates of multi-factor productivity growth by sector.

COMPARATIVE GDP AND PER CAPITA INCOME PERFORMANCE

The growth acceleration of the Dutch economy has now been well documented, and is confirmed by the most recent estimates of growth rates of GDP and GDP per capita for the Netherlands and the averages for Northwest Europe, the European Union and the OECD presented in Table 7.1. Compared to Northwest Europe, growth of real GDP per capita in the Netherlands has been one percentage point higher between 1987 and 1996.

Table 7.2 presents corresponding figures in terms of relative levels. Whereas GDP per capita in 1996 was still around five per cent below the Northwest European average it came up from a level as much as 11 percentage points below the Northwest European level in 1987. In 1987 Dutch GDP per capita was at the bottom of the league of the eleven Northwest European countries, whereas in 1996 it was in eighth place behind Norway, Switzerland, Denmark, Belgium, Austria, France and Germany, although the differences between the latter five countries and the Netherlands were within a range of 7 percentage points. The estimates clearly lead to the conclusion that between 1987 and 1996 the Netherlands has been in the process of making up for what it had lost in terms of relative wealth compared to the rest of Northwest Europe in the late 1970s.[3]

Table 7.1 Growth of GDP and GDP per capita (1960-1996)

	Netherlands	NW Europe[a]	EU[b]	OECD[c]
GDP (constant prices)				
1960-1996	3.1	2.9	3.3	3.5
1960-1973	4.8	4.5	5.3	5.3
1973-1979	2.7	2.3	2.7	2.8
1979-1987	1.2	2.0	1.9	2.2
1987-1996	2.7	2.0	2.4	2.4
GDP per capita				
1960-1996	2.3	2.2	2.8	2.7
1960-1973	3.6	3.7	4.6	4.4
1973-1979	1.9	1.7	2.1	2.0
1979-1987	0.9	1.5	1.6	1.8
1987-1996	2.2	1.2	1.9	1.8

Notes:
a Northwest Europe, unweighted average for Austria, Belgium, Denmark, Germany (since 1991 incl. East Germany), Finland, France, Netherlands, Norway, Sweden, Switzerland and the UK.
b European Union, excluding Luxembourg.
c Unweighted average for 20 OECD member states (pre-1995 membership, excluding Luxembourg, Ireland, New Zealand and Turkey).

Sources: 1960-1990 from Maddison (1995), linked to 1990-1996 from OECD (1998k), with 1993 GDP in national currencies converted to US$ with EKS PPPs.

Table 7.2 Relative Level of GDP per capita (Northwest Europe=100)

	Netherlands	NW Europe	EU	OECD
1960	96	100	79	87
1973	95	100	85	92
1979	95	100	86	93
1987	89	100	85	93
1996	95	100	88	95

Source: See Table 7.1.

It should be emphasised that this process of convergence towards the Northwest European average has not been an automatic process. Indeed, as we show in the third section, it is our contention that the relative decline of the Netherlands was reversed due to the combined efforts of trade unions, employers' organisations and government. The very bad economic situation at the beginning of the 1980s created the right conditions for a change in wage and governmental policies. Indeed, it could be argued that a crisis was perhaps a necessary (but not a sufficient) condition for these changes to take place. However, despite a quick return to real output and per capita income growth by 1984, it was not until 1989 that the per capita income level began to rise relative to the Northwest European average.

Table 7.3   Analysis of strong recovery periods in Northwest Europe

| | Period with % GDP growth above 'NWE avg.' | | | | % inflation rate above 'NWE avg.' | |
| | 'above NWE avg. Growth'[a] | in given period (column 1) | in subsequent five years | differential (3)-(2) | in given period (column 1) | in subsequent five years |
	(1)	(2)	(3)	(4)	(5)	(6)
Austria	66-77	1.1	-0.2	-1.3	-1.5	-3.0
Belgium	66-74	0.7	-0.4	-1.1	-0.8	-8.1
Denmark	64-69	0.5	-1.5	-2.0	1.7	1.1
Denmark	82-86	1.2	-1.8	-3.0	1.1	-0.3
Finland	79-89	1.6	-4.8	-6.4	1.5	-0.2
France	61-78	0.8	-0.1	-0.9	0.3	3.6
Germany	67-73	-0.3	0.0	0.3	-1.7	-4.8
Germany[b]	88-92	1.9	-1.5[c]	-3.4	-0.9	0.0
Netherlands	62-71	1.4	0.2	-1.2	0.5	-0.5
Netherlands	73-78	0.6	-1.3	-1.9	-1.4	-2.9
Norway	74-81	2.3	1.7	-0.6	0.4	2.4
Norway	83-87	1.8	-0.4	-2.2	2.9	2.9
Switzerland	67-71	0.1	-3.2	-3.4	-0.1	-2.7
Switzerland	85-89	0.2	-1.0	-1.2	-1.4	0.5
UK	83-88	1.1	-1.0	-2.1	0.5	1.8
Average		1.0	-1.0	-2.0	0.1	-0.7

Notes:
a Periods of five or more years during which GDP growth was above Northwest European average or not less than –0.5 per cent below Northwest European average.
b Only West Germany.
c Only 1993 and 1994.

Source: For GDP see Table 7.1, inflation rates from IMF (1997a).

An important question is how long 'above average' growth can continue if one assumes that it is just a reflection of a movement around an average Northwest European growth rate. At some stage a slowdown in the growth rate may then be expected. Column (1) of Table 7.3 shows the periods during which Northwest European countries achieved an 'above average' growth. Column (2) shows the average growth rate above the Northwest European average. On average this growth surplus amounted to about 1 percentage point. Column (3) shows the average growth rate above (or below) the Northwest European average in the subsequent five years. It shows that on average the growth rate is 1 percentage point below the Northwest European average during these years. If we impose this outcome on the Dutch 'above average' growth rate from 1989 to 1996, the implication is a GDP growth rate of 1 percentage point below the Northwest European average once the convergence process has been completed.

Of course, the reasons for acceleration and slowdown vary across countries and across periods. However, as we include in Table 7.3 only periods with 5 or more years of 'above average' growth, the reasons are mainly structural and not cyclical. We checked this by calculating the inflation rates during the periods with above average growth as well, from which no clear pattern emerges (see columns (5) and (6) in Table 7.3). In eight cases (Denmark (twice), Finland, France, Netherlands (1962-1971), Norway (twice) and the UK) inflation is above the average of NW Europe during periods with a relatively good growth performance, while in the other seven cases inflation is below the average inflation in NW Europe. This suggests that the periods that we have figured out are not just strong cyclical recovery periods.

There are two arguments against drawing too many inferences from the past growth experience in Northwest Europe for the future growth perspective of the Netherlands. First, the 'convergence hypothesis' may be too conservative, as the reforms in labour and product markets may have moved the Netherlands on a structurally higher growth path compared to neighbouring economies. The impact of the reforms on growth in the Netherlands is the topic of the third section. Second, a comparison with the average of Northwest Europe (or any other average) as the yardstick might be less useful in the case when the Netherlands and Europe as a whole have a potential for faster growth relative to, for example, the United States. This possibility will be analysed in more detail in the fourth and fifth sections.

STRUCTURAL REFORM IN THE NETHERLANDS

Since the beginning of the 1980s the economic policies of many OECD countries focused on structural reform. According to the OECD, structural factors 'refer to the capacities of economies, institutions and societies in general to adjust to changing circumstances, to create and exploit new opportunities, and on that basis deploy and re-deploy resources. It is not possible to put a number on this capacity; and its relation to macroeconomic performance is clearly one of interaction, rather than mechanical causation' (OECD, 1987a, p. 16).[4] As pointed out by the OECD, various structural impediments for continued strong economic growth developed during the period when performance was still good, including the weakened capacity of collective bargaining to generate wage settlements consistent with economies' aggregate capacity to pay and the growth of the public sector, implying high marginal and average tax rates.

Two structural changes in the Netherlands are often referred to when explaining the 'Dutch miracle', namely wage cost moderation and liberalisation of markets. With the Wassenaar agreement (1982) between trade unions and employer organisations a policy of moderation of wage costs was introduced. Generally, the share of labour income in GDP is regarded as a useful proxy for the moderation of wage costs. In the 1970s labour income rose to over 80 per cent of GDP (excluding mining) in 1980. Thereafter it declined to just over 72 per cent in 1996 (IMF, 1997b). According to a study by the Netherlands Bureau for Economic Policy Analysis (1991), the enormous improvement in terms of employment growth over the period 1983-1990 was related to the moderation of average wage increases and to the de-linking of the minimum social benefit from contract wages. According to this study, if there had been no wage moderation and no delinkage, employment would have been 400,000 persons lower in 1990. Delinkage accounted for 150,000 jobs, while wage moderation accounted for some 250,000 jobs.

However, a recent study of the IMF criticises these findings, arguing that 'any autonomous contribution of wage moderation to employment growth in the Netherlands, over and above what would have been implied by underlying fundamental trends and policy changes ... appears to be negligible' (IMF, 1997b, p. 74). This conclusion is based on a simple model for the employment growth in which the replacement rate, the change in payroll taxes and social security contributions, the unemployment rate, the rate of change of population at working age and the rate of growth of real GDP relative to trend are the explanatory variables. According to the IMF study there is no effect of the Wassenaar agreement over and above these explanatory variables, because the coefficient of real wage growth is insignificant if it is added as an explanatory variable. However, there are various reasons to doubt this conclusion. First, the estimation period (1975-1995) in the report is too short to test for the impact of the Wassenaar agreement. Second, the Wassenaar agreement has not only directly affected wages, but may also have had an indirect impact on some of the other explanatory variables. Third, as Figure 7.1 shows, manufacturing unit labour costs in the Netherlands have developed vary favourably in comparison to those of Northwest Europe, which no doubt has had a positive effect on employment growth. Without wage moderation this improvement in competitiveness would probably not have been realised.

Wage moderation was stimulated through the pegging of the Dutch Guilder to the German mark since 1983. Indeed, ever since, the fluctuation margin of the Guilder - D Mark exchange rate was much less than the margin allowed for by the Exchange Rate Mechanism (ERM) of the European Monetary System (EMS). Even after the turmoil of 1992 and 1993 the Guilder became the only currency that kept the small band that existed in the ERM before August 1993. This strict exchange rate policy can be considered as having some disciplinary influence on wage developments as a loss of market share due to excessive wage claims cannot be recouped by devaluation. On the other hand, a moderate wage growth also enables the Dutch central bank to credibly stick to its policy target. It was widely believed at the time that the Netherlands had to pay a high price for the devaluation of the Guilder in March 1983 in terms of higher interest rates than the ones prevailing in Germany. Indeed, it took some time for the interest differential vis-à-vis Germany to diminish. However, during the 1990s it often turned negative. As inflation in the Netherlands was more or less in line with German inflation and since Germany is still by far the most important trading partner of the Netherlands, the real effective exchange rate does not show much variation since 1982 (see Figure 7.1).

The government encouraged the policy of wage restraint by reducing the level of taxes and social security premiums, which allowed real net incomes to rise, even in the absence of gross wage increases.[5] There was broad agreement that various structural reforms were needed to strengthen the policy of wage moderation. Indeed, independently of the political parties participating in the governing coalitions, the share of government outlays in national income has been reduced since its peak in 1983. Most of this reduction was realised through a decline in transfers to households. Various reforms of social security arrangements (both levels of benefits and eligibility criteria) have had certain effects. For example, Hassink et al. (1997) conclude that after the reform of the disability scheme only 10 per cent of the observed inflow were in fact dismissals, whereas in the past up to 50 per cent of disability enrolment was related to redundancy.

Figure 7.1 Unit labour cost in manufacturing (national currency basis, effective exchange rates, 1982 = 100)

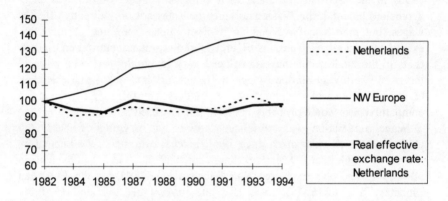

Source: Unit labour cost from Bureau of Labour Statistics, real effective exchange rate (CPI-based) from De Nederlandsche Bank NV.

Apart from fiscal consolidation, the subsequent Dutch governments have also reduced government regulation. This brings us to the second possible explanation for the improved performance of the Dutch economy: less government interference and more reliance on market forces. In contrast to the process of wage moderation described above, it is much less certain what the contribution of deregulation to employment growth has been.

It is widely believed that less regulation and more market flexibility enhances economic performance (Gradus, 1994; Haffner and van Bergeijk, 1997). Despite the difficulties of quantification some scholars have developed proxies for structural reform, which were subsequently used to 'explain' relative economic performance. For example in a widely cited paper, Koedijk and Kremers (1996) conclude that productivity growth during the period 1980-94 in 11 EU Member States is negatively related to overall market regulation. Interestingly, they find that labour productivity growth is significantly related to product market regulation and not to labour market regulation, while the opposite holds for capital productivity growth. This innovative study raises a number of important questions that need further analysis before one may conclude that policy reforms indeed contributed to the recent improvement in economic performance of the Netherlands.

First, the ranking of the Netherlands in terms of market deregulation according to Koedijk and Kremers is rather low. Hence either market deregulation has accelerated recently, or the improvement of the Dutch performance since the late 1980s is due to other factors. Although various product market deregulation measures have been taken recently, it is unlikely that these measures had a large impact in such short time.

This brings us to a second question: is the index of Koedijk and Kremers in line with other indicators for market regulation that have been suggested in the literature? The Appendix to this Chapter shows the original rankings of Koedijk and Kremers and compares them with two other rankings, namely those of Gwartney et al. (1996) and of Holmes et al. (1997). It follows that the ratings of Gwartney et al. (1996) and Holmes et al. (1997) differ quite remarkably from those of Koedijk and Kremers (1996). The ranking of the Netherlands is substantially higher according to these alternative indexes. Although these various indicators do not focus on exactly the same aspects of market regulation, the diverging outcomes warrant further research and should act as a warning signal not to use only one of the indicators as evidence.[6]

Figure 7.2 Employment growth (1981-1993) and ranking of overall regulation

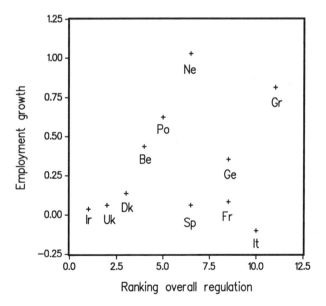

Source: Overall regulation from Koedijk and Kremers (1996); employment growth from OECD (1996c).

In line with Winston's (1993) results for the United States, Koedijk and Kremers find no clear-cut correlation between regulation and employment growth. Indeed, using data from the OECD (1996a) on employment growth, we do not find any relationship between regulation and employment growth (see Figure 7.2). This conclusion also holds for the separate indicators of product market regulation and - more interesting - labour market regulation, which are not shown here.

Table 7.4   Indicators for labour market flexibility in EU member states

	Impact of unemployment on real wages[a]	Persistence in unemployment[b]	Part-time workers as share of total employment	
			1979	1996
Austria	1.43	0.21	7.6	12.6
Belgium	0.65	0.36	6.0	14.0
Denmark	0.66	0.52	n.a.	21.5
Germany	0.55	0.38	11.4	16.3
Finland	0.48	0.78	6.6	7.9
France	2.22	0.88	8.1	16.0
Ireland	0.80	1.16	5.1	11.6
Italy	2.07	0.82	5.3	6.6
Netherlands	0.66	0.80	16.6	36.5
Norway	1.96	0.28	27.3	26.6
Portugal	n.a.	n.a.	7.8	8.7
Spain	0.17	1.11	n.a.	7.7
Sweden	2.31	0.69	23.6	23.6
Switzerland	1.32	0.12	n.a.	27.4
UK	0.98	0.55	16.4	22.2

Notes:

a The first column shows the (negative) influence of unemployment on real wage growth over 1969-85.

b The second column shows persistence in unemployment, i.e. the coefficient of lagged unemployment in a regression for the unemployment rate over 1969-85.

Sources: Layard, Nickel and Jackman (1991, pp. 406 and 413), OECD (1998b).

Still, even without an effect of deregulation being present, the Netherlands might already have had a more flexible labour market than other countries supporting its better employment performance. Generally when economists think of market flexibility they have in mind whether prices (are able to) respond to market conditions. Referring to the labour market: there is more flexibility the more (real) wages are responsive to unemployment and, consequently, unemployment will not be very persistent. Table 7.4 shows some comparative evidence on labour market flexibility based on work by Layard et al. (1991) and OECD (1996c). The second column shows the impact of the labour market situation on real wage growth for the period 1969-1985, while the third column shows the degree of inertia in unemployment. It follows that labour market flexibility at the beginning of the 1980s in the Netherlands was not exceptional: the responsiveness of real wages and the persistence of unemployment in the Netherlands were not out of line with those of neighbouring countries.

An alternative way to analyse labour market flexibility is to focus on the flexibility of labour supply. One indicator is the share of part-time workers as a share of total employment, which is shown in Table 7.4 for 1979 and 1996. It follows that there has been a huge increase in part-time employment in the Netherlands. The effects of changes in labour supply are discussed in more detail in the next section.

OPPOSITE TRENDS IN GDP PER CAPITA AND LABOUR PRODUCTIVITY PERFORMANCE

Rapid increase in labour input in the Netherlands has raised real GDP growth and per capita income. However, at the same time we observe a slowdown in the labour productivity growth rate (Figures 7.3a and 7.3b). Between 1973 and 1987, labour productivity grew at 2.9 per cent per year on average, which was higher than the Northwest European average (2.5 per cent), the EU average (2.6 per cent) and the OECD average (2.4 per cent). Between 1987 and 1996, labour productivity increased at 1.7 per cent per year, which was lower than for Northwest Europe (1.9 per cent), the EU (2.0 per cent) and the OECD (1.9 per cent).

Figure 7.3a   Growth rates of GDP and GDP per hour (1973-1987) [*]

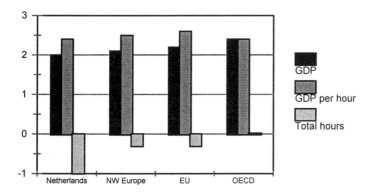

Figure 7.3b   Growth rates of GDP and GDP per hour (1987-1996)

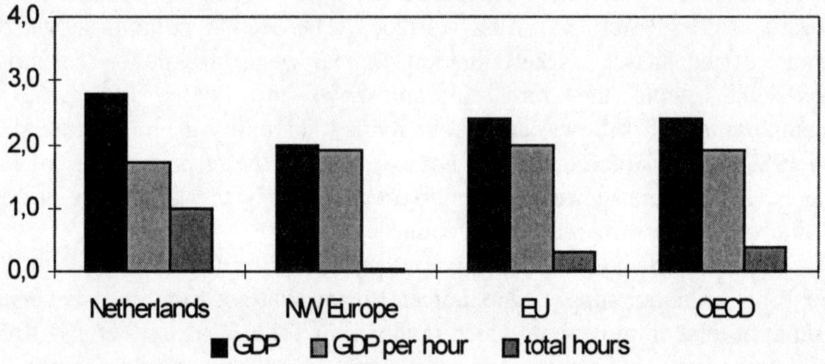

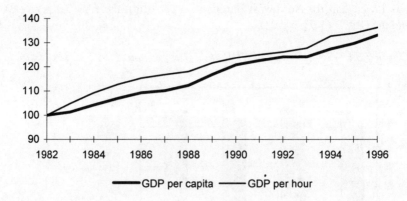

Netherlands   NW Europe   EU   OECD

■ GDP   ▤ GDP per hour   ▦ total hours

Note: * For composition of country groups see Table 7.1.

Sources: GDP see Table 7.1. Employment and hours up to 1992 from Maddison (1991, 1995); employment since 1992 from OECD (1997h, 1997f). Hours updated from 1992 to 1996 with annual hours from OECD (1997a). Where no estimates for 1996 hours were available, we applied the estimate for the most recent year available.

Figure 7.4b shows in more detail the factors that explain the divergent development between the development of per capita income and labour productivity in the Netherlands since 1982, which is exhibited in Figure 7.4a.

Figure 7.4a   GDP per capita and GDP per hour worked, Netherlands (1982=100)

*Figure 7.4b   Effects of working hours and participation on GDP per capita,
                Netherlands (1982-1996)*

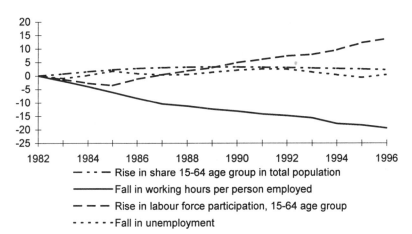

— · · — Rise in share 15-64 age group in total population

————— Fall in working hours per person employed

— — — Rise in labour force participation, 15-64 age group

· · · · · · Fall in unemployment

Sources: GDP per capita and GDP per hour, see Table 7.1 and Figures 7.3a and 7.3b. Labour force participation and unemployment from OECD (1994c, 1997a, 1998b).

During the early 1980s the fall in working hours drove the faster productivity growth, but since 1987 this has been largely offset by the rapid improvement in the participation in the labour force of the population in the age group 15-64 years. As a result productivity growth slowed down relative to per capita income growth. The effects from the fall in unemployment and the rise in the share of the population in the age group 15-64 years on the difference between the per capita income and productivity growth trends were negligible.

As a consequence of the rapid increase of the participation rate, the Netherlands is no longer an outlier in this respect relative to other countries. There is, however, one subgroup in the population for which participation is still exceptionally low. Table 7.5 shows that in all five age groups above 50 years participation is substantially lower than the EU average.

As mentioned in the second section, it may not be all that useful to compare the Netherlands or any other European country with an average for Europe, in case Europe itself would have potential to grow more rapidly as well. Between 1987 and 1996 the average growth of real GDP in Northwest Europe was 2.0 per cent, compared to 2.4 per cent in the USA. This also appears from Table 7.6, which shows that in 1996 GDP per capita in Northwest Europe was only at 75 per cent of the US level. In the European Union it was even lower, namely at 69 per cent of the US level. The

Netherlands was relatively close to the Northwest European average, as the latter was 78 per cent of the US level.

Table 7.5   Participation rates in the EC, Japan and the US (1995)

Age group	50-54	55-59	60-64	65-69	70-74
Belgium	62.1	37.0	11.7	2.9	0.8
Luxembourg	60.7	36.1	11.4	0.0	0.0
Italy	57.3	37.9	18.2	6.0	2.2
Spain	60.2	47.0	26.8	4.3	1.0
Netherlands	67.1	44.4	13.9	5.6	1.5
Greece	62.8	51.0	33.1	13.7	3.5
Austria	72.9	44.8	14.6	7.4	2.3
Ireland	60.3	49.7	35.6	14.8	5.8
France	78.6	52.5	10.8	3.1	0.8
Portugal	72.6	55.3	38.6	23.8	9.4
Finland	81.1	57.2	19.7	6.8	1.4
Germany	79.7	60.0	19.3	4.5	1.6
UK	78.8	64.7	37.2	10.9	2.8
Denmark	81.1	70.2	35.5	8.6	-
Sweden	91.8	82.3	52.0	10.0	-
EU	72.4	53.6	22.8	6.6	2.0
US	-	58.4[a]	-	13.4[b]	-
Japan	-	69.4[a]	-	48.5[b]	-

Notes:
a Age group 55-64 years.
b Age group 65-74 years.

Source: Eurostat (1995).

Table 7.6 also shows that for the Netherlands, Northwest Europe and the EU the gap in terms of labour productivity compared to the USA is much smaller than the per capita income gap in 1996. Labour productivity in the Netherlands is almost the same as in the USA. In Northwest Europe and the EU, the productivity gap with the USA is 11 and 18 percentage points respectively (compared to a gap of 22 and 31 percentage points for GDP per capita). The major part of the difference between the two performance measures is due to Europe's lower labour force participation and to fewer hours worked per person employed. The extraordinarily high share of part-time workers in the Netherlands, in particular among women, is the major explanation for this. About half of the net employment creation of 5.5 per cent among women in 1995 is due to a rise in part-timers. Net employment for men increased at 4.5 per cent, but part-time employment for men increased even faster at 5.5 per cent, whereas employment for full-time men even fell by almost one per cent (European Commission, 1996).[7]

Table 7.6 Relation between GDP per capita and GDP per hour worked in 1996 (United States=100)

	Netherlands	NW Europe[a]	EU[a]	US
GDP per capita	75	78	69	100
GDP per hour worked	99	89	82	100
Overall effect of lower labour input on lower per capita income relative to the US of which:				
- fewer working hours per person[b]	18	4	2	0
- more unemployment[c]	1	2	4	0
- smaller labour force as % of working age population[d]	8	5	8	0
- smaller working age population as % of total population[e]	-3	-1	-1	0

Notes:

a For composition of country groups see Table 7.1.

b Calculated on basis of actual hours worked per person per year.

c Calculated on basis of standardised unemployment rates from OECD (1997h, 1997a).

d Calculated as percentage of population from 15-64 years.

e Calculated as percentage of total population.

Sources: GDP per capita see Table 7.2. GDP per hour estimates obtained with employment and hours for 1992 from Maddison (1995), updated to 1996 on the basis of OECD (1997f, 1997h).

IS THERE A PRODUCTIVITY PROBLEM?

One might hypothesise, on the basis of the previous section, that there is a relation between the acceleration in employment growth and the deceleration in productivity growth. This would be the case if the net expansion of labour input has led to an increased concentration of economic activity in low productivity activities, in particularly in the service sector. This shift would not be a particularly serious problem as long as total GDP continues to increase, i.e. the economy continues to expand by the development of new activities in services at the expense of previous activities in agriculture and manufacturing. A second reason for the productivity slowdown, however, could be a slowdown in productivity growth within the sectors. This in turn could be a sign of stagnation in accumulation of inputs or, when not already embodied in inputs, technological change.

To measure the effect of the contribution of labour input shifts on the overall productivity growth, one may express the productivity for the economy as a whole as the productivity level by sector weighted by the sectoral employment shares:

$$P_m = \frac{Y_m}{L_m} = \sum_{k=1}^{n} \frac{Y_k}{L_k} \frac{L_k}{L_m} = \sum_{k=1}^{n} (P_k S_k) \tag{7.1}$$

with Y and L representing output and labour input by sector ($k=1,..,n$) and the total economy (m), P representing productivity (Y/L) and S representing the sectoral labour input share (L_k/L_m).

In a time perspective this expression can be rewritten as:

$$\Delta P_m = \sum_{k=1}^{n} (\Delta P_k * S_k) + \sum_{k=1}^{n} (P_k * \Delta S_k) + \sum_{k=1}^{n} (\Delta P_k * \Delta S_k) \tag{7.2}$$

In a discrete format the latter can be rewritten into three components as:

$$\frac{P_m' - P_m^0}{P_m^0} = \frac{\sum_{k=1}^{n} (P_k' - P_k^0) S_k^0}{\sum_{k=1}^{n} P_k^0} + \frac{\sum_{k=1}^{n} P_k^0 (S_k' - S_k^0)}{\sum_{k=1}^{n} P_k^0} + \frac{\sum_{k=1}^{n} (P_k' - P_k^0)(S_k' - S_k^0)}{\sum_{k=1}^{n} P_k^0} \tag{7.3}$$

for a current year t and a base year 0.

The first term on the right-hand side of Equation (7.3) represents the intra-sectoral productivity growth, i.e. that part of the overall productivity change that is caused by productivity growth within each of the sectors. The second term is the net shift effect, which measures the effect of the change in sectoral employment shares on overall productivity growth. This effect is positive when labour moves into sectors with higher levels of productivity. In contrast, the second term is negative when the new activities have lower productivity. The third term is the interaction effect, which represents the joint effect of changes in employment shares and changes in sectoral productivity growth. The latter effect can be either negative or positive, depending on whether sectors with a falling share show rising productivity (then it is negative) or sectors with a rising share show falling productivity (then it is positive).[8]

Table 7.7, which is based on a disaggregation to ten sectors (excluding the real estate sector), shows a number of interesting results. Firstly, compared to the first period (1973-1987), the slowdown in the growth of labour productivity during the second period (1987-1995) has found its way primarily into a substantial slowdown in intra-sectoral productivity growth. Secondly, the negative interaction effect is mainly related to a fall in employment shares of agriculture and manufacturing, which both show above-average productivity growth rates, to the advantage of services. As the interaction effect is smaller in the second period, it may be concluded that most of the restructuring of agriculture and manufacturing was realised during the first period, i.e. before 1987. Thirdly, we find that the net shift effect during both periods is positive. The positive sign suggests that the shift of resources between sectors has helped productivity to accelerate instead of decelerate. This perhaps somewhat counterintuitive result can be related to the fact that, even though productivity *growth* in many service sectors was *slower* than in commodity sectors, the absolute *level* of value added per hour in, for example, transport and communication, finance and business services was *higher* than in agriculture or manufacturing.[9]

Table 7.7 Intra-sectoral effect, net shift effect and interactive term on growth rates of labour productivity, Netherlands

	Value added per hour worked		Percentage contribution to labour productivity	
	1973-87	1987-96	1973-87	1987-96
Annual compound growth rate[*]	2.4	1.4	100	100
Intra-sectoral effect	2.8	1.4	117	100
Net shift effect	0.3	0.4	13	29
Interaction effect	-0.7	-0.4	-29	-29

Note: * The estimates of value added per hour worked in this table and in Table 7.9 are based on sectoral accounts. These estimates differ slightly from those for the total economy (Figures 7.4, 7.5 and Table 7.8). Firstly the sectoral estimates exclude the real estate sector. Secondly the trend in sectoral estimates of working hours - which is based on the change in contractual hours - suggest a slower decline of working hours than the trend in actual hours according to Maddison, in particular between 1973 and 1987.

Sources: van Ark (1996), updated. Employment from Statistics Netherlands; hours for 1987 based on contractual hours corrected for sickness and other 'non-contractual' absence from work, extrapolated to other years with trend in contractual hours from Statistics Netherlands (1997a) and updates.

Table 7.7 suggests that there is little support for the view that the slowdown in productivity growth in the Netherlands is related to a rise in low-productivity activities. However, further research is required to settle the issue. Firstly, a more detailed measurement below the level of ten sectors may reveal new information.[10] Secondly, measurement problems may lead to an overstatement of productivity in service sectors with few technological and organisational changes, whereas productivity growth may be understated in sectors that have been more dynamic. Thirdly, the assessment of the productivity slowdown may be expanded to the impact of variables other than the distribution of employment by sector.[11]

Table 7.8 *Labour productivity, capital intensity and various concepts of total factor productivity, Netherlands*

	1973-87	1987-96
Value added per hour worked[a]	2.8	1.7
Non-residential capital stock per hour worked	4.0	1.8
Total factor productivity[b]		
- incl. Non-residential (NRS) capital	1.7	1.1
- incl. NRS capital and human capital	1.1	0.5
- incl. NRS capital, human capital and R&D	0.9	0.3

Notes:
a See Table 7.7 for an explanation of the differences from labour productivity growth rates at the sectoral level.
b TFP estimates were obtained by applying a Tornqvist index based on a Solow-type production function, using average factor shares for each current year and the previous year as weights. For details, see van Ark and de Jong (1996).

Sources: van Ark and de Jong (1996), updated. Capital stock from Groote, Albers and de Jong (1996).

The foregoing analysis suggests that the productivity slowdown is primarily associated with a productivity slowdown across the board. Table 7.8 shows that for the total economy, growth in value added per hour worked slowed down from 2.8 per cent between 1973 and 1987 to 1.7 per cent between 1987 and 1996. To some extent this was accounted for by a slower rise in capital intensity during the second period. However, total factor productivity growth also slowed down. The three bottom lines of Table 7.8 show various concepts of total factor productivity (ranging from including only non-residential capital as an input, to including a variable for human capital and one for the R&D stock) for the total economy as derived from van Ark and de Jong (1996). According to all concepts we observe a slowdown in TFP growth during the second period.

Table 7.9 Sectoral labour productivity, capital intensity and total factor productivity (TFP) growth, Netherlands

	Value added per hour worked		Non-residential capital per hour worked		TFP[a]	
	1973-1987	1987-1996	1973-1987	1987-1996	1973-1987	1987-1996
Agriculture[b]	5.2	6.2	6.6	3.6	2.1	4.5
Mining	3.0	-0.1	8.5	-0.1	-4.9	-0.1
Manufacturing	3.6	2.6	4.2	2.1	2.4	1.7
Public utilities	4.0	4.6	1.1	3.1	3.3	2.6
Construction	1.6	-0.2	4.1	0.1	1.5	-0.3
Wholesale, retail trade	2.8	0.4	4.8	0.8	1.5	0.2
Transport, communication	3.0	3.7	3.2	1.6	1.9	3.1
Finance, insurance and business services[c]	1.7	0.0	d	d	d	d
Other market services	0.1	0.1	1.0	0.7	0.6	0.3
Government services	0.8	1.1	d	d	d	d
Total sectors[e]	2.3	1.4	2.7	1.1	1.5	1.0

Notes:
a The sectoral total factor productivity estimates are of a tentative nature and subject to revision depending on possible correction to the investment data used for estimation of the capital stock and dynamic sectoral weighting systems.
b Includes forestry and fisheries.
c Excluding real estate.
d Included in other market services.
e Productivity growth rates for the total GDP differ slightly from those reported at the aggregate level as explained in Table 7.7.

Sources: GDP and employment from van Ark (1996), updated; working hours from 1987 to 1996 on the basis of Statistics Netherlands (1997a); trend in working hours 1977-87 are for contractual hours from Statistics Netherlands. Capital stock based on perpetual inventory method using investment in non residential capital stock from Statistics Netherlands for 1921-38 and from 1950 onwards, and from Groote, Albers and de Jong (1996) for 1938-50, which were accumulated on the basis of 39 and 14 years life assumptions for non-residential structures and machinery and equipment respectively. TFP on the basis of Cobb-Douglas production function with fixed sectoral labour compensation weights averaged over 1990-1996.

Table 7.9 shows that the slowdown in labour productivity growth was concentrated in manufacturing, construction, trade and finance, insurance and business services. The latter sector, which was the sector with the most rapid increase in labour input, even experienced a productivity standstill after 1987. A correction for the continuous fall in annual working hours leads to slightly higher growth rates, in particular in services, where a lot of part-time labour has been created.

Sectoral estimates of the capital stock in the Netherlands are still difficult to obtain because of serious data problems concerning the time series on investment. The capital stock figures used for the construction of Table 7.9 are based on provisional estimates by Ronald Albers (Netherlands Central Bank) and Joost Beaumont (University of Amsterdam) using the perpetual inventory method and (mainly) official investment data from Statistics Netherlands.[12] The figures on capital intensity in Table 7.9 suggest that the accumulation of fixed capital per hour worked slowed down across the board since 1987.

However, during the period 1987-1996 a dichotomy arose between agriculture, manufacturing, public utilities and transport and communication on the one hand, where capital intensity continued to increase at an above average rate, and major parts of services, including trade, finance, insurance, business services, other market services and government services, with below average capital intensity growth. Strikingly, TFP during the period 1987-1996 also grew substantially faster in the first group (between 1.7 and 4.5 per cent) than in the latter group (between -0.3 and 0.3 per cent).

This outcome suggests that the productivity problem cannot be exclusively interpreted as a problem of insufficient technology creation. Sectors that include most technology producers still perform above average, whereas major technology users perform below average.[13]

CONCLUSION

In this Chapter we argue that the recent improvement in economic performance of the Netherlands needs to be seen in the light of the losses that occurred during the previous period, in particular between 1973 and 1987. The increase of the participation rate (except for people of age 55 or more) is an important factor behind the improvement in employment and per capita income performance. The 'convergence' of the level of per capita income towards the Northwest European average has of course not been automatic. It is the result of combined efforts of trade unions, employers' organisations and the government. It has led to a moderation in the growth of wage costs and inflation, a strict exchange rate policy and a reduction in the budget deficit and the size of government. Consequently, the position of the Netherlands in terms of GDP per capita relative to Northwestern Europe is now more or less the same as it used to be in the 1960s and 1970s.

Our analysis of past growth performance suggests that it is highly unlikely that a country will experience substantially higher growth rates over a longer-term period than surrounding countries. Although structural reform has taken place (and was, no doubt, necessary) our analysis does not indicate that it will enable the Netherlands to reach a structurally higher rate of growth than other Northwest European countries.

We also observe a decline in productivity growth since the mid 1980s. Although still ahead in comparison with the average for Northwest Europe, the productivity advantage in terms of the level of GDP per hour worked in the Netherlands has eroded. This deceleration of productivity growth occurred across the board: in most sectors of the economy growth in labour productivity and total productivity slowed down. However, the productivity problem should not be mixed up with a technology problem 'per se'. Apparently capital intensity and multi-factor productivity growth was weakest in sectors which mainly consist of technology users, whereas technology producers (such as manufacturing, transport and communication) continued to show an above average performance in capital intensity and TFP growth.

APPENDIX - HOW REGULATED IS THE DUTCH ECONOMY?

This Appendix provides a comparison of the indicators of Koedijk and Kremers (1996) with a number of alternative so-called 'economic freedom' indicators. The index for product market regulation of Koedijk and Kremers refers to regulation for business establishments, competition policy, public ownership, support to manufacturing companies, regulation of shop opening hours, and the implementation at the national level of the European Single Market programme. Their overall index is the total of their product and labour market indices. Gwartney et al. (1996) used 17 measures in four broad areas (money and inflation, government operations and regulations, 'takings' and discriminatory taxation and international exchange) to measure economic freedom. They rated 102 countries on each of these measures on a scale of 0-10. A crucial issue is how these measures are weighted.

In Table 7.10 we show the ranking - adjusted to make them comparable with those of Koedijk and Kremers - in which money and inflation is given a low weight. An important conclusion is that the ratings of Gwartney et al. (1996) differ quite substantially from those of Koedijk and Kremers (1996).

The rankings of the Netherlands is substantially higher both in 1980 (in parentheses) and 1995 according to the index of Gwartney et al. (1996). We have also calculated the rankings for one of the subgroups of the Gwartney data set, i.e. those referring to government operations and regulations (group 2). Again this yields a different position for the Netherlands. A similar conclusion follows from a comparison with the indicator of Holmes et al. (1997).

Table 7.10 A comparison of liberalisation indicators (1=free; 11=not free)

	Koedijk and Kremers		Gwartney et al.			Holmes et al.
	product markets	overall	total 1995	1980	group 2 in 1995	total 1996
Ireland	1	1	2	5	6	6
UK	3	2	1	4	3	2.5
Denmark	5	3	6	7	4	2.5
Belgium	6	4	4.5	1	5	4.5
Portugal	4	5	10	11	9	8
Spain	2	6.5	8	8.5	8	9.5
Netherlands	9	6.5	3	3	1	1
France	7.5	8.5	7	6	7	7
Germany	7.5	8.5	4.5	2	2	4.5
Italy	10	10	9	8.5	10	4.5
Greece	11	11	11	10	11	11

Sources: Koedijk and Kremers (1996), Gwartney et al. (1996), Holmes et al. (1997).

NOTES

We would like to thank Ronald Albers, Willem J. Kooi, Erik J. Monnikhof and Peter Hein van Mulligen for their assistance in data collection and processing. We are grateful to Ronald Albers, Palle Andersen, Bas B. Bakker, Simon Kuipers, Henry van der Wiel and to participants in the conference on 'The effects and policy implications of structural adjustments in small open economies' on 29 and 30 October 1997 in Amsterdam for comments.
1. Our Northwest European average includes Austria, Belgium, Denmark, Germany (since 1991 including East Germany), Finland, France, Netherlands, Norway, Sweden, Switzerland and the UK. See the section on structural reform in the Netherlands for more details.
2. See also van Zanden (1997) for a historical assessment of the Dutch growth performance.
3. The selection of the sub-periods is based on the identification of turning points in an international comparative perspective (see Maddison, 1995). For the Netherlands, the period 1979-81 was a more crucial turning point in growth experience than 1973.

4. Van Bergeijk and Haffner (1996, p.5) define structural change in a broad sense as the reform of policies and institutions to promote economic growth. As far as policy concerns it includes privatisation, and de- and reregulation, competition policy, fiscal consolidation and tax reform.
5. See also Chapter 3 and 4 in this volume.
6. See also Kuper and Kuipers (1996) who show the lack of statistical robustness of the country sample in the estimates of Koedijk and Kremers.
7. Recent measures from Statistics Netherlands (1997a), however, show a reversal of the declining trend of full-time employment since 1997.
8. See van Ark (1996) for a detailed assessment of the shift-share method.
9. See van Ark and de Haan (1996), Diagram 2, for a comparison of labour productivity levels by sector as a percentage of the labour productivity level of the total economy.
10. Compare, for example, with Netherlands Bureau for Economic Policy Analysis (1998d) that shows a small negative net shift effect, which therefore partly explains the slowdown in labour productivity growth. However, the main explanation for the productivity slowdown according to this study is the decline in 'within-sector' growth rates.
11. Netherlands Bureau for Economic Policy Analysis (1998c, 1998d) also accounted for shift effects from changes in composition of educational levels, age, sex and the share of part-time labour in the labour force. These estimates suggest some small negative shift effects for the 1980s (in particular in services), but since 1990 the shift towards more highly trained people and a more experienced labour force positively contributed to labour productivity growth.
12. The estimates are subject to revision in particular because the official investment figures pre-1987 and post-1987 are not fully consistent and require further adjustment (see Netherlands Bureau for Economic Policy Analysis, 1998d).
13. Clearly, while drawing these conclusions, we need to remain aware of the serious problems in estimating services output and the output of high-tech products (such as computers) which are used as inputs by the technology users.

8. Productivity, Wage Moderation, and Specificity in Factor Inputs

Eric J. Bartelsman

INTRODUCTION

This Chapter provides an empirical evaluation of the macro-economic importance of specificity in factor markets. I compare the model of specificity with a base model by considering the different short- and medium-term effects on productivity growth of wage moderation that took place in the Netherlands after 1982. An analysis also is made of differential behaviour under the two models of a collection of indicators on investment, employment, and capital stocks in individual industrial firms in the Netherlands. In particular, observed behaviour of capital investment at the micro level allows one to distinguish between the two competing hypotheses.

The first model is based on a production structure with technology embodied in vintage capital. In this model, wage moderation leads to a transitional reduction in productivity growth. The mechanism is that reduced wage pressure reduces incentives for firms to invest in new capital, and delays scrapping of old capital, thus allowing a decline in the capital-labour ratio. The second model has a similar vintage production structure, but posits the existence of a rent-appropriation, or hold-up, problem associated with specificity of labour and capital in the production relationship (see Caballero and Hammour, 1998). In this model, wage moderation via consensus acts as a fortuitous institutional advance that reduces the appropriability problem. In the model, reductions in specificity curb opportunism and pull resources into production, thus increasing productivity. In this Chapter, the empirical distinction between the two models is not based on estimation of a structural model of firm dynamics. Instead, analysis of carefully selected indicators provides support for the macro-economic importance of specificity as described by Caballero and Hammour, and points towards a significant role of wage moderation in boosting employment as well as productivity.

Although the Chapter is primarily concerned with evaluating the relevance of specificity problems in macro-economics, it does so by considering the effects of wage moderation. A short digression on the institutional setting of wage moderation and on the manner in which wage moderation can be modelled is thus in order. Wage moderation has been credited with the extraordinary growth in hours worked in the Dutch economy since 1983. During the first Lubbers administration, wage bargaining between social partners was replaced with consensus building over common policy goals. The social partners (confederation of unions and employers organisation) provided qualitative recommendations on specific issues, while sectoral trade unions took into account sector-specific conditions that allowed variation within the central guidelines. Wage moderation affects more than 80 per cent of workers who were directly covered through collective agreements or through mandatory extension (see Netherlands Bureau for Economic Policy Analysis, 1997a). Following the 'Agreement of Wassenaar' of 1982, the common policy goal became employment creation, and the common vehicle wage moderation.

The operational definition of wage moderation to use in a model is intertwined with the type of economic interaction that determines wage setting. The wage itself is an endogenous variable in most economic models. In a neo-classical labour market with perfectly elastic labour supply, wages are determined by workers' reservation wage. Wage moderation could be achieved by lowering workers' outside options, for example through reductions in unemployment benefits. With perfectly inelastic labour supply, wages depend on the state of labour demand and the level of labour supply. A helicopter drop of highly educated workers would lower wages, all else equal. In a model with wage bargaining, wage moderation could denote any action that weakens the position of labour in bargaining, e.g. helicopter drop of workers, reductions in benefits, posting of employment bonds by workers, reduction in workers' share of negotiable surplus. In order to compare the effects of wage moderation in the two models, we need to find a description of wage moderation that can be applied in both. A reduction in benefits, such as occurred when policy makers decoupled benefit levels from minimum wages, is an exogenous event to both models.

The policy debate surrounding wage moderation that took place in Dutch economics journals in the early and mid-1980s is summarized nicely by Bovenberg (1997). According to the arguments, three main channels exist through which lower wages led to employment growth. First, profitability of firms improved, creating the financial room and incentives to invest. Next, the competitive position of firms improved on world markets, raising exports. Finally, production became more labour intensive. While the effects on employment are clear, the effects on total factor productivity (TFP) are not. In a vintage capital model with embodied technology, the first channel leads to more new capital, thus to higher TFP. The second channel is ambiguous, because it is not clear which firms raise output to meet export demand. If existing firms with old technology increase utilisation and output, or delay scrapping, TFP will be held back, while if firms with new capital gain market share, TFP will improve. The third channel lowers labour productivity, and may retard TFP growth if increased demand is met by adding labour to existing capital (with old embodied technology).

The combined effect on productivity (TFP) of wage moderation through the three channels above is ambiguous. The analysis is clouded because two different models underlie the descriptions of employment and capital growth following wage moderation. For example, the first channel only makes sense in a model with a production surplus, where the share going to labour through bargaining decreases with wage moderation.[1] The second channel, the competitive effect, is only operative in an open economy and will depend on the size and time-structure of the export demand elasticity. I will argue that the direction of TFP growth following wage moderation can be used to distinguish between the two stylised models and can test whether specificity plays an important role. I will look at the macro, sectoral, and micro-level implications of wage moderation under the two competing models. I will show why sectoral data cannot be used to disentangle the effects of wage moderation on productivity. Instead, I will assess whether findings from the micro data are consistent with the implications of one of the two hypotheses.

The organisation of the Chapter is as follows. First, the two models are presented. Next, a macro and sectoral overview is presented of wage moderation and its implications under the competing hypotheses, followed by implications at the micro level. The empirical section starts with a discussion of the macro and sectoral evidence, or lack thereof. Finally, summary statistics on investment behaviour and age of the capital stock, and some indicators of TFP and capital growth are shown which are consistent with the model of specificity. A final section concludes and sketches an outline for a structural model that nests the two hypotheses.

PRODUCTIVITY AND FACTOR INPUTS: TWO MODELS

What are the determinants of technological change? For both models, the growth rate of available technology is assumed to be exogenous. We further assume that available technology is embodied in capital, and that all investment is in new capital that embodies the best available technology. Once capital is in place, it cannot be shifted costlessly to another use. In other words, a proportion of the investment is sunk. The vintage structure of capital, the embodied nature of technology, and the sunk costs are common to both models. In both models, wage moderation is taken to mean an exogenous increase in effective labour supply elasticity, for example through reductions in unemployment benefits.

First, the model of Caballero and Hammour (1998), hereafter the CH model, will be introduced. This model highlights the role of specific investments made by capital and labour in order to produce jointly, the effect of the sunkness of these investments on the bargaining which takes place ex-post, and the macro-economic consequences of decisions made by factor inputs. Next, a more traditional vintage model will be introduced and the differences with the CH model will be noted.

The CH Model: Specificity in Input Markets

In a production relationship, capital and labour join forces to produce more output than they could generate independently. The production function, with its associated properties of scale and substitution elasticities and diminishing marginal returns, has been well described in the literature. More recently, another aspect of joint production has come to the forefront in (macro-) economics, namely the temporary nature of the production relationship. Jobs are created and destroyed, firms come and go, capital is put in place and scrapped.[2] Each discrete decision has irreversible elements because investments in the relationship are sunk. Besides obvious reasons why a portion of capital investment may be sunk, for example underground cables, specificity may arise from hiring (and firing) costs, and investment in training. Specificity for labour may arise from search costs and from acquisition of firm-specific knowledge. Net specificity combines the outside options and potential losses from separation, and points to the factor that is subject to appropriation, or opportunism, by the other factor.

The costs incurred in the specific relationship need to be recouped during the lifetime of the joint effort; when the relationship is broken, a remainder is lost. The economic problem is that it is difficult to form ex-ante contracts to cover the division of the flow of rents which are generated to cover the fixed costs. In the words of Caballero and Hammour (1998), the '... specific quasi-rents may not be divided *ex post* according to the parties' *ex ante* terms of trade.' This problem, known in the literature as the 'hold-up' problem, occurs when one party to a transaction can appropriate a portion of the quasi-rents associated with the relationship.[3]

In a particular market, the hold-up problem leads to an under-commitment of resources, because the factor is concerned that future quasi-rents may be appropriated by others. An introduction of a new technology which is profitable given factor prices may not lead to adoption if the benefits cannot be shielded from future opportunism of other contracting parties. Institutional arrangements are thought to evolve in order to compensate for the hold-up problem, although they are generally acknowledged not to solve the problem completely.[4] In the empirical section of this Chapter, we examine whether wage moderation in the Netherlands in the years after 1982 can be seen as an institutional change that reduced the hold-up problem in the eyes of the market participants.

In the model of Caballero and Hammour the hold-up problem plays a central role in the functioning of the macro-economy. In particular, '... a highly inefficient macro "solution" to the unresolved microeconomic contracting problems' results as the problem of deciding on investments and sharing the benefits on an individual level spreads throughout the economy. The basic macro implications are that the market for the appropriating factor is segmented and that the productive structure is sclerotic. In other words, if workers attempt to get more than what was predicated on their ex-ante terms of trade, involuntary unemployment will occur and too many low-productivity units will be kept in operation. The ingredients of the CH model, taken nearly directly from Caballero and Hammour (1998), are presented in Appendix 1, together with some of the main results. Below, a verbal description of the model is given. Because no formal testing of the models takes place in this Chapter, a verbal description of the predictions of both models following wage moderation should suffice in order to evaluate the empirical evidence.

In the CH model of the economy there are two factors of production that can either produce in autarky or commit to joint production relationships with partly irreversible fixed costs. The ex-ante terms of trade are derived from their autarky options and determine the factor supply curve; when operating jointly the factors are complementary and cannot be given payments based on marginal products. The quasi-rents arising from a specific relationship consist of the difference between the value of the joint product and the sum of the autarky products. The hold-up problem occurs because a party can threaten to break the relationship, leaving the other with a loss. In the equilibrium outcome, division of rents and allocation of factors to joint production is such that no party has an incentive to deviate from its choices, given the choices of others. In the general framework of the CH model, the factors labour and capital are symmetrical. They differ only in the proportion of investment that is sunk and the supply elasticity derived from the value of the outside option (autarky). These differences together with a parameter of bargaining strength determine net specificity, or which factor receives more in joint production than in autarky. An interpretation of the autarky option may be unemployment with benefits for workers, and flight to international assets for capital.

The CH model is further akin to the vintage model, described below, with a distribution of productivity among the existing production units, a lower bound on productivity below which the unit is scrapped, and a free entry condition for creating new units with the best available technology. However, in the vintage model (VM), labour does not sink any resources in joint production, and is not able to bargain away any portion of the production surplus. These assumptions require that two of the parameters of the CH model, φ_j, and β, be set to zero (see Appendix 1).

If the interplay between outside options and sunk costs is such that specificity in factors is not balanced (net specificity points to one factor), an inefficient equilibrium with the following properties will result. First, there will be underemployment (positive allocation of resources to autarky), and market segmentation (the appropriated factor will always receive its autarky marginal product, while the appropriating factor will earn less in autarky). This latter effect can be thought of as involuntary unemployment for the appropriating factor. The number of joint production jobs is limited by the low allocation of the appropriated factor to the joint sector, which is their response to the appropriability problem. Second, with unbalanced specificity the scrapping margin is at a lower level of productivity than would occur if specificity were balanced or if complete enforceable contracts could be made. This happens because resources freed up by scrapping the marginal unit would not receive the benefits from the new technology with certainty, but would have a probability of earning less in autarky. Finally, the model shows that in equilibrium creation will be insufficient and destruction excessive. The latter occurs because the social opportunity cost of labour (return in autarky) is lower than the wage in joint production.

So far, the model does not say much about the capital-labour ratio. The model posits fixed proportions in the short run. In the long run, the model allows for technological choices from a range of proportions, with perfect substitutability. In equilibrium the appropriated factor chooses the technology. The direction of the capital-labour ratio following a change in specificity depends on the extent to which net specificity itself varies with the capital-labour ratio. For example, if specificity is caused by severance pay, a higher capital-labour ratio for a given level of output reduces the magnitude of the problem. In this case an exogenous increase in specificity of capital leads to lower employment and a higher capital-labour ratio for new vintages. If, on the other hand, specificity does not depend on the capital-labour ratio, the earlier described mechanism of withdrawing capital to autarky will dominate after an exogenous increase in capital specificity, reducing the capital-labour ratio of new vintages. In either case, the capital-labour ratio is sub-optimal, given outside factor prices.

Traditional Vintage Model

The vintage model (VM) used in this Chapter is a variant of the dynamic general equilibrium model of Broer (1996) where firms make capital investment, hiring, and vintage scrapping decisions in order to maximise a stream of future expected profits. Some of the assumptions of the Broer model are changed in order to be consistent with the CH model, and in order to better fit a small open economy. First, labour supply is not perfectly elastic; instead the labour supply elasticity is assumed to decrease as unemployment benefits rise. Next, product markets are not imperfectly competitive; instead the world output price is taken as fixed. These two changes in assumptions are complementary in the sense that they cause the level of output in equilibrium to be bounded, albeit in different ways. In Broer, the product demand curve limits the amount of elastically supplied labour that can be put to work at the reservation wage, while in VM, the increasing wages needed to supply more labour restrict the amount of output that can be produced at competitive prices.

In the VM, wage moderation, as modelled by an increase in labour supply elasticity, has a clear transitional effect on the actions of the representative firm. First, the age at which old vintages cease to be profitable, at the margin, increases. Second, all the existing vintages will be used in production with a higher level of associated labour. Output can thus increase somewhat without adding newer vintages of capital with their embodied technology. The lull in new capital spending may be longer or shorter, depending on the speed with which the economy proceeds to the new equilibrium, where output and employment are higher than prior to wage moderation.

IMPLICATIONS OF WAGE MODERATION

This Chapter attempts to assess which of the two models better fits the Dutch economy. The method is to find an economic event that generates a different response under the two models, and to analyse which set of predictions best fits the actual data. The following sections show that the two models predict different outcomes for a few indicators following wage moderation. However, two obstacles cloud the ability to distinguish between the two models. First, what is the nature of the wage reduction? Is it an exogenous occurrence, for example caused by a helicopter drop of highly educated workers? Or is it caused by an institutional change in the way in which wages are negotiated? If so, is the implication that the specificity of labour was reduced? One path for implementing wage moderation is in the lowering of the value of the outside option, which increases the supply elasticity of labour. This would bring net specificity closer to zero in the CH model, but could be interpreted as an effective increase in labour supply, thus resulting in more moderate wages, under VM. Another path is more direct through the belief that market parties have that the consensus agreement will be honoured, and that opportunistic behaviour will be limited. In the CH model, this is brought about by exogenously changing the bargaining parameter, thereby moving towards balanced specificity. However, in the VM model, this path has no operational meaning. The choice made in this Chapter is to study predictions of the models following wage moderation brought about through the lowering of the outside option.

The second obstacle is the level at which the models generate differences in outcomes. Possibly, a difficulty could exist in isolating the theoretical differences in outcomes of indicators from observed differences at the sectoral level. At the micro-level, such problems of interpretation may be less severe.

The importance of micro-level data in distinguishing between sources of changes in aggregates lies at the heart of the above problem. As an example, the evolution of aggregate TFP is broken down into its micro-components. Aggregate or sectoral growth of TFP is the result both of the development of productivity at each production unit, and of the allocation, usually through market mechanisms, of sectoral or aggregate output across firms. Aggregate TFP is thus a weighted average of the productivity associated with technology embodied in each unit of capital, with the weight being equal to the share of output produced by that unit of capital (together with associated labour). Firm level TFP can only change with a change in the age structure of its capital, either through the introduction of new units of capital or the scrapping of old units. Aggregate TFP can increase without changes in productivity at the firm level, for example if highly productive firms gain market share, new firms enter the industry, or less productive firms exit the industry. We will see below how knowledge of micro-level developments in indicators indeed can aid in understanding the channels through which effects occur in the two models.

Aggregate and Sectoral Indicators

Table 8.1 shows the short- and medium-term effect on a selection of macro (or sectoral) variables following wage moderation under the two models, the traditional vintage model (VM) and the model of specificity (CH). The first line shows the effect on output. In the CH model, output grows because of the increase in resources drawn into joint production. Labour increases in VM, through an increase in labour intensity, while employment grows in the CH model because of a reduction in market segmentation. The effect on the capital-labour ratio in the CH model is ambiguous, because even though capital is drawn into joint production, the choice of technique might favour labour if the degree of specificity depends on factor intensity. Labour productivity is depressed in VM because of the higher labour intensity and because of the postponement of purchases of new vintages. In the CH model, labour productivity may decline if the effects of new vintage purchases are offset by the possible decline in capital intensity.

Table 8.1   Aggregate and sectoral indicators

Indicator	VM	CH
Output	+	+
Employment	+	+
Capital-labour ratio	−	±
Labour productivity	−	±
Labour share of income	−	−
Investment	−	+
TFP	−	+

The next line in Table 8.1 shows labour share of income, which is related to the cause, wage moderation, as well as to the effects, output and employment. The fall in labour share resulting from the increase in the labour supply elasticity can be offset partly by the fall in labour productivity under VM, but could be strengthened by an increase in labour productivity under the CH model.[5] The first five rows of the table do not provide indicators that can be used to distinguish between the two models.

The models do have distinct effects on investment spending and TFP. Investment clearly goes through a lull in VM as the stock sits around waiting until the new, increased, obsolescence age is reached.[6] In the CH model, sclerosis is reduced and new vintages are purchased as capital is drawn into joint production. Unfortunately, the very cyclical nature of investment makes it hard to determine whether the movements in investment over time are the results of the change in the labour environment, or because of other (international) macro-economic disturbances. Similarly, the different prediction for TFP, a decline under VM and an improvement under the CH model, may be hard to distinguish in practice because one does not know what the direction of TFP would have been in the absence of wage moderation. Of course, a structural model with appropriate instruments for other effects could be used, but in practice such instruments are difficult to find. Nonetheless, I will briefly describe the aggregate and sectoral indicators, but before doing so I will look at the micro level.

Micro-level Indicators

The richness of micro-level data provides dimensions that aid in distinguishing between the two models. Individual firms vary significantly from each other in many ways, whether size, age, technology, profitability, productivity, cyclicality, etc. This heterogeneity seems to be the one constant found by analysts looking at longitudinal micro datasets, i.e. datasets that cover a large sample of all firms or establishments over time, and that form the basis for the official sectoral and aggregate statistics.[7]

Some of the stylised facts from analysis of longitudinal micro datasets (LMDs) in various countries fit the theoretical constructs in the CH model quite nicely. Table 8.2 shows the direction of certain measurable quantities from the micro data following wage moderation under the two models. Before discussing the table, it is helpful to introduce terminology that has become standard in the analysis of LMDs. First, measurements can take place along the 'within' or 'between' dimension. 'Within' productivity growth, for example, shows a weighted average of firm level productivity, with initial input shares as weights. 'Between' productivity growth shows how much aggregate productivity changes through a shift in output shares, given initial productivity levels. Next, a cross-term shows the contribution to the aggregate of the covariance between changes in productivity and changes in shares. Finally, entry and exit affect aggregate productivity.

Another term to be used is a difference-in-differences estimator (DD). This method looks at differences in outcomes of a group which is influenced by an effect before and after the effect occurred, with differences before and after in a group which is not influenced. A concrete example: if wage moderation can only have influence on a firm's technology choice if they are at the vintage stage where they are ready to implement a new technology, we can compare outcomes of firms which do major re-tooling before and after wage moderation, with outcomes of firms which are not at the re-tooling stage. This technique can be argued to provide a 'control group' to filter out influences of other factors.

First, we review some general features of the data, and what they would look like under the two models. The degree of factor substitutability depends on the dimension along which it is measured. Substitution occurs 'within' micro-units, takes place over time as older units are replaced (entry-exit) or cross-sectionally through reallocation of output shares across micro-units with different factor intensities ('between'). For capital-energy substitution in the US industrial sector it is well documented (see Doms, 1993) that the 'within' dimension shows little action. This fact also fits the modern views in energy modelling (see Koopmans, 1997). Little 'within' substitutability of capital and labour at a particular firm in the short run, and possibly even complementarity, would fit the CH model nicely. In the long run both the VM and CH models exhibit substitutability between capital and labour.

Next, investment behaviour is analysed by counting the number of firms that experience a 'major investment project' in a particular year, where 'major investment project' is defined as investment expenditures that make up a significant portion of total investment spending of the firm over a long horizon (see for example, Dunne and Doms, 1993, or Cooper et al., 1994). Both models should show significant lumpiness in investment, because in a vintage model a period of inaction follows after a new unit of capital has been put in place.

Productivity (TFP) growth changes only in the within dimension following an investment spike of a firm, under both models. Between effects, and entry and exit contributions also play a role in both models.

Table 8.2   Micro-level indicators

Indicators	VM model	CH model
Model features		
Factor substitution		
- short run	Yes	No
- long run	Yes	Yes
Lumpy investment	Yes	Yes
TFP growth		
- within	after spike	after spike
- between, entry, exit	Yes	Yes
Wage moderation		
Firms with spike	–	+
Average age of capital	+	–
Difference in difference estimate of effect		
- TFP growth	–	+
- Capital growth	–	+

The next rows of the table show the effects of wage moderation on certain indicators. The first effect is the number of investment spikes in the years following moderation, which should go up under the CH model as expected realisable profits increase and scrapping age decreases, and decline under VM as more firms will find themselves in the range of inaction. Next, the within measure of the age of the capital stock should decline under the CH model and increase under VM. The lowering of opportunistic behaviour of labour creates an incentive for investments in new, highly productive capital.

Further, the scrapping age decreases leaving many firms with capital that can be scrapped immediately.

An investment spike of a firm gives the econometrician a nice tool to see what choices a firm has made for capital investment and for the implementation of new technology. The last two rows of Table 8.2 show the expected difference-in-differences estimates for the effect of wage moderation on changes in capital and on TFP growth.

The capital stock clearly is boosted following a spike in investment at the firm. Changes in the capital stock in firms in years where no major investment project takes place could be positive if investment is larger than the amount of scrapping, or could be negative, but in any case are smaller than for firms with spikes. Capital stock growth following wage moderation will be different under the two models, and will depend on whether spikes occur. More spikes are expected under the CH model, but even under VM spikes will occur with a positive probability. Conditional on a spike occurring, the growth in capital will be lower following moderation under VM, all else equal, because desired capital stock is reduced. Under VM, capital growth for firms without a spike will be higher than before, all else equal, because the scrapping margin is extended. Under the CH model, growth at firms without spikes will decline, because more scrapping takes place, and growth at firms with spikes will increase because firms desire to draw more capital into joint production. Thus, under the CH model, the relative growth of spike to non-spike firms increases following wage moderation, while it declines under VM. The difference in differences estimate helps in the 'all else equal' clause, because external influences, such as an exogenous increase in the cost of capital, will affect aggregate investment, and the probability of the spike, but will have no, or less, effect on the relative change of spike to non-spike firms.

For TFP, we look at the contribution to TFP growth of the firms with a spike compared with firms without a spike, before and after wage moderation. Although we thereby implicitly take into account the number of firms that have a spike, we are able to correct for underlying differences in technological opportunity because we use the control group of firms without a spike. The expectation is that the relative contribution to TFP of firms with a spike increases following wage moderation under the CH model, and decreases under VM.

EMPIRICAL EVIDENCE

Aggregate and Sectoral Data

The empirical section starts with a cursory glance at aggregate and sectoral data. Sources and definitions of the data are provided in Appendix 2. Figure 8.1 shows four panels with the developments in the industrial sector between 1975 and 1995. The top left panel shows labour share of income on the left scale and the minimum wage (deflated with product prices) on the right scale. These indicators show the policy shift following the agreement of Wassenaar in 1982. The top right panel shows the development of output (the solid line), hours worked (the declining dotted line) and investment. A clear shift takes place in the trend of hours worked, starting in 1985, although an increase in investment is far more prominent. Bottom left, we see the developments of wages and user cost of capital, both relative to the output deflator. The turning point in the trend of product wages takes place in 1985. Wages relative to user cost of capital actually are increasing until around 1985. Disinflation and reductions in nominal interest rates suppress the cost of capital significantly throughout the decade. Finally, the bottom right figure shows the developments in (log) of TFP, (log) of labour productivity, and the capital-labour ratio. TFP shows a noticeable upturn after 1983, although cyclical factors are notorious in bouncing around measured TFP.

Figure 8.2 and Figure 8.3 show the same indicators for selected industries, Metal and electronics, and Food, alcohol, and tobacco. The layout of the figures is the same. It should be noted that the minimum wage is deflated with the relevant output prices deflator, thereby exhibiting a different pattern in each figure. The metal sector shows an earlier turnaround in labour income share than aggregate industry, and also an earlier recovery in investment.

Overall, the data do not provide evidence to support one model over the other. The movement in TFP and investment would have provided evidence, if one had information on their development in the absence of wage moderation. Of course, instrumental variable techniques could provide an empirical means for filtering out unwanted effects, such as exogenous shifts in export demand, consumer confidence, state of the business cycle, and others. While instrumental variable techniques are quite standard in many econometric analyses, direct access to micro-data can provide more robust identification.

Figure 8.1 Industry indicators

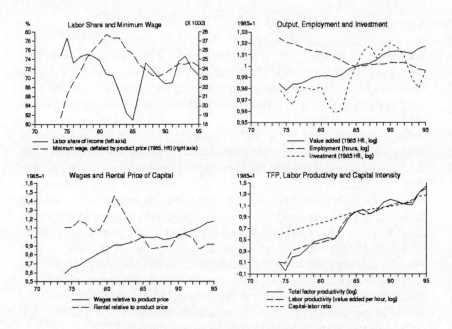

Figure 8.2 Fabricated metal and electrical equipment indicators

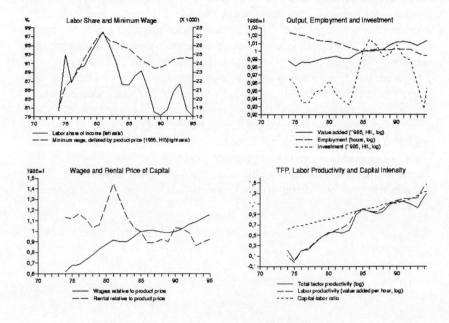

Figure 8.3 Food, beverages and tobacco indicators

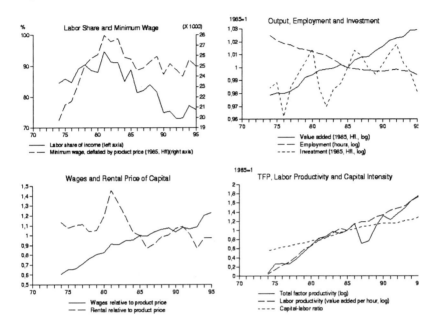

Micro-level Data

The simplicity of the empirical tests applied to the micro-data belies the considerable amount of data manipulation needed to construct the relevant measures. Table 8.3 shows the number of firms with an investment spike in each year. The table is constructed from investment data from a balanced panel of firms, namely firms that occur in all available survey years of the investment statistics database. Next, for each firm a sum is created for real (deflated) investment in transport vehicles and in equipment. A spike occurs if real investment of a firm in a given year on the relevant asset type is more than 25 per cent of the sum of the real investment on that asset type by that firm over time.

It should not be surprising to those who have followed the recent literature on investment that such spikes occur with the frequency they do (see e.g. a survey by Caballero, 1997). In fact, in the Netherlands, half the firms spend more than 25 per cent of their total investment in transport vehicles over a 16-year span in one year. For equipment investment, the size of the median spike is 20 per cent. These figures are roughly the same as for US manufacturing firms, where the median spike is 25 per cent (see Dunne and

Doms, 1993). It is surprising that firm-level data show similar lumpiness to establishment level observations in the US, because firms are able to smooth the necessary lumpiness in plant investment by shifting resources across plants over time, if they want to.

A spike indicator, S_{it}, shows if firm i had a spike in year t:

$$S_{it} = \begin{cases} 1, & if \quad I_{it} / \sum_t I_{it} > 0.25 \\ 0, & if \quad I_{it} / \sum_t I_{it} \le 0.25 \end{cases} \qquad (8.1)$$

where I_{it} measures deflated investment. The spikes column in Table 8.3 below is defined as:

$$Spike_t = \sum_i S_{it} \qquad (8.2)$$

Table 8.3 Investment indicators (1980-1991)

	Transport vehicles		Equipment	
	Spikes[a]	Investment[b]	Spikes	Investment
1980	37	101	20	1215
1981	20	90	17	1093
1982	25	84	10	1103
1983	21	86	12	1260
1984	22	90	18	1876
1985	49	112	26	1947
1986	40	99	31	1947
1987	39	97	32	1613
1988	37	106	29	1535
1989	48	117	33	1880
1990	53	115	55	1955
1991	58	110	40	1954

Notes:
a Number of firms with more than 25 per cent of 16 years of investment in a year.
b Total investment for firms in panel, 1985 guilders.

Source: Author's calculation at CeReM, panel of 1351 firms.

The data in Table 8.3 indeed show a significant increase in the number of firms that have a spike in 1985. This is the same year in which aggregate hours increased, and lags the Wassenaar agreement by three years. The increase in spikes goes against the VM model and is not contradictory to the CH model.

Next, Table 8.4 shows the average age of the stock of transport vehicles and equipment over time. The construction of the age variable is described in Appendix 2. After increasing through 1983, the average age starts declining. The fact that age falls reflects both an increase in investment as well as a reduction of the scrapping age under the CH model. In the previous table we saw that investment does not pick up until 1985; the margin of rejuvenation therefore initially took place through scrapping. It should be noted that aggregate industrial investment picked up sooner than investment in the balanced panel of firms, reflecting the fact that many smaller firms and entrants boosted their investment at an earlier stage.

Finally, Table 8.5 shows the difference in differences estimates of the effects of wage moderation on TFP growth and capital growth. Consistent with the CH model, it is seen that the contribution to aggregate TFP growth of firms in the years surrounding an investment spike minus the contribution of the firms which had no spike in that year increased following wage moderation. Spikes are considered in the years 1979, 1980 and 1981 for before moderation, and in 1983, 1984, and 1985 following moderation; firm level TFP growth (computed from Solow residual) is calculated from the year prior to the spike to two years following the spike.

The row relative TFP change contains the following computations:

$$\hat{\tau}_{s0} - \hat{\tau}_{\neg s0} \qquad \text{and} \qquad \hat{\tau}_{s1} - \hat{\tau}_{\neg s1}$$

where ^ denotes productivity growth of firms, the set s includes firms with spikes in the relevant year, and $\neg s$ firms with no spike. Period 0 refers to any of the years 1979, 1980 and 1981, and period 1 refers to years 1983, 1984 and 1985.

$$\hat{\tau}_{s1} = \sum_{i \in \{I | S_{it} = 1, t \in (83,84,85)\}} \omega_{it} \hat{\tau}_{it} \tag{8.3}$$

where ω is an appropriate weight for aggregating TFP changes, such as net output share.

The difference in differences growth of capital also exhibits the pattern expected under the CH model. In this case, the figures are based on average growth rates of firms in the appropriate set, rather than on contributions to aggregate growth as was used for TFP. In other words, they reflect the within behaviour of capital stock growth for firms with a spike versus firms without. It is seen that changes in growth rates for firms with a spike relative to those without increased following wage moderation, reflecting both a reduction in

scrapping age and an improvement in profitability outlook for investments as
expected under the CH model.

Table 8.4   Average of capital stock (1978-1991)

	Transport vehicles	Equipment
1978	7.9	8.6
1979	8.3	8.9
1980	8.6	9.1
1981	8.7	9.2
1982	8.6	9.2
1983	8.3	9.2
1984	8.2	9.1
1985	8.2	8.8
1986	7.0	8.6
1987	7.6	8.1
1988	7.3	7.6
1989	7.0	7.4
1990	6.6	7.3
1991	6.3	6.9

Source: Author's calculation at CeReM, 1435 firms.

*Table 8.5   Effects of wage moderation, difference-in-differences estimates,
          percentage points*

Indicator	Before moderation	After moderation
Relative change in TFP[a]	0.13	0.42
Relative change in K[b]	8.1	16.0

Notes:
a Contribution to aggregate TFP growth by firms with spike minus contributions to TFP from
firms with no spike.
b Average K growth of firms with spike, minus K growth firms with no spike.

Source: Author's calculation at CeReM, 1350 firms.

CONCLUSIONS AND SUGGESTIONS FOR FURTHER RESEARCH

In this Chapter some preliminary results are presented of an empirical test of the relevance of specificity in macro-economics. The very elegant theory of Caballero and Hammour, of course, is based partly on empirical observation, but, as yet, no rigorous empirical testing has taken place. The preliminary results presented here do not meet standards of rigour, but are suggestive that future research will be fruitful.

The methodology used in the Chapter to assess whether specificity plays a role in macro-economics is to see how wage moderation in the Netherlands has affected productivity (TFP) growth. Using a vintage model (VM) as the null hypothesis and a vintage model with appropriability of quasi-rents (CH) as a description of the world with specificity, we see whether the development of certain indicators leads us to reject the CH model.

The Chapter discusses why it is difficult to make assessments concerning the role of specificity with aggregate and sectoral data. Further a preview is given of the possibilities of distinguishing the models using micro-level data. In particular the ability to make non-standard aggregations and make special queries allows one to tailor series to conform to indicators that are expected to differ between the two models on theoretical grounds. The number of firms that show an unusually large investment in a particular year is such a statistic; the figure would not have been generated through the traditional process of statistics bureaus, but requires retrospective analysis of the micro-data.

The work is still in a very preliminary form. Much work remains to be done to assess the robustness of the indicator on capital age to changes in methodological assumptions, selection of firms, changes in aggregation of asset categories, etc. Further work remains to be done on evaluating the short-term substitutability of capital and labour. Finally, the work still requires some general statistics on the behaviour of the chosen sample compared with the behaviour of the universe of industrial firms, let alone the rest of the economy.

An open question remains whether institutional arrangements in the Netherlands have resulted in balanced specificity, thus solving the macro-economic problems flagged by Caballero and Hammour. It should be clear that in a world with sunk costs, hold-up problems could reduce the efficiency with which an economy operates, and with which it embarks on its path of economic and technological growth. The 'polder model' in the Netherlands, where government facilitates discussions between employers and employees, seems to have provided an environment in which both sides credibly signal not to engage in opportunistic behaviour. Hopefully policy makers will be able to maintain this co-operative behaviour in the future, in a careful balancing act.

APPENDIX 1 - THE CH MODEL

The material presented here follows very closely the description given in Caballero and Hammour (1998). In the model, there are two factors of production, 1 and 2, and one consumption good, which acts as numeraire. Decisions for allocation of the factors are made by optimising agents who derive utility from consumption. Production can take place either in autarky of in joint production, or both. U_i is autarky use of factor i, and E_i is allocation of i in joint production.

Production of output in a joint production unit is given by

$$\tilde{y} = Min(x_1, x_2) \tag{8.4}$$

where x_1, $x_2 > 0$, and $\tilde{y}$ are given by existing technologies. It is possible to generalise the model such that factor substitution is allowed in the long run or even in the short run, under certain conditions. The analysis of the CH model is forward looking, but collapses the future into one future period. E^0 pre-existing production units are already in place, and U_1^0 and U_2^0 of autarky factors are also given. Total supply of each factor is normalised to unity.

The production structure has a vintage nature, with new production units producing y^0 and pre-existing units having heterogeneous production from a distribution which depends on the history of technology adoption and shocks. In the model, the endogenous scrapping boundary, below which units will not operate, is denoted by y^0.

The specificity of the factors is given by the fact that if a *new* production unit is created a share φ_i of each factor is no longer usable if the factors separate; only $(1-\varphi_i) x_i$ of a factor committed to joint production can be used elsewhere.

The factors receive a reward in autarky given by

$$\pi_i = F_i'(U_i) \tag{8.5}$$

A specific functional form can be assumed for the autarky production function:

$$F_i(U_i) = \frac{1}{1+1/\eta_i} \left[1 - (1-U_i)^{(1+1/\eta_i)} \right] \tag{8.6}$$

so that we get a constant supply elasticity η_i for factor i into joint production:

$$\eta_i > 0 \tag{8.7}$$

$E_i = p_i^{\eta_i}$. A lowering of factor rewards in autarky for each given level of U_i is then equivalent to an increase in that factor's supply elasticity.

In an efficient equilibrium, i.e. one where there are efficient contracts so that factors receive ex-post payments in joint production equal to their ex-ante marginal product in autarky, the following holds for the wage:

$$w_i^* = p_i^* \tag{8.8}$$

In the incomplete-contract equilibrium, i.e. where the parties can bargain ex-post, their ex-post opportunity cost is given by $(1-\varphi_i)p_i$. The rents that can be bargained for in such an economy are given by:

$$s'' = y'' - (1-\varphi_1)p_1 x_1 - (1-\varphi_2)p_2 x_2 \tag{8.9}$$

With Nash bargaining, each factor then receives a compensation:

$$w_i'' x_i = (1-\varphi_i)p_i x_i + \beta_i s'' \tag{8.10}$$

where β_i is the bargaining power of factor i with $\beta_1 + \beta_2 = 1$.

The model further has free entry and exit. Factors will join together if

$$y'' \geq p_1 x_1 + p_2 x_2 + \Delta \tag{8.11}$$

where Δ denotes the degree of net specificity. If factors are balanced with each other in terms of what they have to lose, then $\Delta = 0$, and we have *balanced specificity*. The hurdle for entry will be higher if there is an appropriating and an appropriated factor.

Balanced specificity, $\Delta = 0$, occurs when $\varphi_1 p_1 x_1 = \varphi_2 p_2 x_2$, which happens if, and only if,

$$\frac{1}{x_1}\left(\frac{\varphi_2}{\frac{\beta_2}{\beta_1}\varphi_1 + \varphi_2}\frac{y''}{x_1}\right)^{\eta_1} = \frac{1}{x_2}\left(\frac{\varphi_1}{\frac{\beta_1}{\beta_2}\varphi_2 + \varphi_1}\frac{y''}{x_2}\right)^{\eta_2} \tag{8.12}$$

All else equal, the appropriating factor will be the factor with, first, the highest β, second, the lowest specific investment φx, and third, the factor with the lowest supply elasticity, η.

In the model, the following macro-outcomes occur when specificity is not balanced:

- Underemployment, $E_i < E_i^*$, $i = 1,2$.
- Market segmentation; appropriated factor i gets outside option, appropriating factor ($\neg i$) in involuntary unemployment: $w_i^n = p_i$ and $w_{\neg i}^n > p_{\neg i}$.
- Sclerosis: $y_-^0 < y^{0*}$; scrapping margin is lower than in efficient equilibrium.

APPENDIX 2 - AGGREGATE AND SECTORAL DATA

The aggregate and sectoral data are sourced from the sectoral time series database of the Netherlands Bureau for Economic Policy Analysis, and are based on efforts to put National Income Accounts data from Statistics Netherlands on a common basis over time. The capital stock data are created using time series on investment by type and sector from 1950 through 1995, using the perpetual inventory method. Initial stocks (1948) are provided by Statistics Netherlands, along with information on mean service life. The PIM method uses a stochastic mean service life, with a truncated normal distribution centred about the mean life, with a variance of one quarter the mean life, and truncation at 50 per cent above and below the mean. Further, a beta-decay function using • = 0.90 is applied to the remaining stock to reflect efficiency loss. Capital stock by type are aggregated to the sectoral level using expenditure shares, in order to create a measure of capital service inputs, following the methodology of Jorgenson et al. (1987). The data needed to compute user cost of capital is based on a long-bond and equity returns, tax rate information from the Netherlands Bureau for Economic Policy Analysis (1992) macro-economic model FKSEC and sectoral information on tax deductibility, accelerated depreciation allowances, and investment tax credits.

Micro-level Data

The micro-level datasets are available on-site at CeReM, Statistics Netherlands. The data used in the study come from three sets of surveys, the production statistics (PS), the investment statistics (IS) and the capital stock survey (CS). The PS are an annual census of large manufacturing firms, and a survey of small firms (10 employees). Firms are queried about employment (in workers), sales, production, inventories, materials and energy use. Each year, on the order of 10,000 firms are in the dataset. A balanced panel of firms from 1978 through 1993 can be made with about 6,000 firms.[8]

The investment statistics, available from 1980 through 1993, provide information on investment spending by asset type by firm. The survey is smaller, with an integral count of the largest firms (>500). A balanced panel containing observations of a firm for all years results in a selection of about 1,400 firms.

The CS survey is a small sample of very large firms, with information on capital stocks, by asset type and by vintage. The sample is drawn from a rotating selection of industries (SBIs) and contains between 150 and 400 firms per year, from 1983 through 1995. Owing to the sample selection method, only roughly 600 firms are sampled more than once throughout the period, usually with a 5-year span in between observations.

Deflators for output and materials are available at a 3-digit level, from Statistics Netherlands. Investment deflators by asset type also are from Statistics Netherlands.

Construction of time series of the capital stock for as large a group as possible occurs in steps. The reader should be warned that the methodology contains many untested assumptions. Results have not been tested as extensively for robustness to assumptions as I would like.

The first step was to use all firms that were observed twice over time to estimate the parameters for a mean stochastic service life PIM methodology. This can be done by using information on the quantity of capital in firm i of type j and vintage • observed in year t_0 and comparing it to the quantity observed in t_1. This can be done for all $i, j,$ • observed in t_0. Stacking the observations over survey pairs, allowing for differences in time-span between observations, allows one to run a non-linear regression to fit the chosen functional form (Truncated Normal).

The next step is to extend an observed vintage/type capital structure backwards in time for each firm by blowing up observed values with the estimated scrapping function. Then, a beta-decay is applied to vintage structure to create an annual stock for each firm for all years prior and up to the survey year. The average age of the stock of a firm in each year is a (post-decay) stock weighted average of the age of each vintage. For years following the survey date, the scrapping function is applied to earlier vintages, and investment data from IS are used for the latest vintage. All vintage values are then summed, after applying beta-decay. Age is a (post-decay) stock weighted average of age in each vintage. The above process is applied to aggregates of asset type, namely transport vehicles which is a sum of vehicles for internal and external use, and equipment.

TFP is constructed as a Solow-residual, using cost shares rather than expenditure shares as weights for factor inputs. Output is measured as value added, and factors of production are labour, transport vehicle stock and equipment stock.

NOTES

1. This channel could work in a neo-classical setting if we assume that firms are credit constrained, and need cash flow to invest.
2. See Dunne et al. (1988), Davis et al. (1996), and Caballero et al. (1995) for examples of plant dynamics, employment gross flows, and micro capital behaviour.
3. Malcomson (1997) presents an overview of the problem as related to labour markets.
4. See Netherlands Bureau for Economic Policy Analysis (1997a, Chapter 2).
5. The institutional setting of wage moderation in the Netherlands ensured that labour share of income would fall. This occurs because product wage increases are negotiated within boundaries of the 'wage-space,' namely some proportion of labour productivity growth, and agreement was reached to reduce the share going to labour. This story has no meaning under the wage setting set-up under the VM model.
6. In the earlier discussion of the analysis of Bovenberg (1997) on the employment effects of wage moderation, the first channel was an increase in investment. This channel is important when firms are credit constrained and need cash flow for investment. The other explanation for increased investment, namely improvements in expected profits, is related to the CH model.
7. For surveys of the burgeoning literature, see e.g. McGuckin (1995) and Bartelsman and Doms (1997).
8. See Abbring and Gautier (1997) for some notes on panel linking.

References

Aanesland, N. (1990), 'Effektiviseringspotensial i norsk landbruk', *Mimeo*, Ås - Norges landbrukshøyskole.

Aarts, L.J.M and P.R. de Jong (1992), *Economic Aspects of Disability Behaviour*, Doctoral thesis, Rotterdam: Erasmus Universiteit.

Abbring, J.H. and P.A. Gautier (1997), 'Gross Job Flow in Netherlands Manufacturing: A Panel Data Analysis,' *mimeo*.

Adema, W. (1993), *The Beveridge Curve and Institutional Arrangements*, D.Phil. thesis, St. Edmund Hall, Oxford.

Adema, W. (1998), 'What do countries really spend on social policies? A comparative note, *OECD Economic Studies*, No. 28, Paris: OECD, 153-167.

Adema, W. and M.G.K. Einerhand (1998), 'The Growing Role of Private Social Benefits', Labour Market and Social Policy Occasional Papers, No. 32, Paris: OECD.

Adema, W., M.G.K. Einerhand, B. Eklind, J. Lotz, and M. Pearson (1996), 'Net Public Social Expenditure', Labour Market and Social Policy Occasional Paper, No. 19, Paris: OECD.

Andersen, E.S. (1990), 'Effektiviteten i høyere utdanning', *Mimeo*.

Ark, B. van (1996), 'Sectoral Growth Accounting and Structural Change in Post-War Europe', in B. van Ark and N.F.R. Crafts (eds), *Quantitative Aspects of Post-War European Economic Growth*, CEPR/Cambridge University Press, 84-164.

Ark, B. van and J. de Haan (1996), 'Enhancing Growth Through Structural Reform', *SOM Research Report 96C16*, Groningen: University of Groningen.

Ark, B. van and H.J. de Jong (1996), 'Accounting for Economic Growth in the Netherlands since 1913', *The Economic and Social History in the Netherlands*, volume 7.

Ark, B. van, J. de Haan and H.J. de Jong (1996), 'Characteristics of Economic Growth in the Netherlands During the Postwar Period', in Nicholas Crafts and Gianni Toniolo (eds), *Economic Growth in Europe Since 1945*, CEPR/Cambridge University Press.

Armington, P. S. (1969), *A Theory of Demand for Products Distinguished by Place of Production*, IMF Staff Papers no. 16, 159-78.

Bartelsman, E. J. and M. E. Doms (1997), 'Understanding Productivity: Lesson from Longitudinal Mirco Datasets', Proposal for review article.

Bergeijk, P.A.G. van, and R.C.G. Haffner (1996), *Privatisation, Deregulation and the Macroeconomy: Measurement, Modelling and Policy*, Cheltenham, UK and Brookfield, US: Edward Elgar.

Bergeijk, P.A.G. van, and H.A. Keuzenkamp (1997), 'The Macro-Economic Costs of Regulation', paper presented at the international conference on 'The effects and policy implications of structural adjustment in small open economies', Amsterdam, 23-24 October.

Bergeijk, P.A.G. van and J. van Sinderen (1997), 'Models and Macroeconomic Policy in the Netherlands', Paper presented at the 10th anniversary conference of the Tinbergen Institute, Amsterdam, May 14-16, 1997.

Bergeijk, P.A.G. van, R.C.G. Haffner and J. van Sinderen (1997), 'Macroeconomic effects', in R.C.G. Haffner and P.A.G. van Bergeijk (eds), *Regulatory reform in the Netherlands. Macroeconomic consequences and industry effects*, Rotterdam: Ocfeb Research Centre for Economic Policy.

Boles de Boer, D. and L. Evans (1996), 'The Economic Efficiency of Telecommunications in a Deregulated Market: the Case of New Zealand', *Economic Record*, 72, 24-35.

Bollard, A. (1994) 'New Zealand', in J. Williamson (ed.), *The Political Economy of Policy Reform*, Washington, D.C.: Institute for International Economics.

Bollard, A. and R.A. Buckle (1987) (eds), *Economic Liberalisation in New Zealand*, Wellington: Allen and Unwin.

Bollard, A., R. Lattimore and B. Silverstone (1996), 'Introduction', in Silverstone et al. (eds), *A Study of Economic Reform: The Case of New Zealand*, Amsterdam: North-Holland, 1-30.

Bovenberg, L.A. (1997), 'Dutch employment growth: an analysis', CPB-report, 2 (2), 16-24.

Bowden, R.J. (1997), 'The Employment Contracts Act: Common Law and Uncommon Economics', *New Zealand Economic Papers*, 31 (1), 65-83.

Brash, D.T. (1996), 'New Zealand's Remarkable Reforms', Fifth Annual Hayek Memorial Lecture to Institute of Economic Affairs, London, 4 June.

Brash, D.T. (1998), 'New Zealand's Economic Reforms: A Model for Change?' Paper presented to the Waitangi Foundation, the Guildhall, London, 3 June.

Broer, D.P. (1996), On the Theory of Investment in Vintage Capital Models, Tinbergen Institute Discussion Paper Series TI 92-92/4.

Browning, E.K. (1994), 'The non-tax wedge', *Journal of Public Economics*, 53 (3), 419-33.

Bye, T. and T.A. Johnsen (1990), *Effektivisering av kraftmarkedet*, Reports 91/3, Statistics Norway.

Caballero, R.J. (1997), 'Aggregate Investment, a 90's View', *mimeo*.

Caballero, R.J. and M.L. Hammour (1998), 'The macroeconomics of specificity', *Journal of Political Economy*, 106 (4), 724-67.

Caballero, R.J., E.M. Engel and J.C. Haltiwanger (1995), 'Plant-level Adjustment and Aggregate Investment Dynamics', in 'Brookings Papers on Economic Activity', Washington, D.C: Brookings Institute, 1350-68.

Callesen, P. (1997), 'The Policy Experience of Structural Reforms in Denmark', paper presented at the conference 'The effects and policy implications of structural adjustment in small open economies', Amsterdam, October 23-24.

Campbell-Hunt, C. and L.M. Corbett (1996), *A Season of Excellence?: An Overview of New Zealand Enterprise in the Nineties*, Research Monograph 65, Wellington: New Zealand Institute of Economic Research.

Chapple, S., R. Harris and B. Silverstone (1996), 'Unemployment', in Silverstone et al. (eds), *A Study of Economic Reform: The Case of New Zealand*, Amsterdam: North-Holland, 139-72.

Colgate, P. and J. Stroombergen (1993), *A Promise to Pay: New Zealand's Overseas Debt and Country Risk*, Research Monograph 58, Wellington: New Zealand Institute of Economic Research.

Cooper, R., J. Haltiwanger and L. Power (1994), 'Machine replacement and the business cycle: Lumps and bumps', *mimeo*.

Dalziel, P. (1997), 'Evaluating New Zealand's Economic Reforms: a Comment on Evans, Grimes and Wilkinson', Paper presented to Annual Conference of New Zealand Association of Economists, Christchurch, August.

Dalziel, P. and R. Lattimore (1996), *The New Zealand Macroeconomy: A Briefing on the Reforms*, Auckland: Oxford University Press.

Davis, S., J. Haltiwanger and S. Schuh (1996), *Job Creation and Job Destruction*, Cambridge, MA: MIT Press.

Deane, R.S. (1995), 'People, Power and Politics: The Dynamics of Economic Change', Address to the Annual General Meeting of the New Zealand Institute of Economic Research, Discussion Paper No. 39, Wellington, October.

Dixon, P.B. and D. McDonald (1993), 'An Explanation of Structural Changes in the Australian Economy: 1986-87 to 1990-91', Background Paper No. 29, Canberra: Office of EPAC.

Doms, M. E. (1993), 'Inter Fuel Substitution and Energy Technology Heterogeneity in U.A. Manufacturing', discussion paper CES 93-5, U.S. Bureau of Census, Center for Economic Studies.

Duijn, J.J. van (1982), 'Aanbodeconomie in Nederland', in *De economie van het aanbod, preadviezen van de Vereniging voor de Staathuishoudkunde 1982*, Leiden and Antwerpen: Stenfert Kroeze, 1-27.

Duncan, I. (1996), 'Public Enterprises', in Silverstone et al. (eds), *A Study of Economic Reform: The Case of New Zealand*, Amsterdam: North-Holland, 389-424.

Duncan, I. and A. Bollard (1992), *Corporatisation and Privatisation: Lessons from New Zealand*, Auckland: Oxford University Press.

Dunne, T. and M.E. Doms (1993), 'An Investigation into Capital and Labour Adjustment at the Plant Level', *mimeo*, Center for Economic Studies.

Dunne, T., M. Roberts and L. Samuelson (1988), 'Patterns of Firm Entry and Exit in U.S. Manufacturing Industries', *RAND Journal of Economics*, **19** (4), 495-515.

Easton, B. (1994), 'Economic and Other Ideas behind the New Zealand Reforms', *Oxford Review of Economic Policy*, **10** (3), 78-94.

Easton, B. (1996), 'Income Distribution', in Silverstone et al. (eds), *A Study of Economic Reform: The Case of New Zealand*, Amsterdam: North-Holland, 101-38.

Edwards, S. (1989), 'On the sequencing of structural reforms', *OECD Economics and Statistics Working Paper* 10, Paris: OECD.

Ergas, H. (1996), 'Telecommunications Across the Tasman: A Comparison of Regulatory Approaches and Economic Outcomes in Australia and New Zealand', *mimeo*, International Institute of Communications.

European Commission (1996), *Employment in Europe*, Brussels and Luxembourg.

Eurostat (1995), Labour Force Survey.

Evans, L. (1996), 'The Competitiveness of Infrastructure Services', Paper presented to Australia-New Zealand Business Council Conference on 'Past, Present, Prospects and Profitability: Australia/New Zealand Business Competitiveness', Auckland, 26-27 September.

Evans, L., A. Grimes, B. Wilkinson, and D. Teece (1996), 'Economic Reform in New Zealand 1984-95: The Pursuit of Efficiency', *Journal of Economic Literature*, **34** (4), 1856-1902.

Färe, R., S. Grosskopf and D. Margaritis (1996), 'Productivity Growth', in Silverstone et al. (eds), *A Study of Economic Reform: The Case of New Zealand*, Amsterdam: North-Holland, 73-100.

Fay, R.G. (1996), 'Enhancing the Effectiveness of Active Labour Market Policies: Evidence from Programme Evaluations in OECD Countries', Labour Market and Social Policy Occasional Paper, No. 18, Paris: OECD.

Frederiksen, N. K. (1997), *A Note on Interpreting Consumption Tax Incidence in OLG Models*, Mimeo, Economic Policy Research Unit (EPRU), Copenhagen Business School.

Funke, N. (1993), 'Timing and sequencing of reforms: Competing views and the role of credibility', *Kyklos*, **46** (3), 337-62.

Goff, B. (1996), 'Regulation and macroeconomic performance', *Topics in Regulatory Economics and Policy Series*, Dordrecht and London: Kluwer Academic.

Gradus, R.H.J.M. (1994), Nederlandse economie relatief rigide in Europa, *Economisch Statistische Berichten*,**79** (3980), 921-4.

Grafton, R. Q., T. Hazledine and B. Buchardt (1997), 'The New Zealand Economic Revolution: Lessons for Canada?', Working Paper 9705E, Department of Economics, University of Ottawa, May.

Groote, P., R.M. Albers and H.J. de Jong (1996), 'A Standardised Time Series of the Stock of Fixed Capital in the Netherlands', *Research Memorandum GD-25*, Groningen Growth and Development Centre.

Grund, J. (1990), 'Effektiviseringsmuligheter i helsesektoren', *Mimeo*, Norwegian School of Business Administration.

Gwartney, J., R Lawson and W. Block (1996), *Economic Freedom of the World, 1975-1995*, Vancouver B.C.: Fraser Institute.

Haffner, R.C.G. and P.A.G. van Bergeijk (1997), 'Marktwerking in Nederland. Diagnose en consequenties', *Maandschrift Economie*, 61, 143-62.

Hall, V.B. (1996a), 'Economic Growth', in Silverstone et al. (eds), *A Study of Economic Reform: The Case of New Zealand*, Amsterdam: North-Holland, 31-72.

Hall, V.B. (1996b), 'New Zealand's Economic Growth: Fantastic, Feeble, or Further Progress Needed?', *Victoria Economic Commentaries*, **13** (1), 3-13.

Hanneson, R. (1990), 'En samfunnsøkonomisk lønnsom fiskerinæring - struktur, gevinst, forvaltning', *Mimeo*, Norwegian School of Economics and Business Administration.

Hansen, C. T., L.H. Pedersen and T. Sløk (1995), *Progressive Taxation, Wages and Activity in a Small, Open Economy*, EPRU Working paper 1995-21, Copenhagen Business School.

Hansen, E. and D. Margaritis (1993), 'Financial Liberalisation and Monetary Policy in New Zealand', *Australian Economic Review*, 104, October-December, 28-36.

Harbridge, R., A. Crawford and P. Kiely (1997), *Employment Contracts: Bargaining Trends and Employment Law Update 1996/97*, Wellington: Graduate School of Business and Government Management, Victoria University.

Hartog, H. den and H.S. Tjan (1976), 'Investments, wages, prices and demand for labour', *The Economist*, **124**, 497-505.

Hassink, W.H.J., J.C. van Ours and G. Ridder (1997), 'Dismissal through Disability', *De Economist*, **145** (1), 29-46.

Henderson, D. (1995), 'The Revival of Economic Liberalism: Australia in an International Perspective', *Australian Economic Review*, 109, January-March, 59-85.

Henderson, D. (1996), 'Economic Reform: New Zealand in an International Perspective', New Zealand Business Roundtable, Wellington, August.

Hesemans, J.C.M. and H. van Rijn (1986), 'De Ontwikkeling van het Minimumloon', *Supplement bij de Sociaal-Economische Maandstatistiek*, No. 8, 4-20.

Hiorth, O.C. (1990), 'Effektiviseringspotensialer i innenlandsk transportvirks-omhet', *Mimeo*.

Holmes, K.H., B.T. Johnson and M. Kirkpatrick (1997), *Index of Economic Freedom*, Heritage Foundation/Wall Street Journal.

Holmøy, E. (1992), 'The structure and working of MSG-5, an applied general equilibrium model of the Norwegian economy', in L. Bergman and Ø. Olsen (eds), *Economic modelling in the Nordic countries*, Amsterdam: North-Holland, 199-236.

Holmøy, E., G. Nordén and B. Strøm (1995), 'MSG-5 - A Complete Description of the System of Equations', Reports 94/19, Statistics Norway.

IMF (1996), *World Economic Outlook*, Washington D.C., May.

IMF (1997a), *Financial Statistics*, Washington D.C.

IMF (1997b), *Kingdom of the Netherlands. Selected Issues*, Washington D.C.

Industry Commission (1995), *The Growth and Revenue Implications of Hilmer and Related Reforms: A Report by the Industry Commission to the Council of Australian Governments*, Industry Commission: Belconnen Act.

Janssen, J. (1996), 'Labour Productivity - Can we Catch the 'Magic Bus'?', New Zealand Treasury, Internal Note, 23 September.

Johansen, L. (1960), *A Multi-sectoral Study of Economic Growth*, Amsterdam: North-Holland.

Johnsen, T. (1990), 'Effektiviseringsmulighetene i internadministrasjon i offentlig virksomhet', *Mimeo*, Statskonsult.

Jong, G. de (1992), 'Schouten tussen plan en werkelijkheid', in J.H.M. Donders en R.J. Mulder (eds), *In overleg; afscheid van prof.dr. D.B.J. Schouten als kroonlid van de SER*, The Hague: Sociaal Economische Raad, 69-81.

Jorgenson, D., F. Gollop and B. Fraumeni (1987), *Productivity and U.S. Economic Growth*, Cambridge: Harvard University Press.

Kasper, W. (1996a), *Free to Work: The Liberalisation of New Zealand's Labour Markets*, St. Leonards and Wellington: Centre for Independent Studies.

Kasper, W. (1996b), 'Competitiveness and Macroeconomic Performance in Australia and New Zealand', Paper presented to Australia-New Zealand Business Council Conference on 'Past, Present, Prospects and Profitability: Australia/New Zealand Business Competitiveness', Auckland, 26-27 September.

King, M. A. and D. Fullerton (1984), *The Taxation of Income from Capital: A Comparative Study of the United Kingdom, Sweden, and West Germany*, Chicago, University of Chicago Press.

Kleinknecht, A. (1994), 'Oratie - Heeft Nederland een loongolf nodig?', *Tijdschrift voor politieke ekonomie*, **17** (2), 5-24.

Knoester, A. (1989), *Economische politiek in Nederland*, Leiden and Antwerpen: Stenfert Kroeze.

Knudsen, M. B., L. H. Pedersen, T. W. Petersen, P. Stephensen and P. Trier (1998a), *A Prototype of a DREAM (Danish Rational Economic Agents Model)*, Working Paper, Statistics Denmark.

Knudsen, M. B., L. H. Pedersen, T. W. Petersen, P. Stephensen and P. Trier (1998b), *A CGE Analysis of the Danish 1993 Tax Reform*, Economic Modelling Working Paper Series 1998-6, Statistics Denmark.

Koedijk, K. and J.J.M. Kremers (1996), 'Market opening, regulation and growth in Europe', *Economic Policy*, **0** (23), October, 443-67.

Koopmans, C.C. (1997), 'Nemo: CPBs new energy model', *CPB-report*, **2** (2), 34-38.

Krugman, P. (1992), *The age of diminished expectations*, Cambridge MA: The MIT Press.

Kuper, G.H. and S.K. Kuipers (1996) 'Minder regulering, meer prestaties', *Economisch Statistische Berichten*, **81** (4084), 992-3.

Lange, K., L. H. Pedersen and P. B. Sørensen (forthcoming), 'The Danish Tax Reform Act of 1993: Effects on the Macroeconomy and on Intergenerational Welfare', in T. M. Andersen, S. E. H. Jensen and O. Risager (eds), *Macroeconomic Perspectives on the Danish Economy*, New York: Macmillan Press.

Lattimore, R. and P. Wooding (1996), 'International Trade', in Silverstone et al. (eds), *A Study of Economic Reform: The Case of New Zealand*, Amsterdam: North-Holland, 315-54.

Lawrence, R.Z. (1984), *Can America Compete?*, Washington D.C.: The Brookings Institution.

Layard, R., S. Nickell and R. Jackman (1991), *Unemployment. Macroeconomic Performance and the Labour Market*, Oxford University Press.

Lipschitz, L. et al. (1989), 'The Federal Republic of Germany: Adjustment in a Surplus Economy', *IMF Occasional Paper* 64, Washington D.C.: IMF.

Lloyd, P.J. (1997), 'Review' of *A Study of Economic Reform: The Case of New Zealand*, Silverstone et al. (eds), in *New Zealand Economic Papers*, **31** (1), 115-27.

Maddison, A. (1991), *Dynamic Forces in Capitalist Development. A Long-Run Comparative View*, Oxford University Press.

Maddison, A. (1995), *Monitoring the World Economy, 1820-1992*, Paris: OECD Development Centre.

Malcomson, J.M. (1997), 'Contracts, Hold-up and Labor Markets', *Journal of Economic Literature*, **35** (4), 1916-57.

Maloney, T. and J. Savage (1996), 'Labour Markets and Policy', in Silverstone et al. (eds), *A Study of Economic Reform: The Case of New Zealand*, Amsterdam: North-Holland, 173-214.

Martin, J.P. (1996), 'Measures of replacement rates for the purpose of international comparisons', *OECD Economic Studies*, No. 26, Paris: OECD.

McGuckin, R.H. (1995), 'Establishment Microdata for Economic Research and Policy Analysis: Looking beyond the Aggregates', *Journal of Business and Economic Statistics*, **13** (1), 121-26.

McKibbin, W.J. (1994), 'Labour Productivity Growth: Macroeconomic and Sectoral Results from the MSG2 and G-cubed Multi-Country Models', in C. Hargreaves (ed.) *A Comparison of Economy-Wide Models of Australia*, Canberra: Economic Planning Advisory Commission.

McMillan, J. (1997), 'Radical Economic Reform: Lessons from New Zealand', Paper presented to Conference on 'Responses to International Liberalisation', Christchurch: University of Canterbury, 25-27 August.

Murphy, C.W. and R. Brooker (1994), 'Murphy Model and Microeconomic Reform', in C. Hargreaves (ed.), *A Comparison of Economy-Wide Models of Australia*, Canberra: Economic Planning Advisory Commission.

National Bank of New Zealand (1992), 'Is New Zealand's Fiscal Policy Sustainable?' in *National Business Outlook*, July 5-6; and 'Fiscal Policy - Sustainability and Credibility' in *National Business Outlook*, October 5-6.

Netherlands Bureau for Economic Policy Analysis (1991), *De werkgelegenheid in de jaren tachtig*, Working document 41, The Hague.

Netherlands Bureau for Economic Policy Analysis (1992), *FKSEC: A macro-econometric model of the Netherlands*, Nijmegen: Stenfert-Kroese.

Netherlands Bureau for Economic Policy Analysis (1997a), *Challenging Neighbours*, Berlin: Springer Verlag.

Netherlands Bureau for Economic Policy Analysis (1997b), 'Meer laagbetaald werk, minder arbeidsproductiviteitsgroei?', *Macro Economische Verkenning 1998*, section VI.I, 107-17.

Netherlands Bureau for Economic Policy Analysis (1998a), *Macro Economische Verkenning 1999*, The Hague: SDU Uitgevers.

Netherlands Bureau for Economic Policy Analysis (1998b), *Microtax*, The Hague.

Netherlands Bureau for Economic Policy Analysis (1998c), 'Recent Trends in Dutch Labour Productivity: The Role of Changes in the Composition of Employment', *Werkdocument no. 98*, The Hague.

Netherlands Bureau for Economic Policy Analysis (1998d), 'Sectorale productiviteitsgroei in Nederland', Internal document, The Hague.

Netherlands Ministry of Economic Affairs (1997), *Benchmarking the Netherlands*, The Hague.

Netherlands Ministry of Social Affairs and Employment (1996), *Employment and Social Policies under International Constraints*, The Hague.

New Zealand Treasury (1984), *Economic Management*, Wellington, 14 July.
New Zealand Treasury (1996), *Pre-Election Economic and Fiscal Update*, Wellington, 12 September.
New Zealand Treasury (1997), *The Budget Economic and Fiscal Update*, Wellington, 26 June.
Nieuwenhuis. A. and P.A. Terra-Pilaar (1997), 'Marktwerking in beschutte bedrijfstakken: de hoogte van de 'mark-up'', *Onderzoeksreeks directie Marktwerking*, The Hague: Netherlands Ministry of Economic Affairs.
Norman, V., F. Førsund, E. Holmøy, O.J. Mørkved and R. Sørensen (1991), *Mot bedre vitende*, NOU 1991, 28, Oslo: Akademika.
OECD (1983), *Positive Adjustment Policies: Managing Structural Change*, Paris.
OECD (1987a), *Structural Adjustment and Economic Performance*, Paris.
OECD (1987b), *Structural Reform and Economic Performance*, Synthesis report, Paris.
OECD (1990), *Progress in Structural Reform*, Paris.
OECD (1993), *Economic Survey: the Netherlands*, Paris.
OECD (1994a), *Assessing Structural Reform - Lessons for the Future*, Paris.
OECD (1994b), *Economic Outlook*, 55, Paris.
OECD (1994c), *Employment Outlook*, Paris.
OECD (1994d), *OECD Economic Surveys - New Zealand*, Paris.
OECD (1994e), *The OECD Jobs Study – Evidence and Explanations*, Paris.
OECD (1994f), *The OECD Jobs Study - Facts, Analysis, Strategies*, Paris.
OECD (1995a), *Economic Outlook*, 57, Paris.
OECD (1995b), *Historical Statistics, 1960-1993*, Paris.
OECD (1996a), *Economic Outlook*, Paris.
OECD (1996b), 'Interactions between Structural Reform, Macroeconomic Policy and Economic Performance', *OECD Economic Outlook*, No. 59, June, Paris.
OECD (1996c), *Labour Force Statistics, 1974-1994*, Paris.
OECD (1996d), *OECD Economic Surveys - Netherlands*, Paris.
OECD (1996e), *OECD Economic Surveys - New Zealand*, Paris.
OECD (1996f), 'Social Expenditures Statistics of OECD Member Countries - Provisional Version', Labour Market and Social Policy Occasional Paper, No. 17, Paris.
OECD (1996g), *Tax/benefit position of Production Workers*, Paris.
OECD (1997a), *Education at a glance - OECD indicators*, Paris.
OECD (1997b), *Employment Outlook*, Paris.
OECD (1997c), *Family, Market and Community: Equity and Efficiency in Social Policy*, Social Policy Studies, No. 21, Paris.
OECD (1997d), *Implementing the OECD Jobs Strategy - Lessons from Member Countries' Experience*, Paris.
OECD (1997e), *Implementing the OECD Jobs Strategy - Member Countries' Experience*, Paris.
OECD (1997f), *Labour Force Statistics*, Paris.
OECD (1997g), *National Accounts 1960-1995*, Paris.
OECD (1997h), *OECD Economic Outlook*, No. 61, Paris.
OECD (1997i), *The OECD Report on Regulatory Reform*, Paris.

OECD (1997j), *The Tax/Benefit Position of Employees, 1995-1996*, Paris.

OECD (1998a), *Benefit Systems and Work Incentives*, Paris.

OECD (1998b), *Employment Outlook*, Paris.

OECD (1998c), *OECD Economic Outlook*, No. 63, June, Paris.

OECD (1998d), *OECD Economic Surveys - Netherlands*, Paris.

OECD (1998e), *OECD Economic Surveys - New Zealand*, Paris.

OECD (1998f), *OECD Social Expenditure Database 1980-1996*, Paris (CD-Rom).

OECD (1998g), *Technology, Productivity and Job Creation: Best Policy Practices*, Paris.

OECD (1998h), *The Battle against Exclusion: Social Assistance in Belgium, the Czech Republic, the Netherlands and Norway*, Paris.

OECD (1998i), *The OECD Jobs Strategy: Progress Report on Implementation of Country-Specific Recommendations*, OECD Economics Department Working Paper, No. 196, May, Paris.

OECD (1998j), 'The OECD Jobs Strategy', *Meeting of the OECD Council at Ministerial Level: Documentation for Ministers*, Paris.

OECD (1998k), National Accounts 1960-1996, Paris.

OECD (1999), *A Caring World: The New Social Policy Agenda*, Paris.

Øvereng, J. (1990), 'Effektiviseringsmulighetene i den videregående skolen', *Mimeo*.

Pedersen, K. (1990), 'U-hjelp - nytter det?', *Mimeo*, Norwegian School of Economics and Business Administration.

Pedersen, L. H., P. Stephensen and N. Smith (1998), *Wage Formation and Minimum Wage Contracts*, Economic Modelling Working Paper Series 1998-5, Statistics Denmark.

Peters, Hon. W., Treasurer (1997), *The Budget Speech and Fiscal Strategy Report 1997*, Wellington, 26 June.

Peters, Hon. W., Treasurer (1998), *The Budget Speech and Fiscal Strategy Report 1998*, Wellington, 14 May.

Philpott, B. (1994), 'Data Base of Nominal and Real Output, Labour and Capital Employed by SNA Industry Group, 1960-1990', RPEP Paper 265, Wellington: Victoria University.

Philpott, B. (1995), 'Provisional Estimates for 1990-1994 of Output, Labour and Capital Employed by SNA Industry Group', RPEP Paper 273, Wellington: Victoria University.

Pissarides, C. (1998), 'The Impact of Employment Tax Cuts on Unemployment and Wages: The Role of Unemployment Benefits and Tax Structure', *European Economic Review*, **42** (1), 155-183.

Reserve Bank of New Zealand (1996), *Monetary Policy Statement*, Wellington, June.

Robertsen, K. and L. B. Friestad (1990), 'Effektiviseringsmuligheter i grunnskolen', FOU-rapport nr. 72/1990, Agderforskning.

Rodrik, D. (1989), 'Promises, promises: Credible policy reform via signalling' *Economic Journal*, **99**, 756-72.

Rødseth, T. (1990), *Trygd og effektivitet*, Notat 46, Senter for samfunnsforskning.

Savage, J. and A. Bollard (eds) (1990), *Turning it Around: Closure and Revitalisation in New Zealand Industry*, Auckland: Oxford University Press.

Savage, J. and D. Cooling (1996), 'A Preliminary Report on the Results of a Survey on the Employment Contracts Act', Working Paper 96/7, New Zealand Institute of Economic Research.

Shultz, G.P. (1995), 'Economics in Action: Ideas, Institutions, Policies', *American Economic Review Papers and Proceedings*, **85** (2), 1-8.

Silverstone, B., A. Bollard and R. Lattimore (eds) (1996), *A Study of Economic Reform: The Case of New Zealand*, Amsterdam: North-Holland.

Sinderen, J. van (1981), 'Bestek '81 in kort bestek', in *Kabinet Van Agt evaluatie sociaal-economisch beleid*, Rotterdam: Economische Faculteitsvereniging, 43-62.

Sinderen, J. van (1990), *Belastingheffing, economische groei en belastingopbrengst; een evaluatie van aanbodeconomie*, Groningen: Wolters Noordhoff.

Sinderen, J. van (1993), 'Taxation and Economic Growth: some calculations with a Macroeconomic Semi-Equilibrium for the Dutch economy (MESEM)', *Economic Modelling*, **10** (3), 285-300.

Sinderen, J. van, P.A.G. van Bergeijk, R.C.G. Haffner and P.M. Waasdorp (1994), 'De kosten van economische verstarring op macro-niveau', *Economisch Statistische Berichten*, 23 March, 274-9.

Smith, R. and A. Grimes (1990), 'Sources of Economic Growth', Reserve Bank of New Zealand, *Bulletin*, **53** (2), 140-8.

Spencer, G.H. (1990), 'Monetary Policy: The New Zealand Experience 1985-1990', Reserve Bank of New Zealand, *Bulletin*, **53** (3), 252-69.

Spicer, B., D. Emanuel and M. Powell (1996), *Transforming Government Enterprises: Managing Radical Organisational Change in Deregulated Environments*, CIS Policy Monographs 35, St. Leonards and Wellington: The Centre for Independent Studies.

Statistics Netherlands (1997a), Arbeidsrekeningen, Voorburg and Heerlen.

Statistics Netherlands (1997b), *Sociaal-Economische Maandstatistiek*, 14, Voorburg and Heerlen.

Stephens, R. (1996), 'Social Services', in Silverstone et al. (eds), *A Study of Economic Reform: The Case of New Zealand*, Amsterdam: North-Holland, 451-96.

Tinbergen, J. (1955), *On the Theory of Economic Policy*, Amsterdam: North Holland.

Turnovsky, S. (1991), 'Tariffs and sectoral adjustments in an open economy', *Journal of Economic dynamics and Control*, 15, 53-89.

Vennemo, H. (1992), 'Skatter og avgifter: Hvor stort er allokeringstapet?', *Norsk økonomisk tidsskrift*, hefte 4, 267-288.

Visser, J. and A. Hemerijck (1997), *A Dutch Miracle*, Amsterdam: Amsterdam University Press.

Vries, B. de (1995), *Een halve eeuw werk, werk en de werking van de arbeidsmarkt*, Rotterdam: Ocfeb Research Centre for Economic Policy.

VSV (1997), *De Kleine Gids voor de Nederlandse Sociale Zekerheid*, Deventer: Kluwer/Voorlichtingscentrum Sociale Verzekering.

Wagner, G.A. (1990), 'Knopen doorhakken', in: J. van Sinderen (ed.), *Het sociaal economisch beleid in de tweede helft van de twintigste eeuw*, Groningen: Wolters-Noordhoff, 168-75.

Wagner, K. and B. van Ark (1996), 'Introduction' in K. Wagner and B. van Ark (eds) *International Productivity Differences; Measurement and Explanations*, Amsterdam: North-Holland, 1-22.

Wellink, A.H.E.M. (1987), 'De ontwikkeling in de jaren zeventig en tachtig en enkele daaruit te trekken lessen', in A. Knoester (ed.), *Lessen uit het verleden*, Leiden and Antwerpen: Stenfert Kroeze, 333-67.

Williamson, J. (ed.) (1994), *The Political Economy of Policy Reform*, Washington D.C.: Institute for International Economics.

Winston, C. (1993), 'Economic Deregulation: Days of Reckoning for Microeconomists', *Journal of Economic Literature*, **31** (3), 1263-89.

Zanden, J.L. van (1997), *Een klein land in de 20e eeuw. Economische geschiedenis van Nederland 1914-1995*, Utrecht: Het Spectrum.

Author Index

Subject Index